Navigating Nonfiction

VOLUME 2

IN NARRATIVE AND HYBRID TEXT

LUCY CALKINS ◆ KATHLEEN TOLAN

*first*hand

HEINEMANN

DEDICATED TO TEACHERS

This book is dedicated to Zoë Ryder White and Shannon Rigney Keene—with enormous thanks, especially for helping us bring the youngsters to life.

DEDICATED TO TEACHERS

firsthand
An imprint of Heinemann
361 Hanover Street, Portsmouth, NH 03801
www.heinemann.com

Offices and agents throughout the world

"Dedicated to Teachers" is a trademark of Greenwood Publishing Group, Inc.

© 2010 by Lucy Calkins and Kathleen Tolan

The asterisked tradebook titles in this text have been officially leveled by Irene Fountas, Gay Su Pinnell, and their trained levelers. Other systems that use level designations are not equivalent to theirs.

Post-its ® is a registered trademark of the 3M company.

The authors and publisher wish to thank those who have generously given permission to reprint borrowed material:

Material from *Bugwise* is used with permission of Kids Can Press Ltd. Of Toronto, Canada. Text © 1990 Pamela Hickman and the Federation of Ontario Naturalists. Illustrations © Judie Shore.

"A Sea of Headwaiters," from THE WHISPERING LAND by Gerald Durrell, copyright © 1961, renewed © by Gerald Durrell. Used by permission of Viking Penguin, a division of Penguin Group, (USA) Inc.

Reproduced from *Beginners: Cats* by permission of Usborne Publishing, 83-85 Saffron Hill, London EC1N8RT, UK. Copyright © 2003, Usborne Publishing Limited.

"Spill" from *Disasters at Sea* by Andrew Donkin. Copyright © 2001 by Dorling Kindersley Limited. Published in the United States by DK Publishing, Inc. Reprinted with permission from Penguin (UK) Group.

"The Mummy's Curse" from *Secrets of the Mummies* by Harriet Griffey. Copyright © 1998 by Dorling Kindersley Limited. Published in the United States by DK Publishing, Inc. Reprinted with permission from Penguin (UK) Group.

Photographers: Peter Cunningham and Melanie Brown
Cover and Interior Design: Jenny Jensen Greenleaf
Composition: Publishers' Design and Production Services, Inc.

Library of Congress Cataloging-in-Publication Data
CIP data on file with the Library of Congress

ISBN 10: 0-325-03067-7
ISBN 13: 978-0-325-03067-8

Printed in the United States of America on acid-free paper
14 13 12 11 10 ML 1 2 3 4 5

Navigating Nonfiction

VOLUME
2

In Narrative and Hybrid Text

USING TEXT STRUCTURES TO COMPREHEND

Units of Study for Teaching Reading, Grades 3–5

Contents

NAVIGATING NONFICTION IN NARRATIVE AND HYBRID TEXT
VOLUME 2: Using Text Structures to Comprehend

PART TWO NARRATIVE NONFICTION

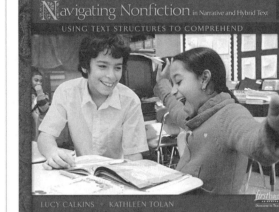

"If you divide nonfiction texts into piles based on how those texts are put together, you'll end up with one pile of true stories (narrative nonfiction) and one pile of all-about texts (little courses on a topic). Readers read these kinds of nonfiction texts in very different ways. When readers know what kind of nonfiction book we have, that helps us decide how to read it. When we know we have narrative nonfiction in our hands, we know we can read it like narrative fiction. A story is a story is a story!"

"You can use the ways of reading narrative even if you don't have a traditional main character in your text. In fact, you can often get to some big ideas by stretching the definition of main character to apply to a different sort of main presence in the text. Doesn't this sound interesting? Soon you'll be able to try it—to see if you can regard a meerkat colony or a venus flytrap or a whole group of people, like the pilgrims, say, as the 'main character' of your nonfiction narrative."

"People write stories to convey ideas. The idea is what allows the storyteller to shape information, experience, into something that fits together so the story is not just a hodgepodge of junky details strung along a line of time. While that is a writer's goal, it is also a reader's goal. Readers have to find the unifying idea behind the texts they read, to make coherence and find meaning out of what would otherwise be strings of events and facts."

"Readers use our sense of how certain types of texts are structured to read disaster and achievement stories, expecting that those common kinds of true stories will follow predictable patterns."

"The most powerful readers don't already know what every single word in a book means. The most powerful readers work hard to figure out what a tricky word means! One of the ways we can do that is to get a picture in your mind of what's going on in that part of the story and to think about what would make sense."

Contents

Narrative Nonfiction

PART TWO

IN THIS SESSION,

you will teach students that first identifying what type of structure a text follows helps readers draw on appropriate skills.

Identifying Nonfiction Text Structures and Adjusting Reading

ears ago, when the idea that writing could be taught as a process first took the country by firestorm, the message was that whether a writer was working on a poem, an editorial, or an essay, the writer would still cycle through the same writing process, shifting between rehearsing, drafting, revising, and editing. Over the past decade or so, as those ideas have been refined, most of us have come to embrace the fact that although it is true that writers rehearse, draft, revise, and edit when working in all sorts of different genres, it is also true that writing a poem is very different than writing an editorial. Because the work a writer does is notably different based on the kind of text the person is writing, I encourage teachers to structure a year-long curriculum that channels youngsters to study and wrestle with the demands of various kinds of texts. Young people in today's writing workshops are growing up knowing that once a writer has determined the kind of text he or she is writing, then the writer has a path to follow.

You won't be surprised to hear that ideas on the teaching of reading have evolved along a similar trajectory. Many educators who believe that reading, like writing, can be taught as a process, emphasize that proficient readers use a set of skills and strategies whether they are reading poems, editorials, or novels. Although there is truth to this, as knowledge about reading processes accumulates, we are increasingly coming to embrace another truth—and that is that the structure of a text influences the way a person reads that text.

GETTING READY

- Bring charts from Unit 2 so they are on hand during the minilesson (such as "To Grow Ideas About Characters, I . . .").

- Bring a small pile of nonfiction texts—including at least one narrative and one expository or "all-about" text—to the meeting area. You'll flip through these in the teaching component of the minilesson, sorting them by text structure.

- Be sure children continue to bring Post-its and pens to the minilesson to use during the active involvement.

- Be ready to create a chart during the link titled "Narrative Nonfiction Readers Notice and Think About . . . ," which will thread through many upcoming sessions.

- Select a narrative nonfiction book that you will read aloud to your class during the active involvement. I've chosen *Secrets of the Mummies*. This text weaves through many minilessons in the unit, and therefore you may decide to use it as well. The text you choose should allow you to pay attention to character traits and its general story line.

We read differently when a text is structured as an expository text—organized to advance ideas, with information divided into compartments—and when a text is organized as a story. Nonfiction texts can be either—or both, combining both expository and narrative structures. Because readers read differently depending on whether we are reading expository or narrative texts, one of the earliest things a

> By helping children think of these nonfiction texts as stories and helping them use their knowledge of story structure to determine importance (and unimportance), you help them synthesize as they read.

nonfiction reader needs to do is to ask, "What sort of text is this?" and then adjust his or her reading accordingly.

Although it is important to teach youngsters to think about the structure of the text they are reading, in the end, this awareness needs to become almost subliminal, with readers adjusting their stance according to a text's structure without devoting a lot of conscious attention to this work. After all, reading, by definition, is all about attending to an evolving meaning and to one's thoughts about that meaning. An awareness of text structure, like an awareness of reading strategies, needs to eventually be internalized.

When the great reading guru, Marie Clay, visited our reading workshops, observing a dozen classrooms across several schools, I asked her for words of advice. She responded, saying, "First of all, these are stellar classrooms. But secondly, I'd worry a bit when teaching crosses a line and becomes too metacognitive. Kids need to *use* strategies and text characteristics, they don't need to *talk* about them."

Marie's advice—that advice and other advice she gave me over the years—has been absolutely essential in the development of the ideas these books contain. I weigh Clay's cautionary note before asking young readers to notice the structure of the texts they're reading. But I'm still convinced that a little attentiveness to structure can help readers synthesize broad stretches of texts and can help them determine importance when confronted with what is often an overabundance of information. And the good news is that by now, readers already know how to bring their consciousness of a text's structure to their reading. Today's session simply reminds them to draw on this ability to recognize the text structure of the nonfiction text they're about to read, and then the session proceeds to focus on narrative nonfiction, reminding children to bring all that they know about reading narrative texts to the narrative nonfiction texts they read.

To show children how to apply a story frame to narrative nonfiction texts, you will probably read aloud one such text. I recommend you select a fairly short, simple text so that in one day you can show readers that they can stand back from the expanse of a whole text and see the pieces working together as a story. Often, when kids read nonfiction, they read as if they're wearing blinders, taking in one specific page of a text at a time, not seeing how that one page links with the broader text. By helping children think of these nonfiction texts as stories and helping them use their knowledge of story structure to determine importance (and unimportance), you help them synthesize as they read.

As you look over nonfiction texts to select your read-aloud, you'll find that you probably have a small cluster of spectacularly beautiful literary nonfiction texts on your shelves. Perhaps you have *14 Cows for America* by Carmen Agra Deedy, *When Marian Sang* by Pam Muñoz Ryan, or

Listen to the Wind by Greg Mortenson. You will probably be tempted to read a book such as those. We were. And we have read both these books to almost every group of children with whom we work—but not on this day, in this session. We made the decision instead to read one of the DK Readers that many children had in their book baggies because we wanted to show readers that there is a story line even in books that look rather informational. We decided it would not be news to kids that our most literary picture books are stories and can be read with a story frame. But when reading other, more fact-laden, informational, narrative nonfiction books, the story line is not so obvious. We wanted to show children that they could find a story line even in these texts.

Your instruction today will be critically important because it stands a chance of helping children synthesize as they read narrative nonfiction. You show children a way in which they can focus on who (or sometimes what) this story is about; what that character is like; what he, she, or it wants; and what the character does to overcome obstacles—all things that children have learned to notice within the context of fiction books.

Expect that when children try to apply this session to their independent reading of narrative nonfiction, some of them will need coaching to keep their eyes on the traits, wants, obstacles, and so forth that their character encounters—especially when the character is not a person but a fennec fox or an oyster or the group of American colonists as a whole. Your children are probably accustomed to focusing on facts rather than story when reading books such as *A Day in the Life of a Lobster*, and you'll be suggesting that rather than gripping onto those facts, they will want to hold onto broader sweeps of text (such as what the character—in this case, the lobster—wants or needs, what causes problems for the character, and what the character does in response to those problems).

MINILESSON

Identifying Nonfiction Text Structures and Adjusting Reading

CONNECTION

Tell an anecdote about one time when you were doing something, and an expert pointed out that you weren't closely matching your technique to the problem.

"Readers, a few months ago, I went fishing for the first time in my life. I thought, 'Hmm . . . There's nothing to this. All I have to do is to stick this worm onto this hook, sink the line, and I'll catch me some supper!' Guess what? Anglers to the left and right of me were catching fish after fish and I got hardly a nibble. And this went on for a few hours until I became quite embarrassed! The fisherman next to me must have noticed because he leaned over and said, 'It's the hook.'

'What about the hook?' I asked him, irritated.

'This is a freshwater lake with small fish,' he told me. 'You'll need an Aberdeen hook to catch these fish." As he said this, he jerked the line out of the water to reveal yet another fish he'd caught.

"'Aberdeen hook?' I asked him. "You mean there are different types of hooks?' I guess my question must have sounded naïve and funny to him because he guffawed with laughter. And then he said, 'Aberdeen hooks, O'Shaughnessy hooks, Kahle hooks, circle hooks. There are dozens of different kinds of hooks. And unless you know which hook to use in which water for which specific fish, you'll keep sitting there till the moon turns blue, but you won't catch yourself any fish.'

"Readers, I changed the hook to fit the fish and made my first catch. And then another. And suddenly, fishing began to make sense to me. I learned a very important lesson that day. We can use different hooks to catch different fish. We can't just cast any old hook into any old water and expect to soon have a bucket of fish. We have to first recognize not only the type of water but also the type of fish in that water, and *then* we choose the *appropriate* hook.

COACHING TIPS

There's nothing magical about these minilessons. You will absolutely replace them with your own, and yours will ring truer for you because they'll reflect your personality, and they'll speak directly to your children. My hope is that as you replace these sessions with your own variations of them, the sessions in these books will function as mentor texts for you. You'll find some of the minilessons will be ones you especially want to study, turning them inside out to ask, "How was this made?" The connection to this minilesson is one of my favorites. It was written by Hareem Khan, coauthor of Constructing Curriculum: Alternate Units of Study *in this series, who lives on the border between Afghanistan and Pakistan and is deeply involved in educating the children (and especially the girls) of her country. She'd written this connection for another purpose and contributed it to the cause, and you'll see that I sewed it seamlessly (I hope) into my minilesson. These aren't my words—and I have actually never done this sort of fishing—but I am totally okay about borrowing the metaphor from Hareem, and in fact, I am especially fond of it because it's imbued with her presence. On your wedding day, you are supposed to wear something borrowed (and something blue.) I love that idea because you carry the owner of that borrowed bit with you, as I carry Hareem with me in this minilesson (and you will sometimes carry me or Kathleen with you). You'll end up sewing your own anecdotes and quotes and tips into these minilessons, and your colleagues', too, and as you teach, you'll feel strengthened by the knowledge that your teaching is stronger because it borrows the wisdom of so many people.*

"You all know that this is the start to a new part of our unit on nonfiction reading—and yet here I am talking about *fishes* and *hooks!* But I've chosen my fishing story for a reason. Many readers sink into nonfiction texts without even thinking about the hook. They think, 'Hmm, it's just reading, anyway. All you have to do is move your eyes across the words on the page.' But we don't read stories the same way that we read a newspaper. We don't read car manual instructions the same way we read fairy tales. Not at all. Like anglers use different hooks for different fish, we readers, too, use different reading eyes for different text structures."

State your teaching point. Specifically, tell kids that readers recognize the type of text that is in front of us and we read accordingly. The way readers read narrative nonfiction texts is not unlike the way we read fiction.

"Just like we have to figure out whether it is big or small fish, freshwater or saltwater fish that we want to catch so that we can decide which hook to use, we have to figure out whether the text in front of us is a narrative or an expository text so we can decide which reading strategies to use. To be really great readers, we've got to be able to recognize text structures and let those structures help us know how to read. When we know we have *narrative* nonfiction in our hands, we know we can read it like narrative fiction. A story is a story is a story!"

TEACHING

Restate to children that it helps to categorize nonfiction into expository texts and true stories, so that we can adjust our reading accordingly.

"I have a big pile of nonfiction texts on my bedside table, and I'm pretty sure many of you have similar piles. We could look at the pile of nonfiction texts that any one of us has, here or at home, and we could divide the texts into two piles—piles that represent different kinds of texts. We might divide the texts into one pile for science books and one for history books. Then again, we could divide the pile into one pile for books and one pile for texts that aren't books. Or we could sort the stack into one pile of texts about living things and one dead things. Those are all possible ways to sort nonfiction books. Today I want to stress that there is one way to sort these books that will be especially important.

The Common Core Standards spotlight that it is important for students to be able to think about how texts are organized, using this awareness of text structures to help them understand how larger portions of a text relate to each other—and to the whole—and to help them vary their reading strategies accordingly.

Note that this teaching point is like a two-scoop ice cream cone. The minilesson requires readers to understand that readers vary our reading based on a text's structure, but the actual emphasis of the minilesson is on the last point—we read narrative nonfiction in a manner that is very like the way we read fiction.

When I'm leading a minilesson, I seize every possible opportunity to use gestures to convey meaning. So when I'm talking about the different ways that children could categorize their nonfiction books, I'll either list the first and then the second and then the third way on my fingers, or I'll act as if the heap of books is in front of me, and I'm shoving some books to my right (say, the books about science) and some to my left (the books about social studies). Gestures make a world of difference. And if you take courses in public speaking, you'll learn that large gestures are more helpful than the little ones you might make if your forearms were glued to the sides of your chest. Try lifting your arms up so there is actually air between them and your chest. In public speaking courses, that air is considered important. It's considered the "air of confidence."

"Listen up. Here's a tip. If you divide nonfiction texts into piles based on how those texts are put together, you'll end up with one pile of true stories (narrative nonfiction) and one pile of all-about texts (little courses on a topic). Readers read these kinds of nonfiction texts in very different ways. When readers know what kind of nonfiction book we have, that helps us decide how to read it."

Demonstrate how you separate books by text structure, doing so with a couple of books on hand. Then recruit readers to join you in sorting books by structure.

"Readers, let's take a moment and look through this small pile of books. Watch as I figure out which kind of nonfiction I've got—whether a text is narrative nonfiction (a true story), or whether it's an expository text." I flipped through a few books, making two piles. As I looked through them, I said, "Oh, this one doesn't have any section headings or chapters. It's more like a story. I'll put it in the narrative pile." Then I said, "Hmmm. This book has sections, and it is telling different things about sharks in each part. It is giving me information, lists of facts. It's an expository book. *[Fig. VIII-1]*

"Readers, did you see how sometimes you can look at a nonfiction book and just tell in a snap if it's a narrative book or all-about book? Well, sometimes it's harder to tell, and you might have to read a little bit to find out. Right now, I'm going to pass out some nonfiction books. I want you and the two or three readers sitting near you to examine the book that comes your way and ask yourself if it is a story (a narrative nonfiction) book or an expository (or all-about) book. If you've got a narrative book, send it back to this pile," I said gesturing to the pile of narrative texts I'd started making. "If yours is an all-about book, you'll put it here." I passed out half a dozen books, one for each cluster of children, and gave them a moment to decide which kind of book they had. "Okay, readers, please put your book in the pile where you think it belongs."

You'll want to decide on the term that you use to describe texts that are not narratives. These texts—imagine them as the ones with headings and subheadings—could be described as *expository*, as *all-about*, as *teaching texts*, as *informational texts*, or as a handful of other names. We decided against using the phrase *teaching texts* because the implication would have been that the other category, *true stories*, *does not teach*.

This part of the lesson is unusual because it recruits kids' involvement before I've done much teaching. It is also optional. Including it in the session made the session a bit longer than usual. If you include this work in your session, be sure it is speedy and streamlined, taking just two minutes. You'll be amazed at how some teachers elongate an activity like this and others accomplish it in a snap. Teach your children to distribute books and to get into and out of partnership conversations quickly.

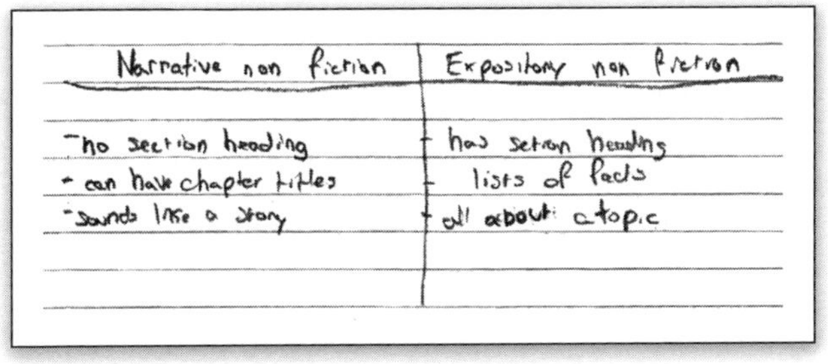

Narrative non fiction	Expository non fiction
- no section heading	- has setion heading
- can have chapter titles	- lists of facts
- sounds like a story	- all about a topic

Figure VIII-1
Children love to sort—baseball cards, stickers, and so on—so sorting and categorizing texts will come naturally to them.

Remind children that readers bring all we know about reading fiction to reading true stories. Specifically, show them that to read narrative nonfiction texts, we pay attention to the character's traits and hold onto the story line that is sometimes buried under facts.

"Remember, the important thing about determining whether a nonfiction text is mostly a true story or an all-about book is that knowing this helps us know how to read the text. This book, *Secrets of the Mummies*, definitely contains a couple of true stories in it. I'm going to read one of those aloud and show you how I read narrative nonfiction, paying attention to who the characters are, what their traits are, what they want, and what gets in the way of them getting what they want. Those are the same things we thought about when we were getting to know Rob and Sistine, remember?"

"You'll see that as I read this, there will be lots of facts, and I want you to notice that I do not try to memorize every fact. Instead, there is a story line buried a little bit under the facts, and it is almost like I reach for and then grab onto that story line and let it carry me fairly quickly through the whole text. So watch what I'm thinking about at the start of the story. Then you'll take over this thinking."

The Mummy's Curse

"I must find the lost tomb."

Howard Carter had been saying the same thing for years. Now it was 1922, the fifth year he had spent digging through sand and rocks in Egypt's Valley of the Kings.

I paused and looked up from the text, clearly thinking, not reading. "Wow. Howard Carter is persistent. Digging through rocks for five years, looking for a tomb."

Name what you have done that you hope children do on other days with other texts.

After a pause, in an aside, I said, "Notice that I am thinking about the main character—like we thought about Rob, in *The Tiger Rising*. Specifically, I'm thinking about what the main character is like, what his traits are. Notice, too, that I am reaching for precise words to capture what he is like: persistent." Then I resumed reading, backing up just half a sentence:

. . . it was 1922, the fifth year he had spent digging through sand and rocks in Egypt's Valley of the Kings. He was searching for a tomb that no grave robbers had ever found—the tomb of Tutankhamun's, the boy pharaoh.

Notice that I tuck in little reminders of the last unit here and there in this part. Children will have an easier time reading narrative nonfiction if they liken it to fiction, thinking about an animal's (or a plant's or a real person's or a group of people's) traits, desires, struggles, and so on.

It's essential to steer children to hold onto the main story line as they begin to read narrative nonfiction, rather than to get bogged down by the tiny, nifty little facts. Later, children will have a chance to notice and record and share facts (we even give this a name: fact dropping). For now, though, they need to learn how to read nonfiction quickly, with purpose, learning big ideas.

I have just demonstrated the fact that as a reader of nonfiction narratives, I name the traits of the main character (or main subject) just as I do when reading fiction. To be explicit, I make a little aside, pointing out to readers that I have done this.

Again I paused to think aloud. "Now I know what he wants—to find the tomb—and I'm wondering if grave robbers are going to pose an obstacle that could prevent him from getting what he wants or what other obstacle might he face." I paused for a brief moment, giving children a chance to reflect.

Recruit children to name what you have done that you hope children will do on other days with other texts.

Then I said, "Tell each other what I have done when reading this narrative nonfiction text that is similar to the work you do when reading fiction. You can refer to our charts of fiction reading if you want to do so. These (I referenced the chart) are ways of reading that you will be using as you read your own narrative nonfiction." I gave children a moment to share their ideas. *[Fig. VIII-2]*

ACTIVE INVOLVEMENT

Continue reading aloud the narrative nonfiction text, this time asking children to jot notes about what they notice about the character and his traits and struggles.

"So let's continue reading this, and from time to time, I'm going to pause and ask you to jot your thinking into your reading notebook. Before I read on, rev up your mind, get your expectations going. Use what you have already heard in 'The Mummy's Curse' and what you know about story structures to help you anticipate what will come next." I gave the children just a little pool of silence. As always, I joined them in silently thinking for a minute—this time, thinking about what was going to come next in the text. Then I read:

> He was searching for a tomb that no grave robbers had ever found—the tomb of Tutankhamun, the boy pharaoh.

> Carter scoffed when he was warned of the curse: "Death comes on wings to he who enters the tomb of a pharaoh."

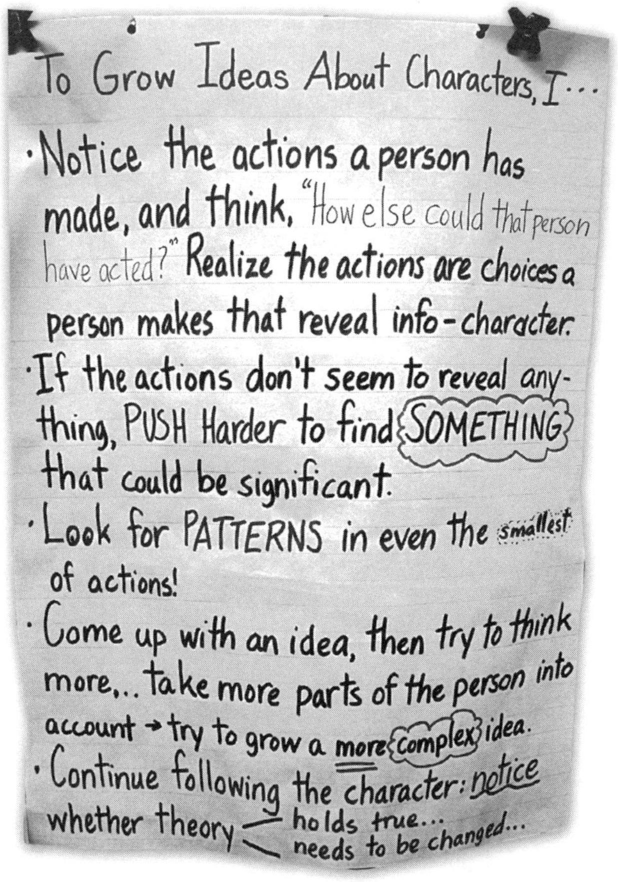

To Grow Ideas About Characters, I...

• Notice the actions a person has made, and think, "How else could that person have acted?" Realize the actions are choices a person makes that reveal info-character.

• If the actions don't seem to reveal anything, PUSH Harder to find {SOMETHING} that could be significant.

• Look for PATTERNS in even the smallest of actions!

• Come up with an idea, then try to think more... take more parts of the person into account → try to grow a more {complex} idea.

• Continue following the character: notice whether theory ⟨ holds true... needs to be changed...

Figure VIII-2
This is just one of the many charts from previous units that you'll reference.

I paused. "Stop and jot." Then, without any time for sharing, I read more. [Figs. VIII-3 and VIII-4]

> Each day, his men worked in the sweltering heat and dust. They seemed to be getting nowhere. Then one morning, as they dug in soft rubble, a shovel clanged.
>
> When Carter arrived, he was met by an excited hush. The men had found a stone step. Another 15 steps were quickly uncovered. Could this be Tutankhamun's tomb?
>
> The staircase led to a sealed door. Carter wanted to open it, but he had to wait. Lord Carnarvon, his patron, had paid for the years of work and wanted to be present at the opening.
>
> Today it would take only six hours to reach Egypt from Carnarvon's home in England, but at that time it took more than two weeks. When Carnavon finally arrived, he hurried to the tomb. Nervously, he fingered the strange symbols, called hieroglyphs, by the door. Then he and Carter opened the door and crept inside.
>
> Carter was the first to look. What he saw left him speechless. Later, he told people that he had seen "strange animals, statues, and gold—everywhere the glint of gold."
>
> When Carter arrived home that night, his servants were wailing and shouting.
>
> "What's wrong?" Carter demanded above the din.

Ask children to jot their thoughts, and then coach into this work, asking children to draw on their knowledge of how stories like this tend to go to help them understand how this one may go.

I lowered the book and again said, "Stop and jot. What are you thinking?"

They have heard only a very few sentences, and I am already suggesting they'll be brimful of insights and ready to jot. There are two reasons why I've paused here. First, I find that when I pause early on in the reading to ask kids to jot or talk, this can remind them that they need to listen actively. But also, I have already read the story, and I know that the fact that people believe anyone entering the tomb of a pharaoh will be cursed is central to the story, so I'm calling attention to that line. This portion of a mini-lesson is a time for providing support. Sometimes the children aren't even aware of our scaffolds.

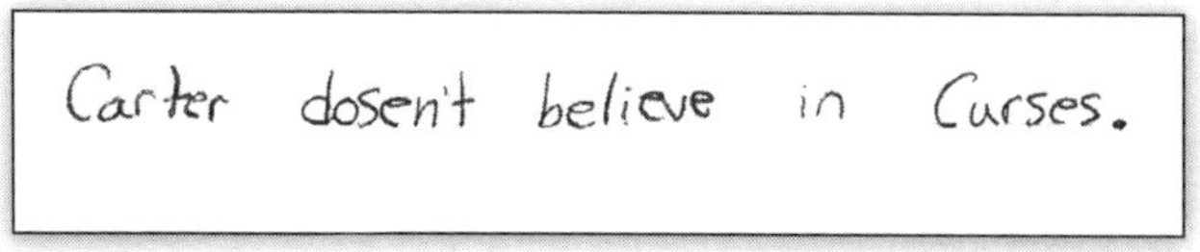

Carter dosen't believe in Curses.

Figure VIII-3
I asked readers to jot reflections because this will turn out to be important.

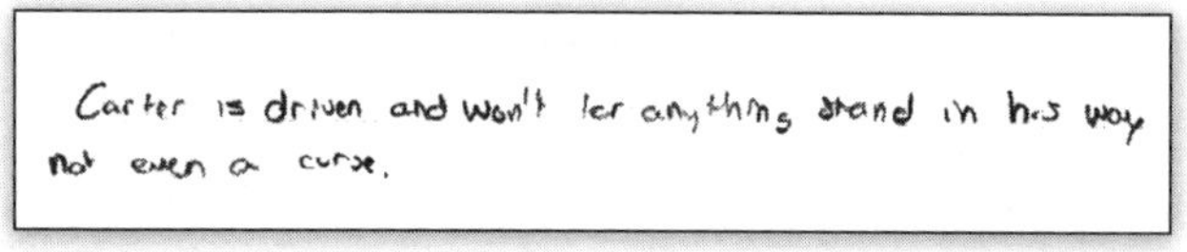

Carter is driven and won't let anything stand in his way not even a curse.

Figure VIII-4
This reader has grasped the central tension in the story.

After children started jotting, I voiced over, "I'm wondering if you are asking why the servants are wailing and how this part of the story will connect to other parts of the story?"

After another moment, I voiced over again, "As you jot, draw on what you know about stories and how they tend to go. If you think about a story as involving a character who wants something, encounters obstacles, then somehow gets past those obstacles, how might the servants and their wailing fit into that? If there are predictable parts to a story, what part of the story might the servants' waiting be? Knowing what you know about stories, what sort of thing will be apt to come next? Are you wondering how Carter's traits, motivations, and choices help shape this story? Keep jotting." *[Fig. VIII-5]*

Continue reading, again asking children to jot their thoughts, drawing on what they know about how stories tend to go.

I continued to read:

> "You have opened the tomb," wept a servant. "We are cursed!" He told Carter that a cobra had swallowed Carter's pet canary at the exact moment the tomb was opened. Cobras were a symbol of royalty in ancient Egypt. They were said to spit fire at a pharaoh's enemies.
>
> Carter was not worried. The next day he began to clear the first room of the tomb.
>
> More than a mile of cotton wadding was used to wrap up the items. Carter's team packed games, clothing, pottery, musical instruments, and statues. Most of these were sent to Cairo, Egypt's capital, by boat. The more valuable artifacts went on a train accompanied by armed guards.
>
> Finally the men were ready to unseal the third door. Slowly and carefully, Carter started chipping away the rocks and plaster. Then he stopped. Before him was a wall of solid gold! Carter was astonished. He knew this was the greatest Egyptian find ever.

"Stop and jot," I said once more. After children started jotting, I voiced over, "Remember what you know about stories. Do you think that at this time, this will become a happy ever after story? If so, what makes you think that? If not, what makes you think that?" *[Fig. VIII-6]*

You may wonder at the text we selected. You may think, "I can understand choosing to read aloud The Tiger Rising *and* Stone Fox, *but this book? Is it really the very best narrative nonfiction text you could find? And the truth is that Kathleen and I rewrote and retaught this unit multiple times, each time choosing different texts to read aloud. At one point, we read aloud a story about Jane Goodall's work with two chimpanzees, Flo and Flint. Another time, we read aloud narrative picture books—beautiful ones such as Adler's* A Picture Book of Amelia Earhart *and Kathryn Lasky's award-winning book,* Monarchs. *In the end, however, we decided that we wanted the text that we read aloud to mirror those that children tended to be reading, and we also wanted to be sure the texts we read aloud had some of the density of information in the raw that characterizes many of the books in this genre. The DK Readers, as a series, seemed to us to be a good place to start.*

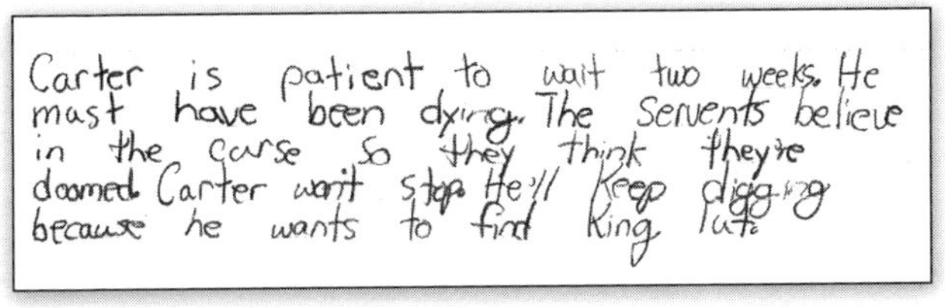
Carter is patient to wait two weeks. He must have been dying. The servents believe in the curse so they think they're doomed. Carter won't stop. He'll keep digging because he wants to find King Tut.

Figure VIII-5
This reader is much more sympathetic to Carter than to the servants!

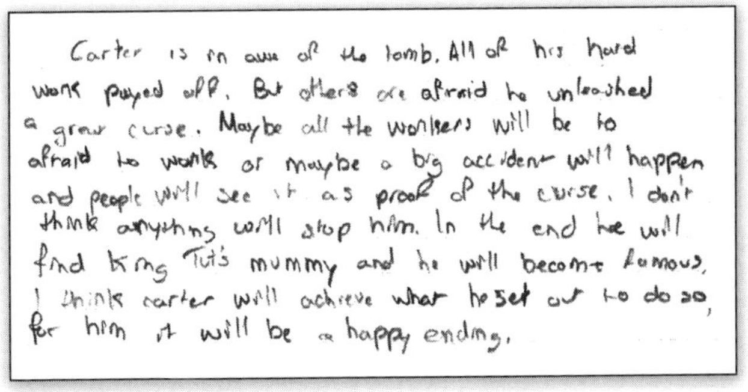
Carter is in awe of the tomb. All of his hard work payed off. But others are afraid he unleashed a great curse. Maybe all the workers will be to afraid to work or maybe a big accident will happen and people will see it as proof of the curse. I don't think anything will stop him. In the end he will find King Tut's mummy and he will become famous. I think carter will achieve what he set out to do so, for him it will be a happy ending.

Figure VIII-6
This reader is doing superb prediction work, speculating among different optons, drawing on what she knows from earlier in the text.

Channel children to turn and talk, using what they know about how stories tend to go to predict upcoming sections of the read-aloud.

After children had another moment to jot, I said, "Turn and talk. Use what you know about how stories go to think together about what will probably happen next."

After children talked for a bit, I said, "Some of you are noticing the title of the story and using that to help you think about the text. That is smart work. Others of you are paying attention to little clues in the book that show what a person is like and using your sense of the people to imagine what they might do next."

"Let me read you the last part of the story."

> But before anyone could investigate further, disaster struck. It began when Carter's patron, Lord Carnarvon, was bitten on the cheek by a mosquito. He accidentally cut open the bite while shaving. The bite soon became infected, and fever set in.
>
> A few days later, Carnarvon's family raced to his bedside. He was very ill. Then, early one morning, it was all over. Lord Carnarvon died.
>
> At the very moment of his death, all the lights in Cairo went out. They stayed out for several hours, and no one could explain why. Back at Lord Carnarvon's home in England, Susie, his dog, pricked up her ears, howled once, then dropped dead.
>
> Other deaths followed. A French scientist who visited the tomb died after a fall. An X-ray specialist on his way to examine Tutankhamun's mummy died unexpectedly. Then a wealthy American died from a virus after visiting the tomb. Were these deaths all coincidences, or was the curse of the mummy to blame? No one knows for sure.

"Now, knowing more about how the story ends, do you see any clues you missed the first time, clues that could have helped you predict how this story would go?"

LINK

Remind readers that they need to notice text structure, varying their reading stance accordingly. Specifically, remind them of the expectations readers can bring to narrative nonfiction texts. Then send them off to read narrative nonfiction.

Teachers, this is an abridged version of the rest of the story.

You will notice, and your children may also, that the setting of this story is a time and place where science and technology do not reign supreme over the way life unfolds. The author takes pains to write that travel to Egypt is a work of weeks. There is as yet no technology to transport people quickly. Later, Carnarvon dies of a single mosquito bite. There is as yet no medicine to save him. In both cases, there is an absence of the enlightened technology we are accustomed to. Does this setting, where nonscientific forces hold sway, help set the stage for the horror of the curse? That is, it is always important for readers to think across elements of a story and, in this instance, across the setting and the plot.

Earlier readers inferred that Carter is, above all, determined and that no curse will turn him back from his quest; no apparent bad omens will halt him in his course. Teachers, you might also want to bring to the children's attention the fact that the author wrote that Carter "scoffed" at the ancient curse that threatened evil to those who would uncover the tomb. What tends to happen to characters who are scornful of ancient sayings or native wisdom? What tends to happen to characters who believe, through their hubris, that they are stronger than gods? As part of the discussion, you may want to remind readers of stories in which bad ends fall to the too proud character.

"So, readers, you see that just like a fisherman needs to think, 'What kind of fish am I hoping to catch?' and to choose a hook accordingly, readers also need to think, 'What kind of text am I reading?' and to vary our stance as a reader accordingly. When we know we will be reading a narrative nonfiction text, then the knowledge that the text is a story can help us discern what is and is not apt to be important. The elements that matter especially in a nonfiction story are those that also matter in fiction." I showed a list I'd made of these on chart paper. *[Fig. VIII-7]*

"So, readers, off you go. Today, as you read, practice bringing the lens of story to what you read. Finish what you were already reading, especially if you are almost done with it anyhow. Then choose a narrative nonfiction text. As you read, use Post-its to mark places where you learn about the characters, the setting, the obstacles and how the characters respond to them."

You will not find many sessions where I assign children specific reading work that I'd like them to accomplish, but today's session is an exception. My larger purpose for doing so lies in my intent to help readers see that reading narrative nonfiction isn't so different from reading fiction.

Narrative Nonfiction Readers Notice and Think About:

- The main character(s) in the true story — traits, struggles, changes, lessons
- The setting and how this time and place contributes to the story.
- The obstacles or conflicts or difficulties and the character's responses to them.

- The kind of story this seems to be, and what is typical of that kind of story.

Figure VIII-7
The last bullet on this list is actually one that will be illuminated in an upcoming minilesson. If you have a chart like this, you'll add the last bullet later.

CONFERRING AND SMALL-GROUP WORK

Help Children Bring Their Familiar Reading Strategies to Narrative Nonfiction

People have always learned through stories, and that is the focus of this new bend in the road. When we meet someone new, the person's statistics alone—the person's age, address, phone number, anniversary—don't tell us much about the person. What we want are the stories. How did you meet your husband? What made you become a teacher? When we hear someone else's story, we can put ourselves into that person's shoes for a while. We learn about that person's life, and we also *understand* what it is like to see the world through his or her eyes.

Even the word hi*story* emphasizes the importance of stories. We can memorize the facts of the Revolutionary War, but when we hear the story of Paul Revere taking his dangerous and insurgent message from back door to back door in the middle of the night, this makes us breathless in a way that helps us truly understand the event and some of the people who took part in it.

> ### MID-WORKSHOP TEACHING POINT
>
> #### Readers Recognize Significant Details
>
> "Readers, have you ever noticed that when you read a nonfiction book about a person, or about a bunch of people, a *ton* of facts come at you as you read? You read 'So and So had three brothers and two sisters. So and so was born in 1972 in Cleveland, Ohio. So and so went to Acorn Nursery School and Big Oak Elementary School.' And it is hard to hold onto all that stuff, isn't it? I don't know what to Post-it or what to record, because there are so many little facts flying at me as I read along, and who knows what's really important and what's not so important?
>
> "Well, if you feel the same way I do, I wanted to tell you about something that might help. The things that turn out to be really important in a story are not the things that are just quick facts that we pass by and leave behind as we read. The things that will be important to a life story are the things that affect not only the past and the present but also the future. Like how the tiger was important in Rob's life because it threaded through his life story and was meaningful in lots of ways, but the tube of ointment he put on his rash—that was just a quick thing that didn't really connect in deep ways to other parts of the story.
>
> "Here's the thing. When reading true stories about people and events that have mattered in history, usually even at the start of the book, you know something about why the person is
>
> *continued on next page*

tive nonfiction. Redirecting the actions of twenty-some students is no small feat. Your library will need restructuring for yet a second time within just a few weeks. As children read independently during this bend in the road of the unit, you'll want the baskets in your classroom to brim with true tales about accomplishments, with problem-solution narratives, with biography, with narrative accounts of animals, plants, or groups of people.

This new bend in the road will require effort, and I can promise that it will be worth it. First, the fact that you are reorganizing the library and redistributing books means that you will have another chance to spotlight the importance of reading "just-right" nonfiction books. Make an extra point to talk up high-interest and accessible nonfiction. Go for the books, too, not the handouts. It is tempting within this unit of study to rely on computer printouts and duplicated passages. Resist that temptation. It is hard to emphasize enough the importance of getting appealing books into your kids' hands, even if this requires that you visit your public library to check out armloads of books.

It is tempting, too, to think, "I don't have many narrative nonfiction books at the kids' levels, but oh well, if the child knows a lot about sports,

Getting Narrative Nonfiction into Your Kids' Hands

Even though you are mid-way through a unit of study, you'll want to shift the work that kids are actually doing so you channel them to read narra-

then he can read a challenging sports book." It is true that a reader's prior knowledge can give that child a leg up on a book that might otherwise be too difficult, but in general, if a child is reading level M/N fiction books, he or she will probably be reading either level M/N nonfiction books or easier ones. Nonfiction is generally considered more challenging than fiction.

You can double-check that a book is accessible for a child by asking, "Will you read me a bit of that?" Then listen to see if the child's fluency and intonation suggest the child understands the book. You can expect the child will encounter unfamiliar terms—the specialized vocabulary related to the subject—and you may want to allow for a little less accuracy than usual (say, 94%, not 96%). You'll want more than mere fluency, of course, but if the child's reading is robotic and lacks the intonation that suggests understanding, then even a tiny episode of reading aloud can serve as a quick way to ascertain that the text is too difficult for the reader.

It's always important for children to read with absorption. Early in the school year, when you had just launched your reading workshop, there were days when you stood back during reading time, scanning the room to see whose nose was in the book and who showed signs of disengagement. Back then, I encouraged you to look for children whose heads were like revolving fans during reading time and to take the time to check whether these readers were reading just-right books. You'll again want to look for signs of engagement and disengagement.

Time and again, we have noticed that during this nonfiction unit, a whole group of children will be reading books that are just plain too hard for them. This may be because the preponderance of photographs in the

---

MID-WORKSHOP TEACHING POINT

continued from previous page

famous or why the event is remembered. That knowledge allows you to sort of guess what the end of the story will say. If this is a book about Arthur Ashe, who is known for being a famous tennis player, then you can guess that toward the end of his life story it will tell about his success at—you guessed it!—tennis! So if you read in Chapter 1 that Arthur's uncle gave him his first tennis racket when Arthur was four years old—pow! That's important. On the other hand, if you read that Arthur liked eating waffles every Sunday morning at 8:30 am, let it go. Unless that detail is written in a way to suggest otherwise, it is probably not so crucial.

"Before you read any farther in your narrative nonfiction text, I want you and your partner to talk about why this person or this event is important enough to have been written about in a book. Talk about the things that you already know about the person or event that make it special enough to have been written about. And then you can review the pages you have already read and see if you can locate passages that look as if they might connect to that important part. If so, pay attention.

"Partners, turn and talk about the person or event in your story. What's the big thing about the person, the event? How does knowing that help you determine what's really important in the story?"

---

book may have led you or someone else to overlook the density of the prose and to mis-level the book. Be cautious as you level your nonfiction books because the large colorful photographs can sometimes lure you into thinking a book is easier than it is! Children also may be holding books that are too hard for them because they haven't read a lot of nonfiction, and therefore their levels of just-right text when reading nonfiction may be different than when reading fiction. Whatever the explanation, it is absolutely crucial that you help children monitor for sense and help them notice their lack of fluency, so the reader learns to say, "This is a bit hard for me" and to shift into a just-right book. They need to devour vast amounts of high-interest, high-success nonfiction reading. If the topics are high-interest ones, you'll find that your readers have no qualms whatsoever about reading "easy" books on a topic, and of course, it makes sense to start with easier ones on a particular subject and to read up the ladder of difficulty on that subject.

As you circle among your readers and the baskets of books, you'll want to give book introductions to the books that you believe will be especially well suited to readers. Do this especially for children who seem to have some trouble engaging with texts. Even if you don't know a book, you can gush over it. "Oh, this looks like a great one, doesn't it?" you can say, and then read aloud a bit of the back cover, an opening passage, a few of the subheads or photo captions. "I bet this book will help you learn. . . ."

As children settle into their new books, encourage them to continue tracking their reading in logs just as they did earlier in this unit and for their fiction books in the character unit, pushing themselves to read long and strong. You might say, "Readers, nonfiction books often take more concentration than fiction, and it's easy to slow down as we read about new subjects. Aim for stamina, pushing yourselves to read further in your books, holding onto new information as you do so." *[Fig. VIII-8]*

Vary Your Conferring So Now You Support Narrative Reading

During this bend in the unit, because your children will be reading narratives, it helps if you confer with your readers just as if they were reading fiction. For example, you can anticipate that as you confer with readers, you will be apt to help many of them grow theories about characters, and you'll help still others envision and predict. When I pulled my chair up next to Kadija, I saw that she was reading a book about Sacagawea "What are you working on?" I asked her.

"Well, I was doing lots of envisioning in my fiction, so I'm trying it out in my nonfiction book, too."

"Yeah! It's totally terrific that you already know that the skills that make your fiction reading strong will also make your nonfiction reading strong! Can you talk me through how you are going about envisioning in a book like this? What kinds of things are you picturing?"

She thought for a moment and then said, "Well, in this part, Sacagawea is in the river. She's really struggling 'cuz the water is coming up—you know, rising? She has a baby on her back. So it's really heavy."

"Wow, yeah. I can see that, too. When you were describing it, you even kind of bent your shoulders, like you were feeling the weight of that heavy baby and feeling how hard it must have been to carry him. You're right that you are reading like a fiction reader, making a movie in your mind. Does that scene make you think something about what kind of character Sacagawea is? What are you learning about her?"

Kadija answered, "I think she's courageous, trying that by herself."

"Hmm . . . I see exactly what you mean. Do you think that there are other places in the book that support your idea that Sacagawea is courageous? If there are, this could become part of your theory about her."

"Oh, definitely!" Kadija started flipping quickly back through the book. "Here, on this page, she was really sick, and she had a bad fever, and she tried to travel anyhow. The whole expedition had to stop and wait for her to get better. I bet she was scared and nervous and thought she would die. You expect floods or whatnot to stop the trip, but sometimes the real dangers are things like sickness."

Figure VIII-8
Because readers often slow down when reading nonfiction texts, this is a time to spotlight their logs.

Not only had Kadija found evidence to support her theory that Sacagawea was courageous, she had also grown bigger ideas, including the realization that Sacagawea's illness stopped Lewis and Clark's expedition—and affected history. I named what she was doing. "Just like in fiction books, in narrative nonfiction books, the characters' actions have consequences. In fiction books, we pay attention to the ways that different characters react to one event, and you are doing the same work in your Sacagawea book. You are making me realize that in nonfiction books, character's actions can have an especially big impact. Sacagawea's sickness changed history. You are so smart to realize that nonfiction readers can also ask the question, 'How did this person's personality and actions make a difference to the people around her, and even to history?'" I left Kadija to jot her idea on a Post-it.

When our teaching transcends even the genre in which children are reading, it gives them more opportunities to practice and develop their reading skills. For example, as I pulled my chair close to Jane, I found her absorbed in the Young Reader's edition of Greg Mortenson's *Three Cups of Tea*. "I've read this book. I was so inspired by it!" I couldn't resist telling Jane head-on. "How's your reading of it coming along?"

"I'm noticing a pattern," Jane surprised me by saying. "This character—Greg—he tries something, but something gets in his way. Then he tries something again, and something makes him fail again. Then he tries again. But I think he will prevail in the end."

Needless to say, I was suitably impressed. Jane had a sound grasp on story structure, noted this book's recurring pattern, and used this knowledge to anticipate the story. At moments such as these in our conferring, we might just congratulate the reader on doing great and move on. But we owe it to our best readers not merely to marvel and gush but to teach them strategies that might take them even further. "It sounds to me like you have a theory about your character—about the kind of person he is," I prodded her.

"Well, he's determined," Jane conceded. "And he's not like other people. He's different, like he lived in his car for a month." I nodded, suspecting that a second or two of quiet would elicit even bigger thoughts. In conferences with strong readers who seem truly engaged with their books, I allow ample space before beginning with my teaching, knowing that merely playing the avid listener at a point when the reading is ripe will often elicit thoughts deeper than the kinds that bubble immediately to the surface. In this case I was rewarded for my patience. "He realizes that he can't carry all this stuff, and he's mad at himself for not planning ahead. Like he doesn't blame others or give up. He just moves on past the problem and gets his hopes up again."

"You're reading your character well." I nodded approval. "I'm hearing a lot of words in what you just said that give me a sense for who Greg is. You've said the words 'determined, doesn't blame others, moves on, gets hopes high again.'

"May I teach you one thing, though? You're nowhere near the middle of your book even, and it sounds like this guy's perfect already. It's like I'm hearing Greg has, at the start of the story, qualities that typical characters might learn to acquire by the *end* of their stories. Maybe the question that I'd ask as I read is, 'How will Greg, who seems so focused and determined already, grow *further*?'"

I knew that in the fiction books that Jane had been reading thus far, the protagonists were children (Rob, Sistine, Willy) who began unsure and gained strength through the book to learn fairly predictable life lessons about courage or relationships. I wanted to alert her, therefore, that the biographies and achievement stories in this bend would chart the growth processes of exceptional protagonists whose claim to fame was often extraordinary heroism. "Unlike much of fiction, which is about relationships or personal growth in everyday situations, the real people about whom books are written are often heroic. They've often achieved big things or historical things. Many have exceptional qualities to start with. That is all the more reason to note a change or growth, and to pay attention to the *new* things they learn along the way because these lessons will not be typical." Hoping that I had alerted Jane to the fact that Mortenson's story might be about *more* than perseverance and determination and setting her up to note even bigger—possibly historical—lessons from his story, I moved on, confident that Jane could rise to the task.

TEACHING SHARE

Readers Retell Narrative Nonfiction in the Same Ways We Retell Fiction

Remind students that they can retell narrative nonfiction in the same way they retell fictional stories.

"Readers, can I stop you?" Once I had their attention, I said, "So, readers, today you all read narrative nonfiction. You all read true stories. You'll remember that when we read fictional stories earlier this year, we learned that it can help to pause from time to time to retell those stories and that one way to do this is to sort of retell from the start, taking large steps through the sequence of events, synthesizing the elements of story as we go—the characters' traits and motivations, the problems and such." I gestured to an old retelling chart, running my hand down the items for a moment. "Right now, decide which partner has read further into your narrative nonfiction book, and whoever has read more of the book, will you story-tell your book?"

If necessary, remind your students to make the texts they are retelling sound like stories.

As the students got going, I walked around the room listening in on their retellings for a couple of minutes. Then I intervened. "Readers, I'm glad your retellings are mentioning these items on the chart. But many of your renditions of your texts don't make the texts sound like stories. Instead, you are talking like this: '*My character is* this scientist named Carter, and *his trait is. . . . What he wants is. . . .*' Try retelling your narrative nonfiction like a story, bit by bit, giving little details to show the important parts about the characters and the setting and the struggles. Right now! Make it sound like a gripping story, not like answers to a ditto sheet of questions."

COACHING TIPS

If your readers struggle a bit and need more support, you could remind them of the ways that they learned to retell their stories in the first unit: by taking big steps across a story or by reaching back to important parts of the story. In this instance, you could simply remind readers of the two strategies for retelling and ask them to do this work in a way that has the ring of story.

The Work that Can Inform—and Transform—Teaching Narrative Nonfiction

The second bend in the road of this unit will focus on narrative nonfiction reading. As you proceed, you'll want to see the extent to which your students access their prior work on reading narratives (stories) and use it within this new context. That is, this bend in the road of your unit will give you wonderful opportunities to assess and support transference. Everything that children learned during the earlier work on narrative reading will be applicable to the biographies and other narrative nonfiction texts that they are now reading, but these new kinds of texts will also be different enough from fictional chapter books that it'll take a leap of creativity and initiative for your young readers to apply their earlier learning in this new context.

Assess To See Whether Children Use Literary Lingo from Their Fiction Reading Within the Context of Narrative Nonfiction Reading

In the context of the fiction work they did earlier in the year, your children probably used a handful of literary terms when talking about their texts. They probably referred to the narrator, the protagonist, the setting, and the character's traits, for example. Many of these terms are equally apt for use in describing narrative nonfiction, and noticing whether your children use this terminology when discussing nonfiction will reveal not only the extent to which your earlier teaching is "sticking" but also the connections that students are making between the two types of texts. Some of those terms will not, in fact, transfer perfectly into narrative nonfiction reading, but even if you need to point out to a student that the main character in a biography is referred to as the subject, not the protagonist, you'll want to celebrate that that reader made the effort to transfer knowledge from one domain to another.

Assess to See Whether Children Bring the Scaffolds that Helped Them Read Fictional Stories into Their Work with Nonfiction Stories

At the start of this new bend in the road, you'll want to tell your youngsters that when reading narrative nonfiction, it helps to pay attention to the elements of story that they see in these books, and then you'll want to notice the extent to which they tap into all they learned earlier about how stories go. For example, you probably taught them to look over a story before they start reading it, thinking, "Who does this seem to be about?" and "What can I glean about how this story goes, just from looking it over?" As you begin work with these new types of texts, notice if your students are carefully reading blurbs on the backs of books. Are they paging through, glancing at chapter titles and pictures? Noting whether or not they are or are not doing these things will help you get a sense of how you might dive in to this work!

Your readers may have developed some habits (and habits of mind) that supported their fiction reading early on. How wonderful it will be to see those things transferring into narrative nonfiction reading. If some of your readers used to keep an index card in front of them, for example, with the words *traits*, *motivations*, *problems*, *changes*, and *lessons* on it, you'll want to take note of whether those readers return to those old scaffolds and dust them off for this new occasion. If some of them used to lean on the prompt "Somebody (who?) . . . wanted (what?) . . . but (what was the conflict?) . . . so (how was the conflict tackled?) . . ." to help them retell a structured summary of the stories they read, will they think to use that same scaffold now when they are reading narrative nonfiction texts?

Watch, too, to see if readers independently initiate the work of rereading their Post-its about a character to sort these into categories. (Remember the lessons you taught about sorting the drawer in your kitchen into winter clothes, office supplies, and other categories?) What a great thing it will be if a child who has been reading Jane Goodall's

The Chimpanzee Family Book pauses in her reading to look back over her jottings about Goodall and begins to sort the ideas about her into piles, just as you taught the class to do with their thoughts about Rob and Sistine in *The Tiger Rising*. This reader might invent the theory "Jane Goodall does things with chimps that most people do with their friends and families—is this partly because she doesn't have many friends or family members of her own?" If a reader invents a theory such as this about the subject of a biography, then you'll want to see whether the reader then reads on with this theory in hand, taking in the upcoming text through the lens of the theory and altering it accordingly.

If you see evidence that readers are applying what they learned earlier in the year to this new work with nonfiction narratives, then you'll definitely want to celebrate this—and you'll want to invite others to do likewise. The important thing to remember is that if your students don't draw on what they learned a month ago while working in the same classroom, with the same classmates, the same teacher, and the same general expectations, then the chances are good that they won't draw on those lessons a year from now when they are no longer in your class! And if you realize that that's the case, don't despair. You have an extraordinary opportunity to rectify this situation. You are not only assessing for transfer, but also teaching for it, which needs to be an important priority.

Assess Children's Use of Reading Strategies, Recruiting Them to Research Themselves

You needn't simply *watch* for the moment when a child reveals whether or not he is transferring strategies learned in previous units into this new unit. You can directly chase after evidence. For example, you can sit beside a child who is about to read a narrative text and say, "Hmm . . . So the first thing I think about when I am about to read a nonfiction text is that I ask myself whether the text is a story or a teaching text—'cause I read those two differently. Would you say that this text you are about to read is a story, or would you call it a teaching text, an expository text?" The child will point out that it is a story. (For this portion of the unit, you'll be channeling narrative nonfiction their way, so the question was really only meant to underscore the presence of that text structure.) Then, once the child has confirmed it is a story, you could say, "Oh, so this is a story. Okay. Right now, get yourself ready to read it, and think aloud as you do this, saying aloud whatever you think as you get ready and start to read."

If the reader doesn't in any way reveal that she's drawing on prior lessons about orientating oneself before reading a story, you probably want to nudge and push a bit before coming to any conclusions. There is always a chance that she is just not articulating her thinking for you. So if the reader is reading away, not revealing that she's growing theories about the main subject, you might start with a general question such as "Can I stop you? What sorts of work are you doing at this point, as a reader?" You might extend your question. "As you get to meet these people, what sort of thinking are you doing? What are you noticing?" You might be angling to learn whether the child is noting that the actions a character makes show something about the kind of person the character is. Does the child pause to realize the character could have acted differently and that this action is probably a window to the character's traits?

There are other ways to learn whether the child is drawing on what she learned during the narrative unit. You might, for example, ask the reader to tell you how she thinks the text might unfold. Of course, an informed reader of biographies is not going to rely only on story structure to produce an answer, but it is probably the case that if this is a book about a person who becomes famous for playing the piano, in the book's first few pages we'll learn the subject's earliest character traits. Was she very musical as a child? What about her perseverance? Almost any character who ends up becoming the subject of a biography will be someone who showed, at a young age, that winning combination of perseverance, industry, and dedication. Presumably, most of us can predict that a biography of that great piano player will not only show the character's traits but will also show ways that she struggled. Was her mother insistent on her becoming a doctor, not a musician? Did she suffer from stage fright? All of us have difficulties on the path to success, and the story of our achievements usually includes the story of those struggles and of our ways of resolving those struggles. Was money for lessons scarce? How did she overcome those difficulties? And in the end, once the person achieved success, did she come to new realizations? New insights? Did she teach lessons the rest of us can learn from?

You could be more specific. You could give the child a short fictional text to read and then ask, as she starts to read it, how her reading is similar to and different from her ways of reading nonfiction narrative.

You could ask a partnership of readers to look between the sorts of Post-its they've been making as they read nonfiction stories and those they made earlier in the year when reading a fiction story, and to have a conversation comparing the ways the lens with which they read is similar and different then and now. Then you can sit back and watch. This invitation will, of course, disrupt the norms of what these children have been doing and thinking about, so it won't reveal what they were already doing before you interceded, but you'll definitely learn from what they say. You'll probably find that the children notice that they used to predict, envision, and grow theories about characters, and now they collect facts and raise questions. And you may find that they think this is par for the course, that nonfiction readers take note of the facts—period. Since you probably worked to move beyond this kind of fact-collecting in the first bend in the road of this unit, this belief may be tempered a bit, but it is still to be expected that most children will hang onto the idea that nonfiction is primarily for collecting facts. Narrative nonfiction will provide a wonderful format in which to challenge this belief.

A few children might volunteer to take a turn as researchers, interviewing others to learn from kids you might not otherwise get to. These mini-researchers can ask questions of each other such as "Can you tell me how you read this narrative nonfiction text differently because of all the work we did earlier with reading narratives?" Or "Here is a chart of the things we learned about reading fictional narratives. Can you tell me which of these things you are still doing now that you are reading nonfiction narratives and show me where you are doing that work?"

My point is that you can specifically set up little investigations like the ones I've described—or devise your own—to understand more about how children draw on their knowledge of fiction reading when they read narrative nonfiction texts.

Shifting from Assessing to Teaching: Begin by Inviting Children to Participate in a Shared Inquiry

If you want to help children transfer more of the reading strategies they used when reading fiction into their narrative nonfiction work, remember that first it will be important to share your research with your children. The fact that you have been studying kids' work with rapt attention, your mind racing a mile a minute, thinking, thinking, thinking all these new thoughts that you never had before—that's impor-

tant right there. If you've done this research without being especially transparent about it, gather your kids close and tell them what you've started to notice as you study their work. Your rapt interest in their thinking, in and of itself, will probably have more of an effect on your kids than any tightly organized minilesson in which you say, "Today I want to teach you that you can transfer all that you learned in the character unit into this work with narrative nonfiction."

Tell kids, "Over the last few days, I don't know if you have noticed, but I have been studying the writing and thinking and talking you do as you read these true stories. I've been trying to understand whether some of you are bringing the stuff that you learned from our character unit into this new unit. My mind has been going a mile a minute because it is *so* fascinating to notice ways your reading is and is not the same now that you are reading true stories, compared to when you were reading fiction. I'm wondering things like, when you read a biography and learn that Abe Lincoln stays up late, trying to read by wavering firelight, do you take that action as a window to the kind of person he is, and do you record your theory about him? Do you think about the work we did earlier on finding more precise words to capture a character? What are you apt to record about the people in these true stories? Do you record your theories about the characters when reding nonfiction, just as you did when you read fiction, or do you record different sorts of things entirely when reading nonfiction?

"I'm telling you this because I'm getting the idea—it's a wild one, but still—I'm getting the idea that maybe you could join me in researching this. You know how you study your volume of reading and how much reading you do at home versus at school and stuff like that? Well, maybe you could study the ways you bring the strategies you learned in fiction reading into your narrative nonfiction reading! And maybe we could even deliberately try to change this—to bring more skills and strategies from one kind of book to the other—and continue researching. I have the feeling we could invent ideas that we might teach to all the other classes across the grade, 'cause I don't think many people have ever researched this. Would you be game?"

I think you'll find there is a thin line between research and teaching—and that what you pay attention to, you support. So what starts as research will end as teaching—teaching tailored closely to the specific needs of your specific students.

Reading Nonfiction Narratives as Stories with Main Characters

IN THIS SESSION,

you will teach students that readers use what we know about understanding fictional characters when we are reading narrative nonfiction.

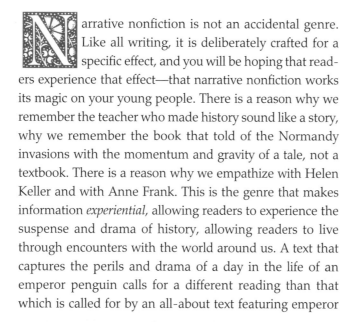

arrative nonfiction is not an accidental genre. Like all writing, it is deliberately crafted for a specific effect, and you will be hoping that readers experience that effect—that narrative nonfiction works its magic on your young people. There is a reason why we remember the teacher who made history sound like a story, why we remember the book that told of the Normandy invasions with the momentum and gravity of a tale, not a textbook. There is a reason why we empathize with Helen Keller and with Anne Frank. This is the genre that makes information *experiential*, allowing readers to experience the suspense and drama of history, allowing readers to live through encounters with the world around us. A text that captures the perils and drama of a day in the life of an emperor penguin calls for a different reading than that which is called for by an all-about text featuring emperor penguins. Narrative and expository texts are written differently, and they call for us and for students to use somewhat different strategies.

It's for all these reasons that readers benefit from knowing whether the nonfiction text we are approaching is narrative or expository: forewarned is forearmed. This knowledge allows readers to reach for the appropriate repertoire of ways to rev up our minds before reading. Just as an avid fisherman knows the precisely right hook to use when fishing in a particular bay of a specific lake, readers work in similar ways, only our tools are mostly invisible.

Part of the challenge, then, during this bend in the road of the unit, will be to help children understand that strategies they learned during earlier work with fiction texts can now be drawn from the repertoire and used again with nonfiction texts that are narratives. During the preceding session, you

GETTING READY

- Prepare to read *The Cactus Hotel* or another narrative nonfiction book that features an animal, plant, or group of people as a main character, as opposed to a single human.

- Prepare to unveil a new chart you've created: "Identifying and Reading Narrative Nonfiction" for use in the teaching and active involvement sections.

- Create a chart that lists the words "Someone . . . Wanted . . . But . . . So. . . ." Be sure to leave large spaces between these words.

- For the mid-workshop teaching point, each child will need a copy of the "Nonfiction Readers Read with Power Checklist." You can find a reproducible version of it on the *Resources for Teaching Reading* CD-ROM.

will have helped children learn to look over a text and determine whether it is a narrative or an expository text, and then, after finding it to be narrative, you will have helped them read it as a narrative. As kids lean into nonfiction bins and peer at books in an attempt to differentiate between narrative and expository texts, you'll see a few furrowed brows. Not every text advertises its text structure clearly!

> *Narrative nonfiction makes information experiential, allowing readers to live through the suspense and drama of history, and to live through encounters with the world around us.*

From their experience of stories thus far, children might have a set image of narratives as containing a protagonist—a character who has a motivation, pursues a goal, and undergoes a struggle to achieve it. Their classification of a story versus a nonstory might simply be based on the presence or absence of this easily identifiable protagonist. And children may not think that animals or plants (who are apt to play lead roles in nonfiction texts) can be main characters. Of course, many fiction stories feature animal-heroes, but those protagonists have often been personified to an extent where they appear to have human thoughts and traits. (Black Beauty, for example, may not wear a coat and pants like Frog and Toad, but Sewell granted her a human voice. Beverly Cleary doesn't give Socks a distinct voice, but she does convey the cat's thinking often enough that she grants the animal a human range of emotions.) The tame, understandable animals of fiction *feel* like characters in a way that animals in nonfiction might not.

You will, then, want to teach children that to read narrative nonfiction well, readers can think of a real-life plant, animal, object, or even a group of any of these as the main character. As long as the text contains a chronology—this and then that, and then, and next—the text has narrative at its core. Although the main character may be unlikely, once he, she, or it is identified, the reader can start uncovering motivations, obstacles, struggles, and possibly, a journey toward resolution or growth. In this session, you will teach readers that not finding a human or human-like main character should not deter them from reaching for a narrative nonfiction reading framework. This framework may well be even more useful and generative with unlikely main characters and uncommon story lines. This juxtaposition of framework with text gives us a new way to think about the text.

MINILESSON

Reading Nonfiction Narratives as Stories with Main Characters

CONNECTION

Recap yesterday's emphasis on the varying demands that different structures of texts place on readers.

"Readers, I think you know that people in a community are not all the same. If a town has a population of 18,000 people, it won't have 18,000 firemen. It will also have teachers, doctors, shopkeepers. . . ."

I signaled for others to add to the list, and children pitched in, "Policemen, electricians, coaches, builders. . . .

"And we've been learning that books, too, even nonfiction books, are not all the same. Some are expository, or all-about, texts, and we've learned to read these looking for the main ideas and the supports. Some are narrative texts, and we've learned to read these like stories."

A narrative may be an eye-witness account, a biography, an autobiography. . . . The Common Core Standards encourage us to help readers compare and contrast narratives that are written from the first-person perspective. You will teach this within the upcoming days.

Bring questions readers raised the preceding day to the fore, especially those revolving around texts that are sequential yet don't star the sort of character that readers have come to expect in stories.

"My hunch is that some of you have been puzzled as you try to decide if a text is narrative nonfiction or not. This morning I talked with Gabe, and he was really puzzled by *Cactus Hotel*. He was trying to figure out what kind of nonfiction it is, and he said, 'I think it's a true story—it's definitely true, but there isn't even a person here to be the main character!' Many of you would probably agree, and you probably have books like this in your bins too—books, maybe, that tell about one day in the life of a beaver or a glacier. You may have thought of those books as being all-about because there is not a person who is the main character."

Even though it's powerful to use a story about a real reader from your class, the most important thing is to show an example of a text that suits your purpose. Don't worry if none of your children actually has a text in his bin that fits the teaching point. Find the book you want to use and then you can say something like, "Class, I was separating books into two piles: narrative nonfiction and all-about books. When I came to this book, I almost put it in the all-about pile. I bet you can see why. This book isn't about a person, it's about a plant! But then, I realized. . . ." You can also, of course, make up a story about a reader from the class next door or a reader who was in your class last year.

Name your teaching point. Specifically, tell readers that stretching the conventional wisdom about what constitutes a main character can allow them to apply a narrative frame to texts that might otherwise not seem to fit that template.

"But today I want to teach you that you can use ways of reading narrative even if you don't have a traditional main character in your text. In fact, you can often get to some big ideas by stretching the definition of main character to apply to the main presence in the text. You can regard a meerkat colony or a Venus flytrap or a whole group of people, like the pilgrims, say, as the main character of your nonfiction narrative."

Teaching and Active Involvement

Ask children to listen as you read part of a narrative nonfiction text in which the main character is a plant or animal. Ask them to consider who the characters are, and what they want, struggle with, and do to overcome obstacles.

"First let's try it together. Listen to this book, and as you listen, ask, 'Is this a story? Might it be narrative nonfiction?' And if you decide it is narrative nonfiction, ask who it is about and what are some traits of that main character. What does the character want—what are its motivations? Its needs? What threats or struggles does it encounter?" As I spoke, I revealed a chart on which I'd written those questions:

Identifying and Reading Narrative Nonfiction

- Is this a story? Might it be narrative nonfiction?

- If it is narrative nonfiction, read asking:
  - Who is it about, and what are some traits of the main character?
  - What does the character want—what are its motivations? Its needs?
  - What dangers or struggles does it encounter?

"Listen, and then in a minute you'll have a chance to share your responses to these questions."

There will definitely be times when you want to elicit big ideas from children, and in those instances, you might merge your active involvement and teaching sections of the minilesson. As you read this section of the minilesson, you'll see that I recruit children to find the narrative structure in this book, and then I teach them how to retell the book in a way that centers on that narrative structure. If I was to divide this minilesson into teaching and active involvement sections, the work would go from teaching to active involvement, then back to teaching and back to active involvement.

You'll notice that Kathleen and I use synonyms to expand children's understandings of key terms. In this instance, we make those words inclusive enough that they will pertain to nonfiction as well as to fiction. It is certainly a stretch to say that a cactus has wants, or motivations, but less of a stretch to say that a cactus has needs. Similarly, if I say that cacti struggle with problems, this may be personifying them in a way that is not scientific, but it is not personifying a cactus to say it faces threats to its existence or dangers.

Cactus Hotel

On a hot, dry day in the desert, a bright-red fruit falls from a tall saguaro cactus. *Plop*. It splits apart on the sandy floor. Two thousand black seeds glisten in the sunlight.

When the air cools in the evening, an old pack rat comes out and eats the juicy fruit. Then he skitters across the sand. A seed left clinging to his whiskers falls off under a *paloverde* tree.

It is a good place for the seed to drop. A spotted ground squirrel looking for something to eat does not see it. A house finch chirping high in the *paloverde* does not see it.

After many dry days, a heavy rain falls on the desert. Soon a young cactus sprouts up from the ground.

Slowly, slowly the seedling grows. The *paloverde* protects it from the hot summer sun and cold winter nights. After ten years the cactus is only four inches high. It is just big enough for desert ants to climb its spiny sides.

Set children up to talk with each other about the story elements found in the narrative nonfiction text.

At that point, I paused and said to the children, "Like many of your books, this does not at first seem to be a story—there is not even a person as the main character—but talk about whether, in fact, the book *is* a story, and then talk about how you can use what you know about stories to retell what you have heard so far, zipping all the elements together."

I listened in as partners talked.

Sam seemed uncharacteristically stumped by the task. "It's hard to say what it (the cactus) wants, but it wants to have a life."

The Cactus Hotel is available in a big book (Henry Holt and Co. BYR Paperbacks, 2007), and you may decide to read that version. It is a favorite for us. Alternatively, if you can do so, you might give the children a typed copy of the text, because it's asking a lot of them to mentally hold onto a nonfiction text after they've heard it just one time. You could also select a different narrative nonfiction text, though you will again want one that doesn't fit tidily into kids' impressions of narrative texts.

Notice that I read just the first few pages of the book.

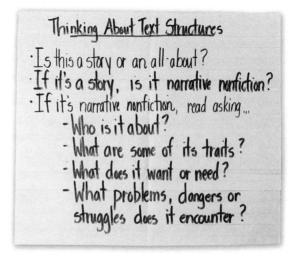

Thinking About Text Structures
- Is this a story or an all-about?
- If it's a story, is it narrative nonfiction?
- If it's narrative nonfiction, read asking...
  - Who is it about?
  - What are some of its traits?
  - What does it want or need?
  - What problems, dangers or struggles does it encounter?

Notice that it's helpful for a chart to have a title that delineates when a reader might use this resource. It's also helpful if charts convey dominant versus subordinate ideas, as this one does.

Aly responded, tipping her head thoughtfully, "Well, the cactus, the cactus, it's struggling with the rat who wants to eat it when it's still a seed. A lot of the seeds don't get roots and grow."

Sam grabbed hold of his partner's idea. "Yes, it's a hard life for a cactus, and it could die." I gave this partnership a thumbs up and moved on to another.

Fallon said to her partner, Josh, "The main character lives in the desert, and it is really sunny, and so it needs shade. It takes a long time to grow!"

Josh piped in, "The cactus is a plant, and the plant is an outdoor plant that lives in a hot, dry place. It wants and needs water and stuff from the earth to grow. It struggles to get the, the, nutrients because it doesn't rain a lot in the desert, so it grows slowly." I noted that these two were expressing their ideas with detail and specificity. Fallon, in particular, had improved in this regard. Josh was a good mentor.

Show children how to produce a synthesis of a narrative text by leaning on the "Somebody . . . wanted . . . but . . . so . . ." scaffold.

"Readers, eyes and ears on me. I think we agree. This is narrative nonfiction, and the main character is not a person but a cactus—a Saguaro cactus! Many of you are talking about what the cactus seems to need. Others of you are talking about what gets in its way, about what challenges its survival. I want to teach you another way you can talk about this."

A reading researcher named Kylene Beers says that one way to retell a narrative well is to use the structure of "Somebody . . . wanted . . . but . . . so . . .": [Fig. IX-1]

Model using the formula of "Somebody . . . wanted . . . but . . . so . . ." to retell a previous read-aloud. Then ask children to use the same structure to retell the book you just read aloud to them.

"So I could retell the story of 'The Mummy's Curse' like this," I said. I pointed to each of the key words of the formula as I spoke. "*Somebody*, specifically, Howard Carter, an archeologist, *wanted* the treasures in the ancient tomb of Tutankhamen, the boy pharaoh, *but* people told him that if he were to open the tomb, he'd be cursed, *so* when he scoffed at their worries and opened the tomb anyway, his canary was eaten and his patron suffered an infection and died.

Figure IX-1
It's so glorious when a teacher has artistic talent and uses it to makes charts like this one!

As I told this, I pointed to the large words "Somebody . . . Wanted . . . But . . . So . . ." on the chart. When reading these words, one after another, be sure that you leave spaces in a way that communicates that the spaces will need to be filled with words based on the children's thinking about their texts, and be sure you say the word so in a way that suggests the upcoming section will crystallize the main character's response to the struggle.

"Can you try retelling the *Cactus Hotel*, as far as we've read in it, using the formula 'Somebody . . . wanted . . . but . . . so . . . '? We haven't finished reading yet, so your ideas will almost certainly change as we keep reading, but still it's helpful to keep the story in mind, even when we aren't finished. Turn and retell the story so far to your partner, all in one smooth retelling." [Fig. IX-2]

LINK

Recap what you have taught about finding and using story elements to better understand a nonfiction narrative starring a plant or an animal.

"So readers, we've learned today that even though you might not consider a cactus or a rocket or even a building a true character, it can be helpful to adopt a story frame and to let the actors in the nonfiction true story assume the role of protagonist in your mind. The cactus in the *Cactus Hotel* did turn out to have certain traits, didn't it? The cactus is resilient, for example. And hospitable. And this cactus is a character who is struggling to live, to survive, in a hot, dry desert. What challenges does it face?"

A couple of children piped in, with excitement. "No water. And the rat comes and eats some of the seeds."

"I had never thought of plants quite this way before, had you?" I nodded and let other children pipe in as well. "So, today and from now on, when you think it might be productive, try thinking of your narrative nonfiction text as being about a character with traits, needs, and dangers, even if (especially if!) that main character is not a person.

"And now you also know another way to help you synthesize narrative nonfiction: the 'Somebody . . . wanted . . . but . . . so . . . ' formula. You can pause as you read, from time to time, and recall in your mind what you have read thus far, and see if it fits into the 'Somebody . . . wanted . . . but . . . so . . . ' string."

It may seem that you haven't read far enough into the text to determine a but *or* so. *However, if readers settle on the cactus wanting to survive, then each of the events in the story becomes a* but, *and each way the cactus does survive becomes a* so. *This can lead to a long series of "*but . . . so. . . .*"*

*When you finish reading the story on another day, you may decide to ask children to extrapolate one "*but . . . so . . . *" It might go something like "*but the cactus is eaten and used by many on the food chain, so it has adaptations that help it survive.*"*

*You could always streamline this minilesson by saving the introduction of the "*Somebody . . . wanted . . . but . . . so . . . *" formula for a later day.*

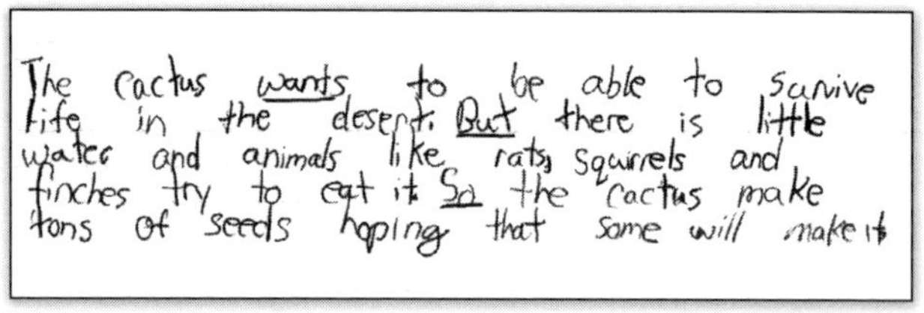

The cactus wants to be able to survive life in the desert. But there is little water and animals like rats, squirrels and finches try to eat it. So the cactus make tons of seeds hoping that some will make it.

Figure IX-2
You always have the option to call "stop and jot" instead of "turn and talk."

CONFERRING AND SMALL-GROUP WORK

Help Children Consider Their Nonfiction in a Narrative Frame

Usually I'd suggest that you approach the reading workshop anticipating that your conferences and small-group work will support not only that day's teaching point but also all the work you've been teaching all year. However, when you've just rallied kids to try a new kind of work, your teaching often needs to make sure that invitation has traction and that kids actually get aboard what you will have talked about and demonstrated in the minilesson. Today, then, you can anticipate that most of your conferences and your small groups will channel children to bring a narrative frame to the narrative nonfiction texts they are reading.

You Might Coach Some Readers to Notice Narratives Embedded in Expository Texts

Then again, you'll find some kids who are not doing what you've encouraged them to do, and you'll need to research the reasons for this and decide upon the best way to respond. For example, on this day, I could easily identify that the book that Kobe was scouring—a book with a robot on its cover—was an expository nonfiction rather than a narrative nonfiction text. Despite the prominently labeled bin of narrative nonfiction that sat center stage in the library area, he'd managed to pluck a book that caught his fancy from the *expository* bin that I'd placed aside at the start of this new portion of the unit. I sidled over to him and started a

casual conversation about the book, hoping to understand why he was reading this book rather than a narrative text.

"It's about *robots*," he was happy to tell me, eyes round and impressed. Kobe may not have been following my recent teaching points on text structures, but he had clearly found a topic with which he seemed to connect. Kobe sometimes seemed detached from books, so this was important. I let him share his excitement about demolition robots and about robot arms that weld metal parts together and about a robot insect before gently interrupting.

MID-WORKSHOP TEACHING POINT

Readers Draw on All We Know to Read Narrative Nonfiction

"All eyes up here, readers," I said and waited for their attention. "Today we talked about two specific things: stretching our idea of what makes a main character and using a little formula to help us retell narratives in a crisp, clean way. I hope you are remembering those things as you read, but more than that, I hope you are remembering *all* that we've talked about this unit. Right now, before we read on, I'm giving you a checklist I've made up based on all we have studied together. Read over the checklist and think, 'Which of these am I doing already? Which do I need to work on?' And then write yourself a self-assignment Post-it, leaving it on the front-right corner of your desk. Then as I come around, I'll help you work toward the goals you set for yourself (or I will question those goals). Then get back to reading."

continued on next page

"This does look like an amazing book!" I pulled it closer to me and turned it this way and that, flipping through the pages as I oohed and aahed over the headings and pictures of robots in space and in offices. "I'm wondering," I finally asked, "if this is expository or narrative nonfiction."

"Expository," said Kobe, the glimmer of guilt on his face suggesting that he wasn't as oblivious to what the rest of the class was reading as I had earlier imagined.

"How can you tell?" I asked, wanting to confirm that this knowledge stemmed from something other than his having read the label on the bin from which he had extracted the book.

"Well," he began with confidence, "It's got real pictures, not—um—drawings," he added, referring to photographs, as opposed to illustrations. "And bolds!" I asked for more reasons, and while Kobe rummaged through his mind for more characteristics of expository texts, I noted that he indeed did have some sense of text structures, albeit cosmetic ones. On his fingers, I helped him list some more features of expository text, moving him beyond noticing surface features such as pictures and bolds into briefly identifying different subtopics, lists and examples, and comparisons and contrasts.

"If this book had been a narrative, I wonder how it might have gone?" I mused.

"It would have been like a . . . a story?" he offered after a minute of thinking. When I nodded for him to continue, he said, "A robot would have been the main character, or an inventor."

I made the decision to leave him with his expository book for the moment even though the rest of the class was busy reading narrative, deciding to return *later* with a few narrative nonfiction books that might appeal to him. "Kobe," I said. "The rest of the class is reading narrative nonfiction. I can see you are really

involved with this, so continue reading it—but would you mind doing some research for me and the rest of the class as you read on? See if maybe, just maybe, there are some tiny stories embedded *inside* this expository text. Like maybe on one page, it will tell the story of how a particular person invented a special robot. And if there are any stories in this book, when you get to those stories, could you see if it helps to read them thinking about 'Somebody . . . wanted . . . but . . . so. . . .'" If you have

continued from previous page

MID-WORKSHOP TEACHING POINT

Nonfiction Readers Read with POWER

* We check that our books are 'just-right' and read **long** and **STRONG**

* We think, "Is this a narrative or an all-about text?" And read differently based on whether it is one or the other.

* If the text is an all-about text, we read expecting to learn the main ideas and supporting details. We use text features to help us find these. We pause at the end of sections to think, "What did I just learn?"

* If the text is a narrative one, we look for the main character (this may be an animal or a group of people) to have traits, motivations, struggles and to do things to respond to troubles and to change and/or learn through the process.

time, after you read this, look back at some of the expository texts you read earlier and see if any of them include stories as well. I might use your research to teach the rest of the class, so be sure to mark pages where you find narratives, and come talk with me about what you find, okay?"

A day later, Kobe and I led a small group, showing a cluster of readers that the new work they'd been learning about reading nonfiction narratives could actually pay off when reading expository texts as well. With Kobe's and my help, the small group of readers each scanned through one of the expository texts that he or she had read earlier, finding small narratives embedded in those texts.

Help Readers Use Specific Names When Thinking and Talking About People and Places in Narrative Nonfiction Texts

I pulled my chair alongside Lily. "How's it going?" I asked.

Lily said, "It's going pretty good. I'm reading about this ship that sank years ago. This guy is studying the ocean to find it because it had valuable treasure."

"So you're reading about a ship. Does the ship have a name?" I asked Lily.

"Sure," she said. "It's called the. . . ." Lily flipped the book over to look at the back cover to confirm. "The *Atocha*," she said a bit uncertainly, like she was speaking the name out loud for the first time.

"Huh. I've never heard that name before," I said to Lily. "*Atocha*," I repeated, for emphasis. I gave Lily a knowing look, like we'd discovered something new and exotic. "So you're reading a book about a guy studying the oceans." I said. "What's the guy's name? What's he like?"

Lily gave me a puzzled look and said, "Well, he's . . . he's Mel, but I never thought of his personality. I just thought it's about a guy who was looking for this lost treasure on a ship, you know?"

I nodded. "I'm asking about Mel's name, the ship's name, and about what Mel and the *Atocha* are like because when you read narrative nonfiction, it can help to think of the characters as having traits and motivations and struggles. At least the guy, and perhaps even the ship, can be thought of that way—like you'd think of Rob and Sistine in *The Tiger Rising*. But here's a tip for you: When you talk about the characters in narrative nonfiction, name them. Be on a first name basis with them, just like you are with the people in your life."

"Ohh," Lily said, catching on. "Okay. The guy, Mel, actually (she looked at the back cover of the book), an archaeologist named Mel Fisher was really eager to find the . . . *Atocha*, which is a ship that sank a long time ago. Which would make him kind of lonely."

"How does it feel telling the story like that?" I asked.

"Well," Lily said. "It's like the story's more real now. And it's making me want to learn more about Mel Fisher and the *Atocha*."

I smiled at her newfound ease with naming the characters in her book.

"That's a great idea, Lily. You could do a research study of the sinking of the *Atocha* and Mel Fisher's attempt to find the sunken treasure. There are probably lots of books written about the topic because readers love learning about sunken treasure."

"Yeah," Lily said.

"So remember, as you continue reading this book or other books on this topic, that instead of talking about a guy, looking for any ol' ship, you'll want to talk about Mel Fisher, an archaeologist, who was looking for the *Atocha*. And you can use precise names for other things too—for places, for example. He was looking for the *Atocha* that sank off the coast of Florida about 400 years ago. Do you see how differently we feel and think when we are on a first name basis with something?"

Lily nodded enthusiastically.

"So this is another choice readers make. We can live and read, being just *vaguely familiar* with whatever is in our lives and in our books, or we can be on a *first name basis* with the people in our lives and the subjects of our books. I make sure that I don't come in here and say, 'Hey you with the yellow sweater.' Or, 'You! Boy on the left! Stop talking.' I make sure I know my kids on a first name basis as soon as possible."

Lily laughed and I moved on to confer with another child.

You Might Help Some Readers Bring a More Flexible Sense of Story to Their Narrative Nonfiction Texts

While some of your proficient readers may have developed an internal sense for these text structures, others may have never thought about them. It can help these readers to become more aware of text structures if for no other reason than that then they can use these when they write their own nonfiction texts using those structures. Also, there are microstructures within the overall structure of expository texts, including, for example, cause-and-effect, compare-and-contrast, and define-and-exemplify structures, and when readers understand that writers employ this full palette as they write, this allows readers to read with more awareness and control.

When I approached Izzy, I expected that I'd be able to use my conference with her as a time to show her an array of text structures that all fall within the general categories she'd learned about. I found her thumbing through a book entitled *From Cocoa Bean to Chocolate*. The pages inside were dominated by photographs depicting various stages in the chocolate-making process, and the book was clearly easy for Izzy. Just as I was deciding how best to move her into challenging concepts, she said something that caught me off guard. What, she wanted to know, was an expository text like *From Cocoa Bean to Chocolate* doing lying around in the narrative nonfiction bin? Since the text structure in the book was obviously narrative in nature, I was surprised at Izzy's confusion. This was, after all, one of my relatively stronger readers holding a book that was simple for her.

"That's interesting," I replied. "Tell me why you think it is an expository text."

Izzy had plenty of logic to support her assertion and was ready to school me on this. There's no person or main character, she told me. It's got facts and photographs about what goes on in a factory. She flipped to the table of contents, where chapter titles began "Cocoa Beans Grow . . . ," Workers

Open the Pods . . . ," and "The Sun Dries the Beans . . ." and ended with "The Chocolate is Wrapped . . . I Eat My Favorite Treat."

Of course, I could see at once that the unlikely hero of this "story" was the cocoa bean, and the "story" chronicled the journey of this "hero" from its birth as a cocoa bean to its death as a piece of chocolate that is eaten. But I could also see her point. Not only did this text have a technical, expository *feel* to it, but the main character was treated as the *object* rather than the *subject* all through the book. The workers who open the pods, for example, looked more prominent than the bean. Similarly, the machines that mashed and the sun that dried appeared like the main movers and shakers, while the bean didn't really sit up and claim any wants or struggles. What's more, the hero's metamorphosis from unopened pods to beans to a slushy cocoa mixture to a wrapped candy bar made it hard to maintain a feel that this shape-shifter was one and the same "hero." It was clear that Izzy needed even more scaffolds to understand the structure of narrative texts.

"Have you heard the story of the frog that turned into a prince?" I began. As Izzy nodded, I continued, "That's what I like to call a transformation story. Where the hero starts off like a beast, for example, and something happens along the way to turn him into a prince. Or the story of a raggedy girl sitting in the cinders? Along comes something that—poof—turns her into the belle of the ball, right? Or even a shy boy like Rob who starts off friendless, scratching a rash, but things happen to him along the way, and he turns into someone who is suddenly surrounded by the truest of friends, right?"

By now, Izzy was looking at me with rapt attention, and I added, "Or some *beans* that start off growing invisibly in pods in a South American jungle but end up packed in foil as *chocolate* in an American kid's hand." I noted the dawning awareness on Izzy's face as she registered what I had just said and began staring at the book anew.

"May I teach you one thing?" I asked. "A way to determine if a text is narrative is to ask yourself, 'What happened first? What happened next? And next? And what happened in the end?' And if you ask yourself, 'Who or what did all this happen to?' you'll be able to identify the hero or the main character in the narrative."

"So the little cocoa bean is the hero of this story!" Izzy said, sounding victorious, as if she alone came to this conclusion. I nodded and smiled as I got up to move on to confer with another reader. As I was leaving, I heard Izzy mumble, in a mournful tone, "I just think it's a sad kind of hero, though, because it gets eaten in the end."

TEACHING SHARE

Readers Think About Main Characters Even in Narrative Nonfiction

Ask readers to reflect on their learning and to consider the most important parts of the day's reading. Then ask children to share that information in a succinct, powerful way.

"Readers, I've got to stop you. I am so blown away by the feel in this classroom right now. It's as if we have all these different experts in the room. There are people here who are deeply involved with sports heroes. You are practically taking courses in how to grow up to be a pro. And some of you are all fired up about becoming protectors of endangered species. We've practically got a Protect the Dolphin Club right here.

"You are reading true stories, and you are learning from all these amazing characters who have opened trails of possibility, who have shown the way for the rest of us. How about if we take some time to share, not our books, but our characters—and the things we are learning from those characters? In a minute, I'm going to ask you to share your character and your learning. Think what you'll say." I gave them some time. "Now think about how you can share what you've learned with pizzazz, so it sparkles, and yet so it is brief—just two or three sentences at most."

COACHING TIPS

Rallying your children's enthusiasm at the beginning of a new bend in a unit is critical. Describing children as experts, fired up and deeply involved, inspires them to fill those shoes. Asking them to talk about what they've learned with pizzazz will build palpable excitement in the room.

Ask children to share brief insights about their characters by pointing to them one by one, as if you are the conductor.

"Okay. I'm going to be like the conductor in the symphony, and when I point my baton toward you, name your character and name what you are learning. If you don't have anything to say yet, gesture 'pass,' and I'll move on to someone else."

Grace went first, "I read about C. J. Walker. She had three husbands and didn't like any of them." I pointed my baton to another reader.

"Well, I learned," Malik began, "about a person named Hershey who invented chocolate. I learned they get chocolate powder from a plant. You need milk and the powder to make chocolate. It made me hungry!" he confessed, rubbing his stomach and smacking his lips.

I waved the baton.

Sarah said, "I learned Helen Keller went blind and deaf from just a fever, and it did not stop her from hardly anything!" I pointed to the next reader.

"I read about P.T. Barnum. He is the guy who started Ringling Brothers and Barnum Bailey circus. He walked twenty-one elephants across the Brooklyn Bridge to prove it was safe," said Josh, looking around at his classmates with an enormous grin. (Giggles broke out around the meeting area while other children called out things like "That's so weird!")

This little ritual—pretending you are the conductor and tipping your baton gracefully to indicate that one, then another person add to the symphony—can be exquisite and can be used in zillions of ways. Watch a conductor so you remind yourself of how it feels.

I swirled my baton in an ending flourish, signaling to stop the symphony. Then I said, "Remember—the things that people did are windows to their character. Remember earlier, when Rob was brave enough to try rescuing Sistine, we said, 'That shows the sort of person he is.' The things your people do show the sort of people they are—and show why, years later, they are the subject of books. Malik, you could be thinking, 'Hershey was a really creative, inventive person,' and Josh, when you read that P.T. Barnum walked those elephants across the Brooklyn Bridge (Can you imagine herding twenty-one large animals across a bridge?), you might be thinking, 'That P.T. Barnum was one resolute guy. He must have had a really strong passion to carry out his vision.' All of you, remember as you read to think hard about the character whose story you're studying. When you learn what your characters do, those actions are clues to their personalities, and if you are reading a biography, there are clues, too, to tell you why that person became famous."

Reminding children of the character unit of study will keep the content you taught earlier alive for your children. It is very important to teach children the way a reading curriculum cumulates, leaving the reader with a repertoire of skills and strategies. This share gives you a chance to convey the cumulative nature of your teaching.

Seeking Underlying Ideas in Narrative Nonfiction

ll of us who teach have gathered children close and said, "I want to tell you a story. . . ." Then we have told a story about a particular moment in our own lives. Recently, I told children the story of visiting my mum when she'd just been released from the hospital after yet one more operation on her hip. After my return flight to New York City, I walked through La Guardia airport, thinking, "These halls are so very long, so hipachingly long." Then I said to the children, "That's how it goes in life. We care for someone who is different from us and then end up seeing the world through that person's eyes. I walk the halls of the airport differently now that my mother struggles to walk; I see those halls through her eyes."

But, of course, I had a reason to tell the story. I was using it as almost a parable about reading. I followed the story about my mother with a larger point. "When I read, I find myself seeing the world through the eyes of the characters I come to know. I read about a librarian in Iraq, trying to save precious books from the perils of fiery war, and end up listening to the news about the Middle East differently because I'm cheering for that librarian. When I read, I come to identify even with a cactus, rooting for it to survive, to thrive, despite the odds. When we read, we come to care about characters that are different from us, and this expands our view of the world."

When we, as teachers, tell stories like these to our children, we are creating narrative nonfiction texts, and we are using those texts, as writers do, to make a difference. Nonfiction stories are not just true accounts. They are stories, and as such, they are held together by ideas and told to effect readers—listeners. In her book, *A Writer's Guide to Nonfiction*, Elizabeth Lyon writes, "How many articles, essays, or books have you read and forgotten the instant you

GETTING READY

- Prepare an anecdote from your own class in lieu of the sample anecdote written in the connection. (As in the connection, you'll need to tell it with no unifying idea, to offer a contrast.)

- Be prepared to read a passage from *Secrets of the Mummies*. If you choose a different nonfiction text to read aloud, select a text that supports children in reflecting on the unifying idea behind the story.

- Create a chart to display during the active involvement titled "How Can We Find Unifying Ideas in True Stories?"

- Be ready to read the passage "Spill!" from the DK Reader *Disasters at Sea*. If you choose an alternate text, be sure to read a passage where a character makes a choice that ends up being consequential to the unifying ideas of the text.

finished reading them?" Then she addresses the authors of nonfiction narratives and says sternly, "Readers and writers, if, at the end of reading your writing, your reader has not been changed, then you have made no difference whatever. A waste."

In my little story about visiting my mother and then finding that I walked the halls of the airport differently because I saw the airport through her eyes, the meaning of the story

> *When we read, we come to care about characters that are different from us, and this expands our view of the world.*

is revealed to children, my "readers," by the narrator of the story (me), who tells not only of a sequence of events but

also of a dawning realization. In the story, the character realizes that she sees the airport halls differently because she sees through the eyes of another person. Often, the main character in a story learns something, and those of us who are coming along for the ride learn with that character.

In many true stories, an individual copes with a problem, overcomes an adversity, or handles a challenge. In such stories, the main character meets the challenge, overcomes the obstacles, and reaches the goal. But the important thing is that the individual meanwhile learns something fundamental about himself, herself, or about life.

Readers of narrative nonfiction can learn in lots of ways. Many children are accustomed to reading narrative nonfiction like I eat chunky-chocolate almond moose ice cream. I scoop for the chocolate bits; they scoop for the facts. When one does that, the main substance is overlooked (whether it is ice cream or the story). In this session and the ones surrounding it, you help readers understand that learning does not mean accumulating factoids. Readers learn by being immersed in another time and place, by experiencing something alongside the main character, and by coming to understand and to think about the ideas that provide cohesion to the sequence of events in the narrative. And teachers need to avoid channeling kids to mine for facts in ways that divert them from following and learning from the story and its underlying ideas.

MINILESSON

Seeking Underlying Ideas in Narrative Nonfiction

CONNECTION

Remind readers that we've learned that nonfiction writing can be divided into narrative and all-about texts and that the narrative texts tell us about a subject doing a sequence of actions.

"Readers, over the past few days, we talked about the fact that nonfiction texts can be divided into two main piles: some are stories; some are all-about texts (in other words, expository texts, or classes on a topic). We also realized that sometimes the nonfiction texts that are stories are stories of an animal, a plant, or a group of people. Those stories tell about how a central character did one thing, then the next thing, then the next."

Illustrate the characteristics of narrative nonfiction by writing "in the air," deliberately creating a text that lacks detail and a unifying through-line.

"We could write a true book, a *narrative* nonfiction text, then, about our class, and we could tell what we did Monday, Tuesday, Wednesday, today. I'm going to try to make up a true story about our class over the past few days, and I want you to tell me if my text sounds like a narrative nonfiction text. If something is missing, let me know what it is. Ready?"

I stepped into the role of storyteller and proceeded to ramble through a loose collection of things the class had done:

> Two days ago we had social studies and we watched a movie and we also had recess and yesterday we worked during writing time on writing essays and it was John's birthday and today we came into the class at 8:00. . . .

COACHING TIPS

Of course, during the preceding days you will have told kids more than just this. You generally recap the content that will function as a foundation for the new learning you plan to support.

Notice that this connection in some ways resembles the active involvement section of many minilessons. You have recruited readers to assess whether the story you tell does or does not fit the criteria of narrative nonfiction, and soon you will ask them to advise you on ways to make the story better fit the genre. Their engagement in this work will simply set them up to be ready to hear what you will teach them today. Make this snappy, light, fun. Your efforts to tell a true story should be problematic in highly exaggerated ways.

Elicit feedback from the class. Was the text you created narrative nonfiction? Recruit children to add the missing elements: meaning and coherence.

Stepping out of the storyteller role, I said to the class, "So was that a true story, a bit of narrative nonfiction?"

Children in unison called, "Nooo."

I asked what was missing. Joel suggested that there had been no facts, no information. I nodded, and tried again, this time deliberately studding the text with irrelevant facts.

> Two days ago, at 9:37, Class 203 studied Chapter 8 in the social studies book, which is four pages long, and then watched a black-and-white movie called *The Reasons for Conflict.* After that we went to recess and five kids wore brown coats and nine wore blue coats. . . .

"Am I on my way toward 'writing' a good narrative nonfiction text about our class?"

Again the class let out a resounding, "Noooo."

Feigning shock, I asked, "What was wrong? I told one thing we did, then the next, then the next, and I included *lots* of specific information, facts, and figures."

Josh called out, "But what's it about? It doesn't really say anything."

I pointed to what he'd said, repeating it with enormous emphasis, nodding ferociously. "'It doesn't really say anything.' Exactly."

Name your teaching point. Specifically, teach children that readers need to find the unifying idea behind the texts they read, to make coherence out of all the events and information.

"What I want to teach you today is that people write stories to convey ideas. The *idea* is what allows the storyteller to shape information, experience, into something that fits together so the story is not just a hodgepodge of junky details strung along a line of time. While that is a writer's goal, it is also a reader's goal. Readers have to find the

Of course, the children could catch you off guard and call out, with equal fervor, "Yessss!" You can ask the question with a tone that makes this unlikely to happen, but if it does and you find yourself needing to take command of the discussion and to show them what you think and why, then do so directly. Don't rely on a whole chain of questions meant to elicit the answer you have in mind. Simply say, "You know what I think? I think. . . ."

Time and again, you will see that I use counter examples to pop out whatever I want to highlight.

As you proceed through the minilesson, you'll see that the teaching component does not rely on demonstration as the method of teaching, but rather on "explain and show an example." This makes that aspect of the minilesson talky. I decided to actively involve students in the connection to offset that upcoming aspect of the minilesson.

Students usually know when I am purposefully messing something up to make a point. That doesn't detract from the glee they take in pointing out my mistakes.

unifying idea behind the texts we read, to make coherence and find meaning out of all that would otherwise be strings of events and facts."

TEACHING

Refer to quotations from a nonfiction writer who has said that without meaning, there is no story. Tell how that writer imbued one story with meaning, with a theme.

"Writers, I've been reading a chapter in *Telling True Stories: A Nonfiction Writers' Guide* by Mark Kramer and Wendy Call, one of our country's greatest nonfiction writers, and he says this: 'To write a good narrative, you must be able to answer the question: What is the story about? The idea, the concept, is critical to narrative journalism.'

"That is important information because lots of people think that when you write a nonfiction account of an event, a true story, the writer just tells what happened. But you watched as I told what has happened in our class over the past few days, and my account sounded like a hodgepodge of junky details, strung along a line of time. I believe that Josh, Mark Kramer, and Wendy Call are all saying the same thing: to write a true story, there needs to be a unifying idea, a central concept.

When I describe my story as "a hodgepodge of junky details, strung along a line of time," I am imagining the details strung as if on a line of Christmas tree lights. I write this a day after I helped my Dad unwind his Christmas tree lights from the blue spruce outside the farmhouse in which I was raised, and I think that line of lights has influenced my imagery. You, like me, will find ways to convey concepts that are important to you, and you will draw on your own history, your own experiences, to do so. If you liken a text to something physical in the world, be sure you help children imagine what you are imagining by using your hands to gesture as you talk.

The teaching method that I am using in this minilesson is not that of demonstration, which is the usual mode for teaching reading strategies. Instead, the teaching method is "explain and show an example." Halberstam cited several examples, and I selected the story of the World Trade Center disaster because I know that story is important, a story that touches all of us, and I wanted to refer to an example that would draw listeners into this bit of teaching. I wanted to make this bit of teaching memorable, and I am aware that often telling and showing examples is not an especially powerful way to teach.

"Let me share one more example. This one is from David Halberstam, a great nonfiction writer. After the September 11 attack on the World Trade Center, he decided to write a book, *Firehouse,* in which he told what those days before, during, and after the tragedy were like for the firehouse in his neighborhood of Manhattan. Halberstam said that he couldn't just write *everything* that happened to the people in that firehouse. One person ate pizza; one fed the dog; one answered the phone; one climbed the tower stairs. He couldn't tell it all. He needed to develop an idea of what he wanted his story to say. He ended up deciding to show, in his story, that relationships in the firehouse are especially intense. Men sleep there; they eat together; they risk their lives for each other.

And then he showed the terrible price that this one institution paid that day—twelve men from this one firehouse died that day—as a way of showing the price that the whole city paid. Halberstam said, 'I thought I could measure some of the pain inflicted on the city by looking at that firehouse.'

"Halberstam's point was that until he decided that this would be the idea behind his story, until he knew that this was the overall concept he wanted readers to grasp, there was no story. He says, 'The book is the idea. Once you have the idea, it just flows out.' He also said, 'You must be able to point to something larger.'"

ACTIVE INVOLVEMENT

Remind children of a recent read-aloud, asking, "What was that story aiming to show? What's the unifying idea underpinning all its parts?"

"Readers, let's think back to *Secrets of the Mummies*. I'm going to reread the start of that book, and I want you to think, 'What might the unifying idea be behind this story?'

"As you think about this, remember the personal narratives you have written in the writing workshop. Remember how you ask, 'What is the heart of my story?' Remember how you stretch that part out, telling it in detail, adding in what people say and think? When an author includes details, those details are often there to build up what the author believes is the heart of the story and to convey the message, to teach the lesson, that the author wants readers to get. Okay, listen to the story again. (I'm going to start at the beginning but skip a few parts.)"

The Mummy's Curse

"I must find the lost tomb."

Howard Carter had been saying the same thing for years. Now it was 1922, the fifth year he had spent digging through sand and rocks in Egypt's Valley of the Kings. He was searching for a tomb that no grave robbers had ever found—the tomb of Tutankhamen, the boy pharaoh.

Carter scoffed when he was warned of the curse: "Death comes on wings to he who enters the tomb of a pharaoh."

Each day, his men worked in the sweltering heat and dust. They seemed to be getting nowhere. Then one morning, as they dug in soft rubble, a shovel clanged. . . .

Notice that during the teaching section of minilessons, kids are actually given tips. Some teachers think that the fact that there is one teaching point in a minilesson means that there is only one sentence or two worth of content in the minilesson. Kids won't listen if our teaching doesn't help them learn, and their learning needs to continue past the moment when we cite the teaching point.

I try to make it easy for kids to practice the work I have just described, so I read aloud in ways that highlight one unifying idea or another. Slow down as you read the parts you want the children to notice. Show them that you are mulling over certain parts by pausing for an instant and thinking aloud about them.

There is no one right answer to the question "What ideas are especially foundational to this story?" Readers will have to interpret for themselves. To support children having different interpretations, I read with awareness of the several ideas they may find in the text. I pay special attention to the various details that show how easily it would have been for Carter to be convinced that he should not go ahead: The search took years; the people claimed anyone opening the grave of a pharaoh would be cursed; signs showed that in fact the curse could be coming. But Carter carried on. There is probably no message that is more common in stories such as this message—"Don't give up." And readers can sensibly take that message from this text. After all, no harm came to Carter himself, despite the curse, and he did earn himself the treasure in the end!

On the other hand, the unifying idea of the text could be "Too much pride leads to trouble." After all, Carter's actions, in scoffing at the curse and forging ahead, seemed to cause an ominous city-wide blackout as well as the deaths of a canary, a dog, and a loyal patron!

When Carter arrived, he was met by an excited hush. The men had found a stone step. Another 15 steps were quickly uncovered. Could this be Tutankhamen's tomb?

Carter was the first to look. What he saw left him speechless. Later, he told people that he had seen "strange animals, statues, and gold—everywhere the glint of gold. . . ."

When Carter arrived home that night, his servants were wailing and shouting.

"What's wrong?" Carter demanded above the din.

"You have opened the tomb," wept a servant. "We are cursed!" He told Carter that a cobra had swallowed Carter's pet canary at the exact moment the tomb was opened. Cobras were a symbol of royalty in ancient Egypt. They were said to spit fire at a pharaoh's enemies.

Carter was not worried. The next day he began to clear the first room of the tomb.

More than a mile of cotton wadding was used to wrap up the items. Carter's team packed games, clothing, pottery, musical instruments, and statues. Most of these were sent to Cairo, Egypt's capital, by boat. The more valuable artifacts went on a train accompanied by armed guards.

Finally the men were ready to unseal the third door. Slowly and carefully, Carter started chipping away the rocks and plaster.

Then he stopped. Before him was a wall of solid gold! It was the front of a huge, golden shrine. Carter was astonished. He knew this was the greatest ancient Egyptian find ever.

Inside the golden shrine were three more shrines. And inside the last one was a sarcophagus—a stone coffin. But that was not all. Within the sarcophagus were three more coffins, each fitting snugly inside the other. The final coffin was made of solid gold. Inside it was the mummified body of Tutankhamen.

But before anyone could investigate further, disaster struck. It began when Carter's patron, Lord Carnarvon, was bitten on the cheek by a mosquito. He accidentally cut open the bite while shaving. The bite soon became infected, and fever set in.

It will help if children are aware of the three questions that you'll suggest they ask. Knowing those questions are coming will help you highlight certain aspects of the text as you read. So, gesture to a written record of those questions as you read aloud.

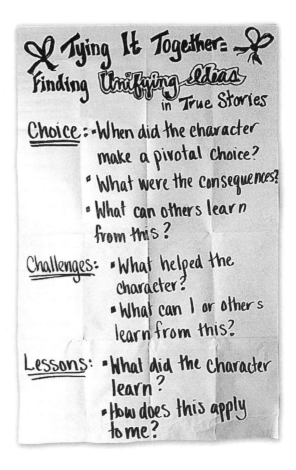

Tying It Together: Finding Unifying Ideas in True Stories

Choice: • When did the character make a pivotal choice?
• What were the consequences?
• What can others learn from this?

Challenges: • What helped the character?
• What can I or others learn from this?

Lessons: • What did the character learn?
• How does this apply to me?

A few days later, Carnarvon's family raced to his bedside. He was very ill. Then, early one morning, it was all over. Lord Carnarvon died.

At the very moment of his death, all the lights in Cairo went out. They stayed out for several hours, and no one could explain why. Back at Lord Carnarvon's home in England, Susie, his dog, pricked up her ears, howled once, then dropped dead.

Other deaths followed. A French scientist who visited the tomb died after a fall. An X-ray specialist on his way to examine Tutankhamen's mummy died unexpectedly. Then a wealthy American died from a virus after visiting the tomb. Were these deaths all coincidences, or was the curse of the mummy to blame? No one knows for sure.

"What might the idea be that this text is conveying to us? Turn and talk."

Break into children's conversations to add tips for finding the big message in true stories. Specifically, tell them that one way readers find unifying messages in stories is by focusing on several aspects of the character.

After children spoke in partnerships for a bit, I said, "Can I have all eyes on me? I want to share with you a couple of techniques that are sometimes helpful when thinking about the meaning in a narrative nonfiction text." I revealed a chart I'd made earlier and asked children to read it to themselves and to draw on it in their partnership conversations.

Ask partners to tell each other the unifying idea they found in the text you read aloud.

"*Now*, let's see if these pointers (on the chart) can help you find a unifying idea in this true story. Think back to 'The Mummy's Curse.' What pivotal choice did Howard Carter make? What kind of outcome did his choice have?" I pointed to the first tip on the chart, and I gave the children half a minute to think. "Now think about this. Could there be a lesson in this story for us all?" Then I said, "Turn and share."

I walked around and stopped to listen in on Izzy and Emma's conversation.

Izzy turned to Emma and said, "I wrote on my Post-it that Howard Carter knew about the curse, but he decided to open the tomb anyway, which was brave of him."

How Can We Find Unifying Ideas in True Stories?

- *Find the time in the story when the main character had to make a pivotal choice. What kind of consequence does the choice have? Is there a message or idea for everyone in this?*

- *When the character meets challenges, what helps? Is there a message or idea for everyone in this?*

- *Did the character learn a lesson? Does this lesson apply to us?*

Don't be surprised if your students have trouble doing this. That's why you proceed to give them some helpful pointers.

Emma added, "Kinda, but I think he didn't believe in the curse, so it wasn't really brave. I wrote that he was determined to see if he had found the tomb of King Tut even though some people believed there was a curse."

"Yeah, but his decision led to all of those deaths," said Izzy.

"I think it was a coincidence, but he was seen as the person who caused everything bad to happen," said Emma.

"Maybe the lesson is that you have to take responsibility for your actions," said Izzy.

LINK

Send children off to read, highlighting the related work of maintaining a good pace, of holding onto the storyline, and of asking, "What's the unifying idea in this nonfiction text?"

"Readers, you'll continue reading your true stories today. First, remember, you are reading long and strong. You should actually read these books like you read fiction books, feeling lost in the story. Don't be afraid that you may miss some bit of information or that you might not remember some fact. Instead, try to get caught up in the story line of your text and to read strong and long. The important facts will connect with the ending of your story anyhow, so they won't be apt to get lost. (You can always reread for specific facts later if you want to do so.)

It is important to notice that reading skills are deeply interconnected. If you see children creeping slowly through their nonfiction texts and reading with blinders, only attending to the current page, then you will need to nudge them to accelerate their reading. But this will not work unless you help those readers know what readers need to collect, to hold onto, if we want to take in broader expanses of text. Here you will see that I channel readers to stop obsessing over facts. I convey this message not because facts do not matter, but because I am convinced that readers won't learn facts unless those facts are lodged in underlying concepts, in stories, and in meanings. One way to break a focus on small facts and to support a focus on wider spans of text is to encourage faster reading.

"And second, try to see the underlying idea that is there in your text. It might be buried a bit, but you know some tips to help you interpret what that idea might be." I pointed to the chart "How Can We Find Unifying Ideas in True Stories?"

"And finally, most of all, be thinking, 'What lesson could this story hold for us all?'"

This work—reading at a brisk pace and attending to the story (and to the story's underlying idea, which in nonfiction is sometimes hidden under a covering of little facts)—is necessary if readers are going to read well. That is why this link sends readers off with so much work to do, all at once.

CONFERRING AND SMALL-GROUP WORK

Support Children in Taking Their Next Steps by Cultivating Your Own Responsiveness

Don Murray, the Pulitzer Prize–winning writer who is regarded as the "father" of writing process, once said, "I do not want to write what I have said before and write it in the same way. In emptiness, I find a new beginning." Murray's words have helped me to write better because I have often found that when I am faced with an empty page, words that I've written before, thoughts that I've shared before, rise to the surface within me, and I'm tempted to fasten them to my page and go from there. If I start with the words and insights from other days, other texts, then I can evade the terror of the blank page.

But Murray, who died a year ago, is still with me, whispering into my ear. "In emptiness, I find a new beginning." And so I resist the temptation to write what I have already said. I reach inside myself, push aside those preformed words like one might push aside the leaves on the surface of the well, and I wait, knowing there will be clear water, a new beginning.

I'm telling you this because I think you can tap an important source of fresh thinking in your conferring and, indeed, in your reading instruction, if you allow yourself to sit alongside a child, wordless for a while, unsure what to say or how to help. Usually when you aren't quite sure what to say or to teach, the words you've already taught rise to the surface within you, crowding out the empty space. And so, for example, when teaching children to grow ideas, if you see that the child's work is a mere approximation of what you want, then all too quickly, you have your suggestion in hand. "One thing you could try is you could use thought prompts such as, 'The idea I'm having about this . . .' or 'The surprising thing about this is . . . ,' and see if those transitional phrases will help you grow ideas."

Granted, that is one acceptable way to teach children to grow ideas. But the truth is that you've probably already taught that scaffold to the young reader sitting in front of you.

It is not surprising that in that moment of emptiness when you think, "It's my turn to talk now. I'm supposed to help. Geez. What do I say?" the words that will surface are the old words, the words you have used before. The important thing to remember is that your teaching will tap a well of freshness if you push aside the hackneyed teaching as one pushes aside the leaves on the surface of the well, and wait for clear water, a new beginning.

> **MID-WORKSHOP TEACHING POINT**
>
> ### Readers Study Characters' Central Choices to Learn Lessons from the Text
>
> "If you have not already been watching for the central decisions that your characters have been making in the nonfiction narratives you have been reading, try doing this now. Look back over what you've already read—if you have finished one book, look back over it, too—and see if you can identify the moment or moments of choice that are central to the whole story of a narrative. Thinking about the choice and its consequences may help you figure out a unifying idea in your nonfiction text, and even a lesson that everyone can learn.
>
> "If you are seeing tons of little choices, but you are not sure which is key, think for a moment about your character. What is the main thing this character wants? How does the character meet obstacles? Usually important moments of choice lie close to the character's main motivations and struggles. Someone once said, 'When we go over the bumps, what's inside spills out.' I think that means that when we meet obstacles, those are times when our insides are revealed. Decisions in the face of challenges are ones to pay close attention to because they are revealing!
>
> "Jot your thoughts about what characters (or what you) are able to learn from the decisions that are made and then keep reading, thinking about this. You may decide you need to get farther into your story line to address this, in which case, read on, read on."
>
>

To Teach Responsively, You Need to Study What Children Are Doing and Almost Doing

You'll find that when you don't rely on the preformed teaching points but reach instead to teach in fresh ways, you need to take more time to study the reader's work.

I had already heard Aly and Fallon describing their reading work and knew they were each reading a biography—Aly was reading on Ben Franklin and Fallon on Barack Obama—and each had been writing their ideas on Post-it notes. Just a quick glance at their writing about reading showed me that they'd each found ways to attach one little Post-it to another. Before she recorded an idea, Aly had fastened her Post-its alongside each other like bricks on a cobblestone road, so that her four-square Post-it cobblestone provided more breathing space. Fallon had written one Post-it at a time on the run as she flew through the pages of her biography, and then when she finished a section of her book, she'd attached one Post-it onto the bottom of the next so they appeared as if they were strings of thought (though actually it was more than the different colors of ink that gave away their disjointed nature). Neither reader seemed to have used very many thought prompts (although absolutely they wrote with a few "on the other hands" or "It is interesting that . . ."), and neither reader seemed to have paid attention to my suggestion that it can help to think about moments of pivotal choice or to lessons the character learned. Although they hadn't seemed to rely on my teaching, their work was impressive enough that I wasn't sure how to help.

Aly, for example, had written on one of her Post-its, "I bet there were many families that were divided during the Revolutionary War. Some of them were probably loyal to King George, while others probably wanted independence. It must have been hard considering you were not allowed to divorce back then. Or say bad things without getting hurt or maybe even killed." Clearly, something in the Franklin biography had sparked this idea.

As a teacher, it takes some discipline to actually take in what children write on their Post-its. You and I can only hope to teach responsively if we can take ourselves in hand and say, "Actually read this. Don't just check off that the child wrote a thought. Take in the thought." Join me, now, in actually reading Aly's Post-its and thinking, "What does this suggest I could do to help her move forward?" *[Figs. X-1, X-2, and X-3]*

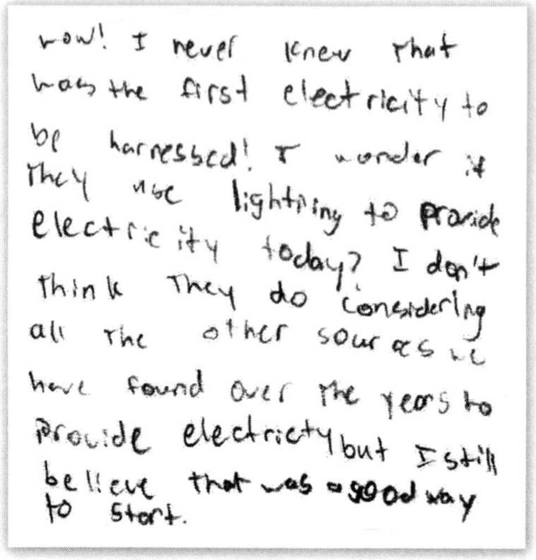
wow! I never knew that was the first electricity to be harnessed! I wonder if they use lighting to provide electricity today? I don't think they do considering all the other sources we have found over the years to provide electricty but I still believe that was a good way to start.

Figure X-1
It is interesting that Aly leaves Ben Franklin behind, thinking more about electricity than about its inventor.

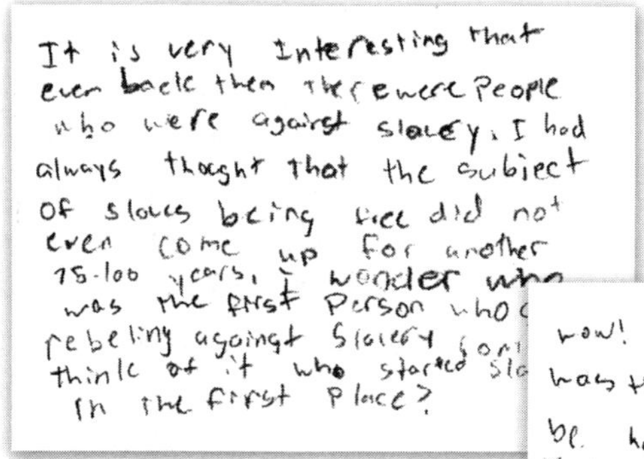
It is very interesting that even back then there were people who were against slavery. I had always thought that the subject of slaves being free did not even come up for another 75-100 years. I wonder who was the first person who c[...] rebeling against slavery [...] think of it who started sl[...] in the first place?

Figure X-2
Aly has taken on a whole other topic that the Franklin biography sparked in her.

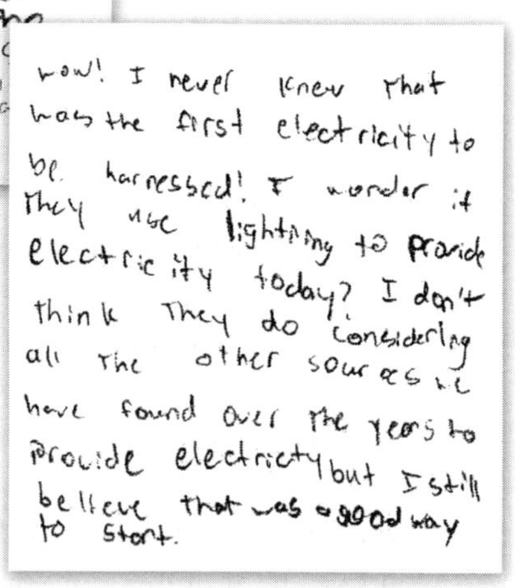
wow! I never knew that was the first electricity to be harnessed! I wonder if they use lighting to provide electricity today? I don't think they do considering all the other sources we have found over the years to provide electricty but I still believe that was a good way to start.

Figure X-3
The level of thinking Aly does here is far richer because of the phrase "On the other hand. . . ."

I thought, "Hmmm. What can I make of these?" Before settling on a thought about Aly's responses, I decided to take in what Fallon had done. Maybe a pattern would emerge.

Fallon's response to the Barack Obama book relied less on contextual information and more on her emotional connection to him, but again, her Post-it captured many of her ideas on the run. *[Figs. X-4 and X-5]*

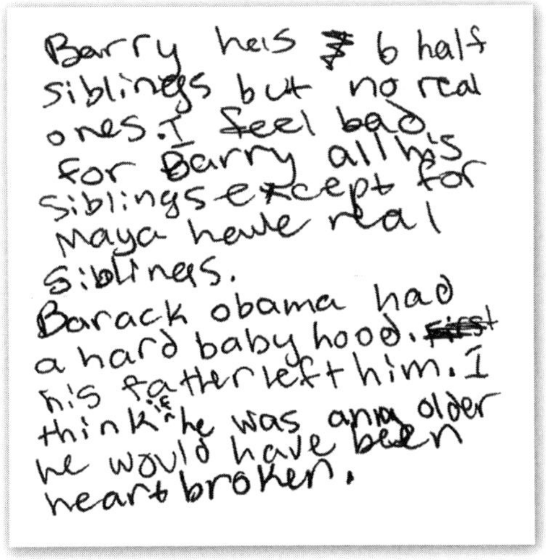
Barry has ~~7~~ 6 half
siblings but no real
ones. I feel bad
for Barry all his
siblings except for
Maya have real
siblings.
Barack obama had
a hard baby hood. ~~first~~
his father left him. I
think if he was any older
he would have been
heart broken.

Figure X-4
The thinking is a bit convoluted, but Fallon's empathy is clear.

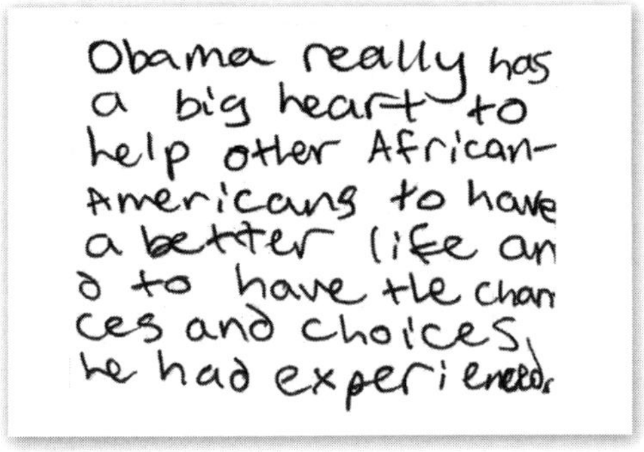
Obama really has
a big heart to
help other African-
Americans to have
a better life an
d to have the chan
ces and choices
he had experienced.

Figure X-5
Fallon is reading with her heart on her sleeve.

What to say? What to teach? Nothing came quickly to my mind, save perhaps the obvious idea that these girls were confined by the size of Post-its and needed to remember that as authors of their reading lives, they could choose where and how to write about their reading. Did they want to record their ideas on the pages of their reading logs rather that squeezing them onto little Post-it notes? And if they did want to write long and strong, they could always rely on the chart of thought prompts to extend their thinking.

I pushed that idea aside. These girls had no trouble priming their thought pumps. They'd long since gained whatever advantages one could gain from those transitional phrases. So, again, what to say? This was taking me too much time, but when I invent conferences that break new trails, the conferences open new frontiers.

To Teach Strong Readers to Outgrow Themselves, It Can Help to Think, "How Might I Have Done This Work?"

When I am unsure where to take strong readers, I sometimes think, "What would the best reader in the world do if he or she was asked to do similar work?" Until I'm clear about the goal toward which I am teaching, it is hard to take readers toward that goal.

I sat, mulling that over, looking at Aly's and Fallon's work, until eventually I felt a thought surfacing.

When we ask readers to grow ideas as they read narrative nonfiction (or probably expository nonfiction, too), we are involving them in a trajectory of work that at its best is interpretation. And one big difference between the work that Aly and Fallon had done and a mature interpretation is that Aly's and Fallon's ideas tended to be localized, page-specific reactions to this or that bit of the biography. Just as children's predictions tend at first to come out of the specific page they are reading rather than drawing upon patterns of evidence that have emerged across many preceding pages, so, too, these readers' ideas seemed to come from the specific page they were on, and each idea seemed to flash across each reader's mind for just an instant.

One way to help Aly, Fallon, and readers like them, then, might be to suggest that they try to generate ideas that relate to more parts of the text. Earlier they had learned that big ideas about a fiction book tend to involve more than just one character and to thread through more than just one section of the book. Similarly, big ideas about a biography tend to involve more than just one time period in a character's life. As I mulled over this insight and looked again at the children's work through this lens, I also noticed that the readers' ideas tended to involve *either* the historical context (such as Aly's ideas about slavery or about families being torn apart during the Revolutionary War), *or* they involved the character's personality and personal life (such as Franklin's relationship with his son), and it also occurred to me that really effective big ideas about a biography tend to involve *both* the person and the historical content.

I was beginning to develop a sense for specific strategies that Aly and Fallon could use that might lead them to develop a few bigger, more interpretive ideas. I figured I could suggest they reread their local, fleeting ideas and see ways in which some of these might fit together into a pattern of thought. Aly's idea about families being torn apart during the Revolutionary War surely relates to her thoughts about Ben Franklin's troubles with his own son, for starters, and both of those ideas could also link to other Post-its Aly had collected as she mulled over Franklin's inventive problem-solving nature (Why was it hard for him to invent ways to solve the tensions in his relationship with his son?). Surely there would be some ways for Aly to link ideas (as Fallon had done with stick-um but as neither child had yet done with thoughts). Then it would be not only *their Post-its* but *their ideas* that they would cobble together. If they did this cross-Post-it, cross-idea thinking, might they develop an idea that wove like a road, taking them and the rest of us on journeys of thought that spanned their texts!

Looking at Aly's and Fallon's work, it also seemed to me that they needed some mentor texts or images of possibility that they could reach toward, so they could have a sense of what it means to do a stellar job of growing ideas within narrative nonfiction. I vowed to do some of my own writing that evening and to bring this to them and to search through files of work that middle school children have produced that could function as mentor texts.

As I vowed to write and find mentor texts, I thought about the fact that right now, these readers didn't seem to be working to outgrow their abilities as readers. They were *using* those abilities, but not aspiring to outgrow themselves. That wasn't surprising because they are proficient readers and writers about reading, but even our strongest readers need to be on fire with resolve to get stronger. Perhaps if these girls had more models of excellence to work toward, they'd experience a bit more disequilibrium, and therefore be a bit more ready to draw on strategies that I was teaching them.

I was reminded that I've often said that teaching kids to monitor for sense as they read is fundamental because unless a child spots confusion and is alarmed by it, that child won't have a reason to reach for fix-up strategies. A fair portion of teaching reading involves making sure kids have reasons to reach into the tool kits we give them. Aly and Fallon are both facile enough as writers about reading that they can easily do work that at least at a glance appears to be "good work," so it is not surprising that they don't find themselves feeling stuck enough that they take my pointers for how to grow ideas seriously. Yet the ideas I'd taught that day could, I thought, help them develop a new sense of criteria through which to assess their own thinking about texts.

After Generating One Way to Help Strong Readers Outgrow Themselves, We Can Develop Other Ways, Sometimes Storing These to Teach Another Day

By this time, I'd formed both an immediate short-term and a longer-term plan for how I could teach Aly and Fallon and was tempted to just deliver my short-term teaching point and move on. But I know that once I am really wrestling with children's work, and the new ideas are surfacing, this is not a time to grab one idea and run with it. If I linger just a bit longer and think a bit more deeply, I can often develop another idea or two or three, and even if I don't teach those today, I can store them away for another day when I may not have as much time to study the children's work.

So I continued poring over Aly's and Fallon's jottings and trying to imagine what I would do if I were in their shoes and had been asked to look across my Post-its and to grow bigger, more encompassing ideas. As I began to do the thinking that I hoped they would do, I spied on myself and quickly realized that what I was doing was reaching for big ideas that are already out there in the world of literary theory, attaching those big ideas to these particular texts. For example, when I saw that Fallon had written a number of Post-its about the people who helped Barack Obama, I found myself saying a big idea that I'd heard before: people who become famous rarely get to those heights without a lot of help from supportive others. How interesting this was. I'd begun this work with Aly and Fallon determined to push aside premade ideas about what to teach them, and here I was discovering that the way I grow interpretive ideas about a text is to reach for premade ideas that can be attached to the text. Of course, this is not as contradictory as it seems. All of us learn to confer by listening to a child's work and then thinking, "What do I already know that I can bring to this child?" and then we function almost as an old-fashioned switchboard operator, attaching the child to the preformed strategy or suggestion. Although I was trying to grow new ideas in response to what these children had done, their work also reminded me of strategies that were already alive in the classroom.

So now I proceeded to study Fallon's Post-its, trying on the idea that one way to grow big, interpretive ideas is to attach the ideas that are already out there in the world to specifics of one person—one text. I saw Fallon's Post-its about Obama's childhood struggles and imagined that she could generate ideas such as these: the hard times in

our lives often end up giving us strengths that we draw on later, or, when people are challenged, we find we have strengths we didn't know we had. Presto! My thought was working. I began to think about the fact that it might help these readers if they could be immersed in other people's big ideas about narrative nonfiction texts, so they could become insiders in those conversations, eventually drawing on those prior conversations as they reached for thoughts in response to texts.

We Can Also Grow Ideas for New Directions by Cross-Fertilizing the Work of One Reader with that of Another and By Helping Youngsters Do the Same

Of course, once I've developed a handful of new ideas in response to the work that a couple of children have been doing, I carry those ideas and those children with me as I continue moving around the classroom, working with youngsters. On this particular occasion, after sharing some of my thoughts with Aly and Fallon and storing others away for future days and future minilessons, I drew a chair alongside another fairly strong reader, Sarah. How fascinating it is to contrast one child's ways of working with another's! On every few pages of her text—*Charlotte Bronte and Jane Eyre*—Sarah had deposited a tidy little Post-it, organized in boxes and bullets, capturing her idea and her evidence for that idea, with those ideas accumulating information she'd gathered from reading at least several pages. Other Post-its laid out the supports in similar ways. *[Figs. X-6 and X-7]*

The marvelous thing about an independent reading workshop in which children are invited to dig in is that one child ends up doing work that is distinctly different from that which another child does, and the mix is a heady, provocative one. A good part of teaching is playing the role of Johnny Appleseed, identifying wonderful ideas and bringing the seeds of those ideas to new places.

Before long, Aly and Fallon were teaching Sarah what I'd taught them about growing interpretive ideas, and Sarah, meanwhile, showed the other girls her technique for creating almost little essay plans to capture her ideas.

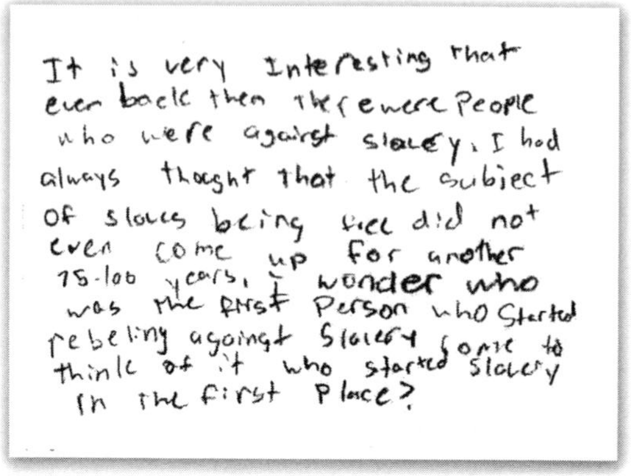
It is very Interesting that even back then there were People who were against slavery. I had always thought that the subject of slaves being free did not even come up for another 75-100 years. I wonder who was the first Person who Started rebeling against Slavery. Come to think of it who started Slavery in the first Place?

Figure X-6
Sarah has internalized the boxes-and-bullets structure of expository texts.

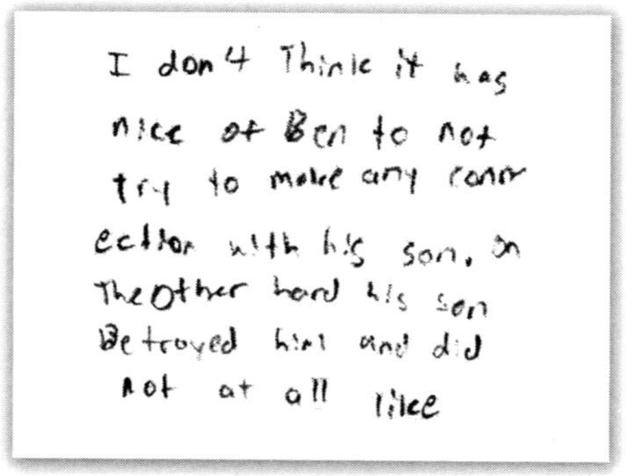
I don't Think it was nice of Ben to not try to make any connection with his son. On The other hand his son Betrayed him and did not at all like

Figure X-7
Sarah has become accustomed to having a thought and then supplying evidence.

TEACHING SHARE

Readers Look to Key Choices Characters Make to Uncover Unifying Ideas

Read an excerpt from a narrative nonfiction text that clearly describes a character making an important choice.

"In a minute, you'll have a chance to talk with your partner about the underlying ideas that you think your nonfiction narrative is conveying, but first, let's practice thinking about this by listening together to one story, 'Spill!' from a DK reader, *Disasters at Sea*. Listen carefully for a moment to note where the character makes a choice that ends up being extremely consequential, and think about how that can help us figure out some underlying ideas in the story."

Spill!

The gigantic ship moved slowly underneath the clear night sky. The *Exxon Valdez* weighed more than 200,000 tons, and was 987 feet long. It had just left Valdez in Alaska carrying a huge cargo of crude oil to California.

The massive vessel, known as VLCC or Very Large Crude Carrier, had a crew of 20. She was under the command of Captain Joseph Hazelwood, an experienced sea voyager.

"Captain, there are some growlers ahead!" warned the officer on watch.

Growlers are small icebergs. They weren't large enough to sink the *Exxon Valdez*, but they could dent her hull.

"Radio the coastguard," ordered Captain Hazelwood.

The *Exxon Valdez* was given permission to change shipping lanes and go around the icebergs.

Ahead now lay the dangerous task of steering the huge ship through the narrow seaway between Busby Island and Bligh Reef. Bligh Reef is covered with jagged rocks and it is a dangerous place for ships. Yet the Captain chose this moment to hand over command to the ship's third mate, Greg Cousins.

COACHING TIPS

By now, you should be accustomed to the pattern that is evident in this bit of teaching. Before reading a portion of a text aloud, I almost always set listeners up with an angle from which to listen. If I simply read aloud and then, afterward, asked listeners to talk about a particular subject, this would be much more challenging. In minilessons, I'm trying to provide youngsters with scaffolded practice. The fact that I clarify the angle of listening before I launch into the read-aloud is one way to support listeners. Of course, one can always read aloud in ways that emphasize bits of the text you especially hope students notice, providing yet another way to scaffold children's work.

How Can We Find Unifying Ideas in True Stories?

- *Find the time in the story when the main character had to make a pivotal choice. What kind of consequence does the choice have? Is there a message or idea for everyone in this?*

- *When the character meets challenges, what helps? Is there a message or idea for everyone in this?*

- *Did the character learn a lesson? Does this lesson apply to us?*

You'll want to gesture to this chart reminding readers that when characters make pivotal decisions, readers can often glimpse the underlying ideas in a text.

"I'll be in my cabin if you need me," said the Captain as he left the bridge.

The ship sailed on through the cold night. Just after midnight, Cousins saw that they were getting close to Bligh Reef and ordered a small course change. He began to plot the new course but when he checked again two minutes later, he saw to his horror that his order had not been properly obeyed. The ship was now directly over the sharp rocks of Bligh Reef!

Cousins tried to contact Captain Hazelwood. Even as he did so, a terrible shudder ripped through the ship.

"Rocks!"

The rocks were only 50 feet below the surface of the water, but *Exxon Valdez*'s hull went deeper than this. The ship had run aground.

As the ship continued forward, the rocks tore open 11 giant cargo tanks full of crude oil. The sticky black liquid began to gush out of the ship's hull.

The crew members were powerless. All they could do was radio for help.

Ask partners to talk about an important choice made by the character you read about. Ask partners to discuss how that character's choice may point to an underlying idea in the story.

"Now, turn and talk with your partner. Was there a moment in which a character made a key choice, a choice that ended up being extremely consequential?" I gestured for them to turn and talk.

Kadija said to Isaac, "I think the captain made a big choice when he went to his cabin instead of making sure the ship got through the rocks."

"Yeah," Isaac said. "It's like Captain Hazelwood went to bed or something instead of keeping the ship safe. He, like, gave all his responsibility to the third mate, and it was like no one would listen to that guy's orders. It's the same as how none of us listen when there's a sub."

"I bet if the captain gave orders to change the course, the people who worked on the boat would have followed *his* orders," Kadija added.

I voiced over the class, "Next, ask your partner more questions that readers ask: 'Could that choice help us understand the unifying idea in this story? Is there a lesson in this for us all?'"

Notice that you have just read about a monumental choice that one of the characters made. The ship was making its way through an especially difficult area, and this was just the time when the captain headed off to bed! If you want to provide lots of support for your children, you'll show, as you read this, that you are flabbergasted by this decision.

You'll later do some vocabulary work with the word hull, *so don't highlight it right now.*

Notice that, like so much of the work in this unit, this task draws on many reading skills. To decide which moment in any story represents a pivotal choice takes integrated intellectual work. Readers must monitor for sense, understanding the plot of this small story on a literal level. Readers must be able to bring background knowledge to the text to understand the jobs of the ship's crew and the stakes of the oil spill. Also, they must determine which choices in the text are most important and which are of lesser importance. To decide if the character's choice holds any lessons for all readers, they must be able to extrapolate the moral of this story, and they may even critique the practices of the crew represented in the story. Your respect for the intellectual merit of this work will help children respect the work as well.

Isaac said, "Maybe the lesson is about being responsible. If Captain Hazelwood hadn't gone to his cabin, he might have saved the ship from crashing and spilling oil."

"I agree with you, and I also think that the ship's crew wasn't very responsible because they didn't follow Cousins's orders."

"I wonder if they tried to follow orders but couldn't. There was only like twenty crew members, and it was a huge ship," Isaac thought aloud.

I leaned in and said, "Talk more about that. What do you think about responsibility and the *Exxon Valdez*?"

"Well, " Isaac said. "Maybe it wasn't very responsible to have only twenty crew members on such a huge ship."

"Yeah, it would have been better probably to have more crew members or a smaller ship," Kadija added.

Gathering the class, I said, "Wow. It was amazing, listening to how far that question about the captain's choice to stay in his cabin took you—from a simple thing like closing a cabin door all the way to those big questions about responsibility! Can you see how figuring out where a character made a key choice, a choice that ended up being extremely consequential, can help you truly understand the text? Can you imagine doing that in your own nonfiction reading from now on? You are off to a powerful start!"

If children clearly understand both this story and the idea that finding key choices in narratives leads us to the idea holding the story together, you can add an extra layer of complexity to this line of thinking. Whenever we study consequential choices, we can ask readers to think about how it came to be that the character faced this particular choice. What other forces brought this situation together to this one high-stakes choice? In this case, that question would bring Exxon into the discussion, though they are scarcely in this small story. Was Exxon's crew well trained? Was it good policy to use ships of that size, carrying that much crude oil? Asking questions outside of the text is especially important for nonfiction, since it helps us see the larger context of our world.

Achievement Texts, Disaster Texts: Templates in Narrative Nonfiction

IN THIS SESSION,

you will teach students that recognizing common structures in nonfiction narratives can give readers command of texts.

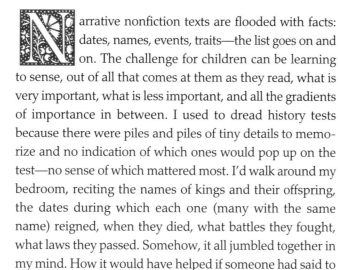arrative nonfiction texts are flooded with facts: dates, names, events, traits—the list goes on and on. The challenge for children can be learning to sense, out of all that comes at them as they read, what is very important, what is less important, and all the gradients of importance in between. I used to dread history tests because there were piles and piles of tiny details to memorize and no indication of which ones would pop up on the test—no sense of which mattered most. I'd walk around my bedroom, reciting the names of kings and their offspring, the dates during which each one (many with the same name) reigned, when they died, what battles they fought, what laws they passed. Somehow, it all jumbled together in my mind. How it would have helped if someone had said to

me, "This is a story of this king's rise to fame," or "This is a story of this king's demise." Then I would have known to pay great attention to every detail that fed into that rise or fall! Without a story line to help me make sense of my reading, I felt that I'd acquired all sorts of little facts but no true understanding.

It doesn't have to be this way. We can scaffold children to read and comprehend nonfiction in ways that help them wade through the details and attend to larger meaning. Luckily for us, many of the narrative nonfiction texts our children read fall into two discernable categories: tales of achievement and tales of disaster. Each of these types of narrative is written in a distinct way, with recognizable patterns of story line and structure that can help children

GETTING READY

- Have on hand two of the nonfiction teaching texts you've used in this unit. One text should represent an achievement story, and the other, a disaster story.

- Invite children to bring the narrative nonfiction books they are reading to the lesson. You will ask each child to sort the books into one of two categories—achievement or disaster. It may be that children's books don't fall so squarely into one category or another, in which case be prepared to talk about that.

- Create the chart titled "Common Features of Achievement Stories," which you will share during the teaching section of the minilesson.

- Prepare two stacks of books so partners can sort the books into disaster stories and biographies.

- For tomorrow's minilesson, you will model how one child used a problem-solving strategy to determine the meaning of an unknown word. During today's conferring, you may consider collecting such an anecdote.

anchor themselves both in the tale itself and in the meaning behind the tale. A reader who recognizes early on that the text she is reading falls into one or the other of these categories will have a way to judge what to pay attention to—a way to estimate what is essential to that text. Of course, this is true for all kinds of texts, fiction and nonfiction, narrative and nonnarrative. Some of the templates are quite appar-

We can scaffold children to read and comprehend nonfiction in ways that help them wade through the details and attend to larger meaning.

ent when you look at stacks of books, like "question-then-answer" texts, or "problem-then-solution" texts. Other templates are deeper within the content of the texts, and the categories are more home-grown, invented by us teachers, like these two templates, "achievement texts" and "disaster texts." You'll no doubt find and name the patterns—the templates—you see in the texts your own students are reading.

As I said above, many of the narrative nonfiction texts (including most biographies) that children read are tales of achievement. The trajectory in such tales is predictable. A person shows great promise at a young age or is affected by something in his childhood and then, despite obstacles, the person grows up to do something remarkable—to achieve something meaningful. You can encourage children to approach such texts expecting to follow the person's path toward achievement. If this is the story of a famous golf player, the reader can approach the book expecting to learn what it was in the person's childhood that set him or her up for excellence in golf. Did the person always have especially keen eyesight? A willingness to persevere? A competitive spirit? Is the character good at scientific research? Finding mummies? Whatever the answer, once the reader begins to learn about a person's special capacities or special opportunities, then the reader can begin to anticipate the trajectory that person will follow. Then, too, readers can also expect that most achievement stories, even the sanitized ones (as biographies written for children often tend to be) will reveal times when the achiever's progress was stymied, when work was hard, and will then reveal the ways the achiever overcame those challenges, often by making a choice or a series of choices.

Children will also read stories of disaster. These books tell the tale of something gone terribly wrong. The disaster may be a natural one—a hurricane or a volcano—or it may be one that occurs because of a sequence of events often involving a fatal mistake (or intentional act of harm) made by one or more persons. (The captain of a boat hands over the wheel to others on his crew, and the boat crashes, killing everyone onboard.) You'll help children understand that just as there is a typical path of achievement, so too, disaster stories follow a path of disaster. These stories are apt to unroll with a sense of rising drama as challenges compound, with a main character relying on resources that he or she never knew were available. Whether the disaster occurs naturally or because of a person's poor choice, there are inevitable lessons to be learned.

There is a related third category, too, albeit not as clearly defined as the others. This category is a combination of the two. That is, some tales of disaster overlap with tales of achievement or heroism. *Firehouse*, for example, which was

introduced in the previous session, tells the heroic tale of the thirteen men of Engine 40, Ladder 35 firehouse in Manhattan, who braved the collapsing World Trade Center towers on September 11, 2001. The event chronicled in Halberstam's book, the attacks on the World Trade Center, is a disaster, but the story of the men themselves and of their courage and sacrifice is the quintessential achievement— or heroism—story. You may want to challenge your children to think about books they are reading that fall into this hybrid category or to present them with stories that may at first appear to be one kind of story but later turn out to be another.

Once children grasp that narrative nonfiction can usually fit into one of these two (or really three) categories and that each one tends to follow a specific structure, you can point out that as readers, we can tap into our déjà vu. We can read thinking, "Oh, this is familiar. This feels like an achievement [or disaster] story. I've read something that goes like this before. I can predict now that young Langton will use his determination and his unique abilities to progress. I know he'll encounter obstacles along the way. I know he'll triumph in the end, though, because of the hints the author is giving me. No sense of foreboding here." That is, we can read in a way that allows us to ready ourselves for, to take in even more deeply, the unfolding story.

Likewise, when we read disaster stories, we can tap into our déjà vu. We can read thinking, "Oh no! I know this feeling. Something's about to go terribly wrong. I can tell from the hints! I bet the lava is going to rise, and the volcano will erupt, and then people will get hurt. Some may lose their homes, and others will even lose their lives! A lot of people will be affected by this in some way. It's going to be a huge disaster."

The more we can teach children how to use their knowledge of story structure, pattern, and order, the better able we will be to give kids footholds as they progress.

MINILESSON

Achievement Texts, Disaster Texts: Templates in Narrative Nonfiction

CONNECTION

Teach children that some narrative nonfiction books can be classified as "achievement stories" or "disaster stories." Set children up to sort their books into one of these two categories.

"I've been talking to some of you, and we've realized that many of your narratives, your true stories, can be divided into two more piles. Right now, I think many of your books are what we can call an 'achievement story.' They tell how someone overcomes all odds and, in the end, makes substantial achievements. And some of your stories are 'disaster stories.' A character gets thrown into a conundrum (that means a puzzle) and is not sure how to proceed. The character makes a decision, proceeds one way or another. Things get worse and worse. In the end, there are lessons to be learned from the sequence of events.

"Look over the book you are reading right now and think, 'Is this an achievement story?' Ask yourself, 'Does this tell how someone got good at something?' If a book is an achievement story, showing how someone learned to do something well, what would you expect will happen later on, as the story progresses?

"If your book is not an achievement story, think, 'Is this a disaster story?' If so, see if you can figure out how disaster stories tend to go. There's a pattern with these stories, just as there is with achievement tales.

"Take a minute to decide which category your book belongs to and to think about how that kind of story tends to go." I gave children a minute to think.

Name your teaching point. Specifically, teach that readers can discern importance if we recognize that a true story seems to be following a familiar template. Readers can expect certain patterns to underlie stories of disaster or achievement.

After today perhaps you'll have a new bin in your library, this one titled, "Disaster Stories."

"Today I want to teach you that if you find yourself flooded with facts as you read and want to discern what is and is not important, it can help to see that beneath the details, many true stories are either tales of achievement or of disaster, and each of those kinds of story follows a predictable path. That path can help readers determine what matters most in the story—which details to pay most attention to and which to pay less."

TEACHING

Model for children how your knowledge of types of nonfiction—achievement or disaster—informs your reading and allows you to notice patterns.

"So let me try this. Listen while I read."

Planting the Trees of Kenya

As Wangari Maathai tells it, when she was growing up on a farm in the hills of central Kenya, the earth was clothed in its dress of green.

Fig trees, olive trees, crotons, and flame trees covered the land, and fish filled the pure waters of the streams.

The fig tree was sacred then, and Wangari knew not to disturb it, not even to carry its fallen branches home for firewood. In the stream near her homestead where she went to collect water for her mother, she played with glistening frogs' eggs, trying to gather them like beads into necklaces, though they slipped through her fingers back into the clear water.

"Okay, readers, I'm going to stop here. I'm already getting a sense of déjà vu, of 'I have seen this kind of story before.' Let me tell you what I'm feeling. First, I'm noticing that this book begins with the account of a little girl. And I know that many achievement stories begin this way. They begin with the achiever's childhood. The author does this to establish some central traits about that person, traits that will serve her as she later sets out to achieve something.

"So here we learn that Wangari respects the sacred fig tree in her native Kenya. We learn, too, that she plays carefully, respectfully, with the frog eggs. In fact, this whole opening is about Wangari's respectful response to nature, to the land where she was raised. Because I am thinking this will be an achievement story, I'm thinking that the

Always remember that a text that you've read aloud to the class can be used again and again. For example, if you want to teach readers to compare and contrast texts that contain similar topics treated differently, you could invite students to look between to texts you've read aloud, say, Planting the Trees of Kenya *and* The Mummy's Curse. *In both texts, the main character comes into contact with something that many believe is sacred—the pharaoh's tomb, the fig tree. Readers could compare and contrast the character's responses to that which some believe is sacred. The Common Core Standards expect fifth-graders to do this work but it is certainly within the grasp for younger students as well. Of course, this is just one lesson you could teach from revisiting read aloud texts and there are scores of others.*

big stuff about this person's childhood will in some way herald her big achievements. I can wisely predict that her big achievements will have something do with nature, with the land she seems to love so much, and with this trait the author has told us about in her, even this early in the book: her respect for nature. I also have this sense of 'expectancy'—the feeling that something is coming or is going to change. Do you know the feeling I mean? Everything is lovely and good in this story so far—pure water, sacred tree, playful girl. Most stories don't go on like that. Something is going to happen to make all this not so perfect. Don't you feel that?" I displayed some features I'd written earlier on chart paper. [Fig. XI-1]

"Let's pause for a minute to return to the story we've read together, *Secrets of the Mummies*, and see if we can tap into that same sense of déjà vu again. Listen while I read.

> "I must find the lost tomb."

> Howard Carter had been saying the same thing for years. Now it was 1922, the fifth year he had spent digging through sand and rocks in Egypt's Valley of the Kings.

"Hmm . . . does it feel like a kind of story we've read before? Does it feed into the path of an achievement story? Well, I think it does. This story does tell us right away that Howard Carter has been at a task for many years. So that establishes a trait: determination. What else? We learn that he's digging in Egypt's Valley of the Kings for a lost tomb. We could have safely bet his achievement would have something to do with the treasures buried in Egypt. (And we know, from having read it, we would have been right.) And I have a sense of expectancy right from the first sentence. He says he must find the lost tomb, so as a reader, I am poised to read about him finding it!"

ACTIVE INVOLVEMENT

Invite partners to determine together if they are reading either a disaster story or an achievement story.

"Readers, we've just talked a bit about the sort of things we can expect to find in an achievement story—the things that will give us that 'Aha, I've see this before' feeling,

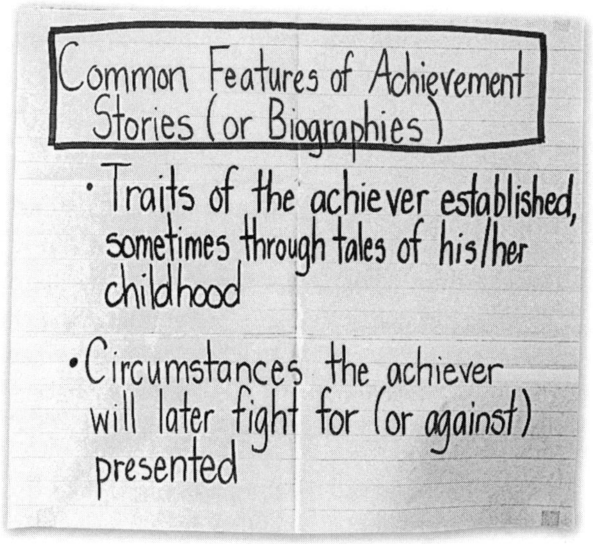

Common Features of Achievement Stories (or Biographies)
- Traits of the achiever established, sometimes through tales of his/her childhood
- Circumstances the achiever will later fight for (or against) presented

Figure XI-1
You'll want the words of your chart either to match the words of your teaching or to capture your children's language.

The interesting thing is that Secrets of the Mummies *is a tale of achievement . . . yet disaster strikes. Sorting texts into categories highlights their complexities.*

that sense of déjà vu. In a minute, I'm going to hand out a book to each partnership, and I'm not going to tell you if it's an achievement story or a disaster story. The two of you will take a few minutes to figure it out, and as you do, jot down the things that tip you off—the features or clues or whatever you notice that make you think it's one kind or another of a narrative nonfiction text."

I handed half of the partnerships disaster stories and half achievement stories. As I handed out the books, I said, "Those of you who are getting achievement stories already have a couple tips (I pointed to the chart 'Common Features of Achievement Stories') to help guide you, but you have the challenge of having to come up with *additional* items to add to our chart. Those of you who are getting disaster stories won't have any guidelines to help you, but you'll have a blank slate for deciding what makes a disaster story. I bet you'll find some characteristics we could record on a chart."

As children opened their books, I called out a tip: "You shouldn't need to read much of the book before you get that déjà vu feeling." After a minute or two, I said, "Put the book down and talk about what you have noticed so far."

After a few minutes, I reconvened the class. "Readers, I just gave you a pretty difficult task, and you really rose to the occasion. Sam and Aly's book was *The Lost Star: The Story of Amelia Earhart*. Sam quickly realized it was a biography and that it was an achievement story. Aly said that she knew that Amelia Earhart died before she could achieve her goal of flying around the world, but she set other records she is known for. That gave them the idea that they would read this trying to figure out what helped Amelia accomplish those achievements and what got in her way.

LINK

Remind children to draw upon a repertoire of strategies they've learned before they go off into their own work of the day.

"As you all continue reading, you have lots of strategies now to draw upon, and all of them, combined, should help you read long and strong while holding onto the parts that matter most in your books. Off you go."

This active involvement section will require that you do a bit of organizational work. You need to collect texts, to distribute them to partners and to re-collect them later. You might well think, "That's too much of a hassle for me." By all means, invent ways to streamline and simplify these minilessons. For example, perhaps instead of this active involvement, the whole class could watch as you or a child scan through a text and then the class could call out or jot down the way to categorize the text.

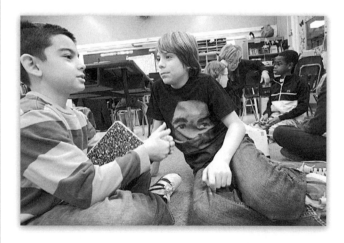

CONFERRING AND SMALL-GROUP WORK

Support Children in the Particular Work of Reading Biographies

Remind Yourself of a Repertoire of Possible Teaching Points You Might Draw upon in a Small Group of Biography Readers

You may want to convene a small group of children who are reading biographies to help them extend their thinking about this kind of narrative nonfiction text.

You will not want to approach this work with only one possible plan of action, but rather with a repertoire of possible teaching points so that you can take note of what the readers are already doing and are wanting to do and can teach in response to what they show you.

You could, for example, let this group of readers know that in biographies (and in life) one really good way to get to know a person is to think about what that person does in response to experiencing difficulties or challenges in his or her life. Earlier I mentioned the adage "When you go over the bumps, what's inside spills out." That can be true for our own lives, and it can also be true for the lives that are featured in the biographies that we read. Every person experiences setbacks and challenges; people who are successful somehow manage to get past the difficulties in their lives. It will usually pay off for

---

MID-WORKSHOP TEACHING POINT

Readers Use Templates to Uncover Structures in Hybrid Texts

"Readers, can I stop you for a minute?" I waited until all eyes were on me and then said, "Jasmine just pointed something out to me that is so interesting. She's been reading a narrative nonfiction book about the *Titanic*, and because she's heard about the *Titanic* and knows it was a ship that sank years ago, she began reading this book, noting the details that relate to that disaster. She paid attention to signs that the ship was going down, that many people were about to lose their lives." I leaned in and said, "But then, as she kept reading, she realized something else was happening in this book. People were helping other people. Men sent women and children into lifeboats first. Molly Brown rowed a lifeboat to safety. Wives stayed with their husbands and died rather than leaving them behind. Jasmine started wondering if maybe this wasn't a story of a disaster so much as a story of achievement. She decided to read with that angle in mind, and sure enough, she began seeing the patterns she'd expected; she noticed that several people struggled against great odds and ended up saving lives. There wasn't one big hero who saved the day, but there were these smaller accounts of quiet heroes.

"Jasmine, I wonder if you realize how huge this discovery is. You've shown us that some books don't just fall neatly into one category. They aren't simply the story of XYZ disaster or of ABC victory. Rather, they are hybrid texts. They are stories of *both* disaster and achievement. Others of you may find books like this, too, maybe not in this classroom or during this unit but in the

continued on next page

---

readers of biographies to notice ways in which the fiber of the person is revealed in times when the person confronts difficulties.

If you've reminded a small group of readers that they can extrapolate aspects of a person's character from watching ways that person responds to difficulties, then you'll also want to remind those readers to read with that theory in hand, expecting to confirm or to revise the theory. They will find evidence either that helps them say, "Yes, I was right!" or that helps them extend or revise their theories.

You could, alternatively, help the group of readers attend to the secondary characters in their biographies. This opens a whole treasure trove of possible teaching points. For starters, you can let readers know that sometimes it is interesting to notice the roles that secondary characters play in helping the main characters overcome challenges. Often in biographies, the secondary character will be a parent, a teacher, or a colleague, and the secondary character will play a big part in the main character's success. As you help readers think about the roles played by secondary characters, you can help them realize that there are *kinds of* secondary characters in books (and in life stories) just as there are kinds of texts. For example, there are *supporters,* that is, people who support the main character as he moves toward his goal. Sometimes these supporters work in quiet ways; they answer questions, offer small bits of counsel, or act as guardians. Other times, they are right-hand supporters, who take a more active role in the main character's life. They forge a path, rally troops of support, or take part in the movement or discovery or solution the main character targets as her life's work. Then, too, there are secondary characters who are adversaries, people who present obstacles for the main character. They may prevent the main character from getting what she wants or fight for an opposing view. They may even try to hurt the main character. They're just as important to the story of the main character's life as the supporters, because often they represent the hurdle the main character has to overcome to achieve something big.

Of course, it is also useful to help readers of biographies step back at some point and ask, "What can I learn from the subject of this text? How can this person's story help me live my own life?" Often children pick biographies of people whose stories touch them in a deeply personal way. Maybe something in the subject's life mirrors something in the child's life, or her achievements match the child's own dreams and goals. In the conference below, notice how I ask Lily to figure out how the things she's noticed about Coretta Scott King, the woman whose biography she is reading, go together to say something meaningful about the whole of Coretta's life.

Anticipate How Your One-to-One Conferences Might Go

I pulled my chair alongside Lily, who was reading a biography of Coretta Scott King. I said, "I'm so glad you are reading about Coretta Scott King.

MID-WORKSHOP TEACHING POINT

continued from previous page

future, when you're reading narrative nonfiction on your own. When that happens, you may want to think about the structure of that kind of text and about what sorts of anchors readers can grab onto to wade through the details to find the big meaning behind them.

"There's another thing Jasmine discovered just now. Sometimes in stories of achievement, there isn't just one hero but many. Often people come together to do great things. Martin Luther King Jr. may have been a prominent leader in the African-American civil rights movement, but he didn't fight that battle on his own. There were many other people who stood by his side, who marched, who spoke up, who risked their lives for a cause they believed in. Rosa Parks, for example. It was like that on the *Titanic,* too."

She's a really important woman. Can you walk me through the thinking you have been doing as you read this book?"

"I'm thinking about the things that show me about her. I have a Post-it here because she was born in April, so that shows me something about her life. And it was the depression, like when lots of people were poor. And the book said that during her life there was segregation."

Sweeping her finger down the page, she found what she was looking for and read aloud to me.

During the 1930s, blacks were segregated, or kept apart, from whites. Because the Scotts were black, they were not allowed to try on clothes in a store where whites shopped, drink from the same water fountain that whites used. . . .″

And then Lily showed me the several notes she'd jotted. *[Fig. XI-2]*

Lily, as always, was noticing some important details about her character and was both jotting notes about those details and clearly absorbing the information. It seemed, though, that her Post-its—while interesting for the most part—weren't being put to their best use. It seemed to me that Lily might be prompted to pause to make more of what she'd already noticed instead of moving along in her reading.

I said, "Lily, as usual, you're noticing some really important things about your book. You're collecting information about Coretta and also about the context in which she lives. I think you are ready to step it up a little bit. You see, when you are reading a story, it is a bit like you are zipping up your coat—bear with me, I'll tell you why—only the zipper is your brain, and you are pulling details of the story alongside each other to hold a big theory together, like a zipper holds together a coat." I tugged on her sweater zipper to show her what I meant. "This is something that you practiced when you were reading fiction books—taking all of the details

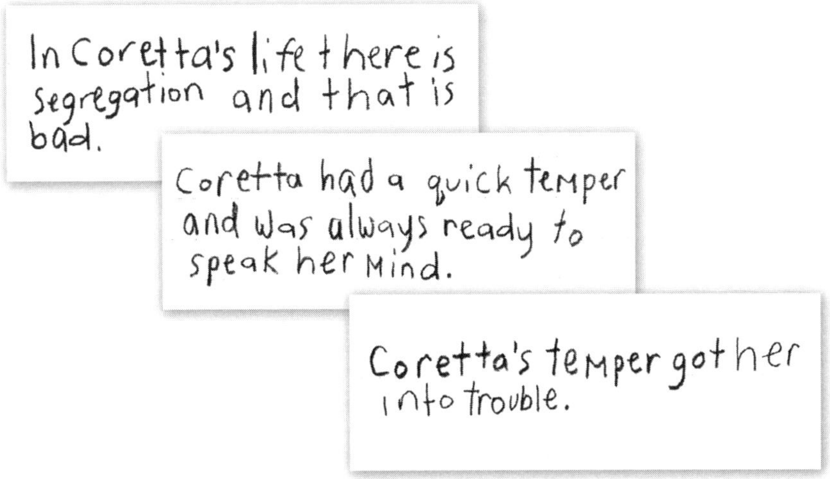

In Coretta's life there is segregation and that is bad.

Coretta had a quick temper and was always ready to speak her mind.

Coretta's temper got her into trouble.

Figure XI-2
In a conference, I nudge Lily to synthesize these thoughts into a theory.

about your characters and seeing how they connected, zipping them up into a bigger idea or theory. Well, no matter what kind of book you are reading, you can always pull your ideas together to make something bigger out of them.

"Let's try now. Reread these Post-its and then talk about how they might fit together to make a bigger idea or theory about Coretta's life."

Lily reread her first two Post-its. She was about to rush on to read yet another Post-it, but I intervened to ask, "Before you head off to another detail, think first about how these two might fit together." I reread them out loud and then said, "I wonder, in this story of her life, what sorts of things might set off her temper."

Lily snapped to it. "Segregation. Because it's not fair. So she probably talked her mind about it and got into trouble."

I nodded encouragingly and then prompted, "And after she got into trouble, do you think she quit trying and gave up and went home to eat bonbons for the rest of her life?"

"No! Well, we know she didn't do that, because there wouldn't be this book about her otherwise. 'Cause she got famous."

"Great. You're noticing another important thing to pay attention to when you're reading biographies. Usually they are about someone who achieved a lot, someone who had to overcome obstacles to get where they got. It's often an achievement story, like we've been talking about.

Whenever you are reading a story—whether it is fiction or true—you can learn a lot from thinking as you read, 'How did this person overcome the obstacles, the hard parts?' And of course, zipping the things you're noticing into a bigger idea about the character is really important, just like you're starting to do. Let's see how the other things you noticed fit in with your idea that Coretta talked her mind about segregation and got in trouble for it."

I paused for a moment to make sure Lily was with me and then asked, "How will you do that as you continue reading this book?"

"I'm going to find out if Coretta did say bad stuff about segregation and whether she got into trouble, and I'm going to see if any of the other things I noticed fit into my idea."

I nodded. "Wise move. And remember to work on jotting ideas that have some weight to them. Jot on Post-its when you see a connection between two observations, or when your mind is thinking something—which you'll want it to do! But you need to pick up your speed a bit so you can reach for and hold onto the story line in your books. Sometimes, like in this book, it is a little bit hidden under a slew of facts. Nice work today. Off you go."

I tucked that point in about speed because while I didn't think it necessary to spend a whole conference on, I had noticed that Lily's pace had gone way down as a reader of expository nonfiction earlier, and I wanted to keep the idea of reading a lot fresh in her mind.

Moving on, I pulled my chair up next to Sam and saw he was reading *Charlotte Bronte and Jane Eyre* by Stewart Ross. I like to let readers know when I have a connection to the books they're reading, so I said, "I saw that you are reading this and I am fascinated. I love *Jane Eyre*. It is one of those books I have read a score of times. How's this going?"

Sam smiled back at that. "Good."

"And what are you working on as you read this book?"

"Well." Sam leafed through the Post-its he'd placed in the book. "I'm working on writing lots of Post-its to make a theory. You see, the publisher agreed Charlotte Brontë could write this book because she tried another book called *The Professor*, but the publisher didn't really like it. And so, he, well, right now this is all about the character in the book, Jane, and how she was at an orphanage, and then they gave her away to a boarding school—"

I put my finger up since Sam seemed to be on a roll, listing every bit of minutiae that he'd read so far. In conferences, I don't have any feeling that I need to let students ramble on and on until they are finished talking. Teaching time is precious. "Can I stop you there for one second, Sam? I feel like you're giving me a lot of information about the book, which is great. But I'm sort of fascinated by what you said about how you were working on using lots of Post-its to make a theory, right? Can we look at those?"

"Yes, these are the ones I wrote so far today," Sam said, and he laid his jottings on the table. [Figs. XI-3 and XI-4]

"So, do you have a theory yet?"

Sam nodded immediately. "Yes. I think that Charlotte is very strong about her writing, and even if someone insults her about it, she keeps on doing it, because in the beginning someone said to her, 'Literature ought not to be the business of a woman's life,' and she got really upset, and so she changed her name to a man's name and started writing again."

"Wow, that's remarkable. What tenacity! It seems like Charlotte was determined to be a writer, no matter what. That's why she kept going even though people discouraged her, even though she had to change her name, even though her sisters were more successful than she was. Have you jotted that theory yet?"

"No, not yet." Sam was already reaching for a new Post-it when I asked him to please jot it now. I gave him a moment to jot. [Fig. XI-5]

I wanted Sam to realize that even though he was working toward a theory, he shouldn't think of it as working toward *the* theory. As readers get more information, our theories usually get more complex or change altogether as another aspect of the character or story becomes more important. I nodded at his jotting and said, "Sam, this is a great theory to start with and to keep in mind as you read on. Let me remind you of something I think you already know, which is that when we make a theory, it's usually not the same on page thirty as it might be on page sixty.

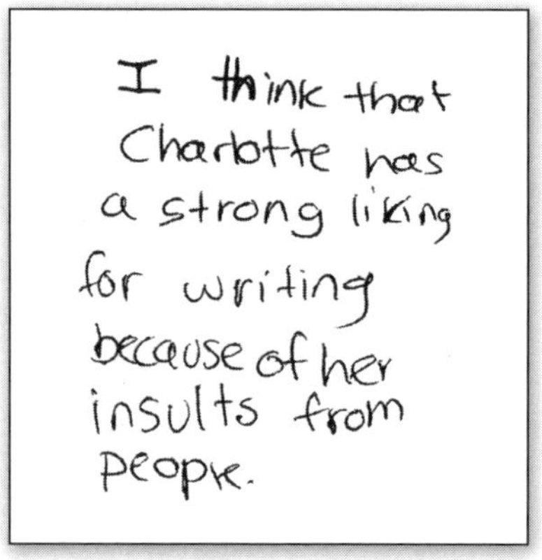

I think that
Charlotte has
a strong liking
for writing
because of her
insults from
people.

Figure XI-5
Sam jotted his theory about Charlotte
Brontë.

I think that
if I read
Jane Eyre
I would
really like the book
too.

Figure XI-3
Who would have thought fifth grade
boys would be eager to read *Jane Eyre*!

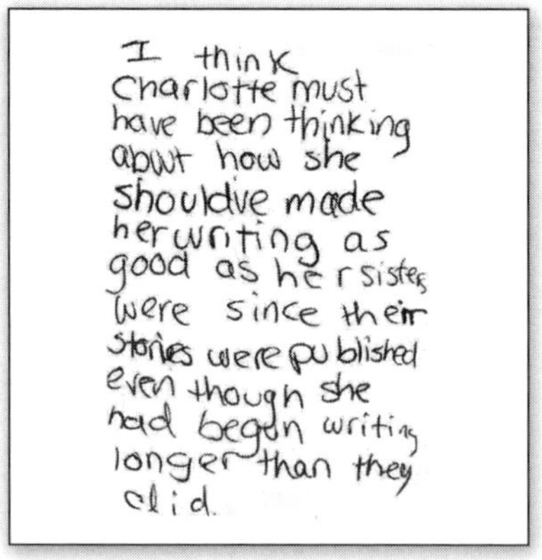

I think
Charlotte must
have been thinking
about how she
should've made
her writing as
good as her sisters
were since their
stories were published
even though she
had begun writing
longer than they
did.

Figure XI-4
Sam's response to Charlotte Brontë and
Jane Eyre

Your theory might become more complicated or change in some way, and you want to be open to that as a reader."

Sam nodded back at me. "Definitely."

"Great. Sam, there's one other thing to think about when reading biographies specifically. Biographies are written about people who have accomplished big things. For example, there's no biography of me in your library, sadly, but this person, Charlotte, has done something big. It's going to be an achievement story. As you're reading it, you already know that her struggle against all that frustration and discouragement was successful. People who make a great impact on the world also impact the lives of those close to them. So you could ask yourself this question as you keep reading: 'What was the impact of Charlotte's life on those around her?' And if you think about that as you read on, it might help you make your theory more complicated or stronger.

TEACHING SHARE

Readers Uncover Text Structures to Anticipate How Texts Are Apt to Unfold

Ask students to tell their partners how they prepared their minds for reading their narrative nonfiction books.

"Earlier, we talked about the fact that nonfiction readers rev up our minds for reading. Right now, tell your partner how you revved up your mind for reading the book you are reading now."

The room erupted into conversation, and I listened in. Brianna said, "When I read about the Beatles, I warmed up by thinking of all the Beatles songs I know. I reminded myself of their songs."

Nearby, I heard Kadija tell her partner, "I was reading *Who Is Maria Tallchief?* so I looked it over and I knew she was a ballerina that had tough times, and I knew the book would tell about those times, and I thought, 'She must of gotten over them 'cause now she is in a book,' so I figured I'd learn how she got past those tough times." Kadija's enthusiasm—both for the work she was doing and for the book itself—was apparent in the way her words rushed out. I whispered to her partner, suggesting she compliment Kadija on how she was using both the information she learned from the book's cover and her prior knowledge to predict what the book would probably be about.

I convened the children. "Wise work. Even before we start reading the actual sentences in a text, we look over the text and think, 'What sort of text is this?' We look at the headings, the pictures, the opening lines, and think, 'How does this text seem to go?' Once we have an idea of the sort of text that this is, and an idea of the subject that the text addresses, we can predict not just the start of the book but the layout of it, thinking, 'I bet maybe the book will go like this.' In our minds, we almost write the text that we are about to read."

Ask students, as they prepare their minds for reading narrative nonfiction, to think about whether the text is an achievement story or a disaster story.

"When we talked about all this prereading earlier in the year, though, we hadn't yet realized that it can help to remember that the nonfiction stories sometimes fit into familiar templates, such as the template of an achievement story or a disaster story, each of which has its own way of unfolding. Look again at your book and think, 'Could this be described

Notice that it's been a long while since you taught students that readers rev up our minds to get ready to read. You'll absolutely want to stitch key points from earlier in the year into your teaching. The whole point is for your teaching to make a lasting impact.

The temptation when listening to a partner conversation is to bypass the listening partner and to respond to whomever is speaking. It is usually more helpful to coach the listener. You'll be amazed at how active listening partners can be, and at the new energy this brings to your class.

as an achievement story? A disaster story? If so, how does that knowledge help me anticipate the way the text will go?' Turn and talk."

After children talked a bit, I intervened. "Some of you realized that the title of the book, alone, clues you in to whether the book follows one of those familiar templates. For example, Kobe is reading *Dare to Dream: Coretta Scott King and the Civil Rights Movement* and *Walking for Freedom: The Montgomery Bus Boycott*. I bet you can guess whether those books are achievement stories or disaster stories."

Tell students to choose new books from their bins and practice preparing their minds to read.

"So you have already learned a lot about how readers go about revving up for reading. Right now, I want you and your partner to take a narrative nonfiction book that you have not yet read out of your bin and use every last drop of what you have learned about reading to get yourselves ready for an amazing read of this text."

IN THIS SESSION,

you will teach students that readers figure out unfamiliar words by envisioning the worlds of our texts and thinking about what would make sense.

Envisioning (and Other Strategies) to Figure Out Unfamiliar Words

t is inevitable. You learn about a subject, and you come away with a new repertoire of terminology. If the topic is horses, people will talk about the girth, the stirrups, the reins, the bridle, the halter, and the lunge line. If the topic is American government, people will talk about the executive, legislative, and judicial branches; about systems of checks and balances; and about the Constitution and the Bill of Rights. If it is geography, people will talk about longitude, latitude, continents, and peninsulas. These words give learners access to the concepts for which they stand. There is no question that readers of nonfiction learn new words as we read. We needn't know every term related to a subject before we open the text and begin the course of study, for there is no better way for a person to enrich his or her vocabulary than through wide reading.

This means that it is absolutely not the case that a reader needs to be pretaught vocabulary words before embarking on a nonfiction text. The text itself can teach words and, more importantly, the concepts for which the words stand. But this only works if the reader is constructing sense. It is the reader's firm hold on the overall meaning of a passage and the more specific meaning of a sentence that allows the reader to imbue unfamiliar words with meaning. Because the unknown words in nonfiction texts will tend to be both unfamiliar and important, it is especially critical that readers of nonfiction texts can hold tight to meaning while reading, using their grip on this lifeline to get them past the hard parts—the tricky words.

So make sure that even when reading nonfiction texts, readers can read with close to 96% accuracy. Perhaps, early in the book, or the text, the percentage might be a bit less as

GETTING READY

- You will need to have collected an anecdote from a child who displayed his or her problem-solving strategies to tackle an unknown word. I chose a child who made a best guess at the meaning of an unknown word using context clues and who read on to confirm the word's meaning.

- Prepare to reread a passage from "Spill!," a narrative in the DK reader *Disasters at Sea*. If you decide to read from a different nonfiction text, be sure to read one that contains technical vocabulary, the meaning of which can be determined making a best guess, using context clues, and reading on to confirm one's guess.

- Prepare a chart titled "Ways to Figure Out What an Unknown Word Means." You will compile this chart with children during the active involvement.

readers take in the new words that will be brought to life within the text. But certainly as the reader moves further into the text, 96% of the words should be familiar to the reader.

Although it is not new for me to say that research is clear that children need to read with 96% accuracy to be able to comprehend and learn from a text, this apparently needs to

> It is the reader's firm hold
> on the overall meaning of
> a passage and the more
> specific meaning of a
> sentence that allows the
> reader to imbue unfamiliar
> words with meaning.

be restated within the context of nonfiction reading because time and again I see that readers who are given just-right fiction texts are given too-hard nonfiction texts. If you see a disengaged reader during this unit of study, chances are extremely good that the youngster will be holding a text he or she cannot handle. You can't see this and simply shrug it off as business as usual, thinking, "Yeah, he's one of my strugglers." Strugglers, like every other reader, need to read books that they can read with enough fluency, accuracy, and comprehension that they can learn from the book they are reading.

It helps to recognize that the illustrations—and other visual trappings—of many nonfiction books often give these texts the feel of being accessible without making them that way. Our aim in this unit is to teach readers to do much more than scan across nonfiction texts. They can scan already! We want to help them build stamina for engagement with longer, denser nonfiction texts than those they have read in the past. To this end, we need to match readers to appropriately leveled books in the nonfiction unit— and more. We need to teach, reteach, and devise specific strategies to help readers be undaunted, and even more, informed, by unfamiliar, content-specific words and phrases.

You'll probably keep a list of these strategies handy as you pull alongside your children and peer into the nonfiction texts that they are holding. "What a super-looking word," you might say, pointing under *archipelago*. "It looks like it's simply itching to be pronounced the way it's spelled. Let's try saying it: Arch-i-pel-a-go! Hmm, what a satisfying mouthful. I wonder what it means." After this nonchalant "wondering," you might wait in brief silence, hoping that the child suggests a strategy for figuring out the word's meaning. It could be a strategy you taught in previous units or a strategy that the child has developed through her own reading experience.

If the child remains silent, you'll know to deliberately insert specific instruction in vocabulary-deciphering. Even in situations when a child uses some strategies, you'll want to introduce yet more ways of pulling meaning from the new word.

The structure of the nonfiction texts you've dealt with thus far in the unit in itself provides a vital scaffold in the comprehension of unfamiliar words. Children can be taught to hold on tightly to the story when they get to unknown words without compromising their overall comprehension of the larger text. This lesson on word decoding, then, is essentially advice to keep on reading past a hard word—not dismissively, but with care and attention to specific clues that will enable us to develop, and later prove, a theory of its possible meaning.

MINILESSON

Envisioning (and Other Strategies) to Figure Out Unfamiliar Words

CONNECTION

Celebrate the way that children are using their sense of how texts are apt to go to help them read, but spotlight your concern that children are also encountering hard words.

"Readers could I have your attention for a bit? I've been watching you read and conferring with a few of you, and I'm noticing: you all have a pretty good idea of what is likely to happen next in your nonfiction stories. Many of you already have a feel for whether your text fits into the template of either disaster or achievement stories, and this is helping you anticipate the direction your story is taking.

"But I'm also noting something else. There are a few hard words in your nonfiction books! And I'm not embarrassed to say, there are one or two words in there that if you all were to ask *me* what they mean, I'd hem and haw, but I probably couldn't answer you. I saw one—okay maybe two, three—words in your books as I was making the rounds that I don't know the meaning of." I threw up my hands and grinned conspiringly, allowing the kids the happy relief of knowing that even the best adult reader isn't a foolproof dictionary. "And so I'm going to tell you an insider secret."

COACHING TIPS

Toward the end of a bend in the road of a unit (and toward the end of this unit as a whole), we find it helpful to take the opportunity to list out, in broad strokes, the ways our children have changed and grown as readers. This helps our community develop a collective sense of "Look how far we've come!" and it gives us a chance to build anticipation (and kids' confidence) for the upcoming work. Peter Johnston writes, in Choice Words, *"Often teachers draw children's attention to their learning histories. Showing children that they have changed as community members, learners, readers, and writers reveals that they are in the process of becoming. It helps to ask questions such as 'How have you changed as a reader?' and 'What do you think you need to work on next?'" The advantage of drawing attention to change in learning and behavior is that children can then project their learning futures.*

Richard Allington says that it benefits struggling readers to have close relationships to richly literate adults, readers who model a disposition toward reading and who can share the enthusiasm and pleasure found in the act of reading and thinking about texts. Of course, this kind of relationship benefits any kind of reader. For some of our kids, we might very well be the primary richly literate adult in their lives. Therefore, it's powerful to find opportunities to share our reading habits, behaviors, quirks, eccentricities, and vulnerabilities. In this connection, I reveal vulnerability. I confide that I also encounter words I don't know—and that that's okay.

Name your teaching point. Tell children that readers need to figure out unfamiliar vocabulary and that one way to do this is to make educated guesses.

"This is the secret that I want to teach you today. The most powerful readers don't *already know* what every single word in a book means. The most powerful readers work hard to *figure out* what a tricky word means! One of the ways we can do that is to get a mental picture of what's going on in that part of the story and to think about what would make sense."

TEACHING

Tell a story about a time when a reader determined the meaning of an unknown word. Describe the child's process in detailed, sequential steps.

"Yesterday, I was conferring with Danny, who was rereading that story we heard the other day—"Spill." And he ran into a couple of words he didn't know. He did really hard work with those words. One of the hard words was the word *hull*. What I want to do right now is to show you what Danny did to figure out what that word probably meant. You'll be researchers, listening to the story of what Danny did, and you and your partner can record strategies he used to help him figure out a tricky word. [Fig. XII-1]

The phrases already know *and* figure out *are in italics for a reason other than that you should stress them while stating this teaching point. A famous study by Stanford researcher Carol Dweck reveals that children who are repeatedly praised for "effort" as opposed to "innate abilities" have significantly higher rates of success at tasks and are more confident at taking the risks needed to learn and improve. Telling a child constantly that he or she is "smart" creates a vulnerability about being exposed as being anything less. Praising a child for trying, working hard, or aiming to figure out something, on the other hand, develops the sense of agency needed to explore and work things out.*

It is important, therefore, that you debunk the myth that good readers possess prefabricated vocabularies that they bring to texts, or that they know a word before they encounter it within the text and that it is this prior knowledge that enables them to make sense of their story. Your emphasis, instead, is that good readers have and learn and make strategies to figure out words, and you will teach some of these.

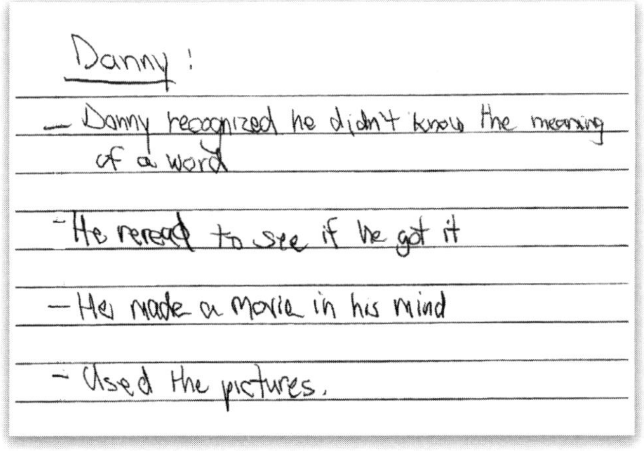

Danny!
— Danny recognized he didn't know the meaning of a word
— He reread to see if he got it
— He made a movie in his mind
— Used the pictures.

Figure XII-1
One child's record of the strategies you dramatize in the minilesson.

"Okay. Here's the story. I have the notes of exactly what he did. First, he was reading along like this:

> The gigantic ship moved slowly underneath the clear night sky. The *Exxon Valdez* weighed more than 200,000 tons and was 987 feet long. It had just left Valdez in Alaska carrying a huge cargo of crude oil to California. The massive vessel, known as VLCC or Very Large Crude Carrier, had a crew of 20. She was under the command of Captain Joseph Hazelwood, an experienced sea voyager.
>
> "Captain, there are some growlers ahead!" warned the officer on watch.
>
> Growlers are small icebergs. They weren't large enough to sink the *Exxon Valdez*, but they could dent her **hull**. [emphasis mine]

"At that point, Danny paused and looked quizzical. 'I'm not sure what *hull* means,' he said and reread just a little bit. It went like this: '. . . they could dent her hull. Okay.'

"I stopped Danny to ask him why he said 'Okay.' He told me that when he got to that part, he knew he needed to picture it. So he worked to make the picture, and when he got the picture in mind, he said, 'Okay.' That meant, 'I'm ready to read on.' When I asked Danny to tell me about how he pictured things, he said, 'I don't know what a *hull* is, so I was picturing the boat moving along in the water. I saw an iceberg—a growler. I guessed if the boat hit one, it would dent the part that's in the water. I know that icebergs are not just on top of the water but they are huge underwater, too. That helped me think where the hull might be that got the dent!'

"I said to Danny, 'It sounds like you made a picture in your mind and that picture helped you think about the hard word.' So class, I'm hoping that you see that Danny made a theory for himself about the word *hull*, and once he had a theory in mind, he was ready to read on, looking for information that might tell him if his theory was right nor not.

In schools today, there is increasing recognition that children need to learn more vocabulary, but there is little understanding of how we can help them to do this. Teachers tend to shower words onto children. In many upper elementary and middle school classrooms, children are given fifteen new words each week in language arts and more in science and social studies. Any one chapter of a social studies or science textbook is apt to contain a score of new words, and often these refer to concepts that are also new—to ideas such as photosynthesis or capitalism. It's no surprise that children don't actually learn vocabulary from this sort of instruction. The sheer volume of new vocabulary would overwhelm anyone.

How important it is for teachers to realize that children benefit from being asked to learn fewer words and to learn those words deeply. Of course, learning any one word deeply ends up meaning that the reader learns more than the one word. For example, if one learns the word scorching, *one might also learn the opposite,* freezing. *One might see* scorching *as part of a gradated line representing temperature. Other words on that same line might include* tepid, lukewarm, boiling, *and so on. Of course, many words represent only one of a set that could be depicted and expanded by a diagram that shows gradations.*

"Then Danny looked ahead in the book, saw pictures of oil spilling everywhere, and said, 'I am pretty sure the hull is the underwater part because it's a disaster story, and so I am thinking what part of a ship would it be the biggest disaster if it got dented by icebergs? I guess the main part—the part that keeps the water out.'"

ACTIVE INVOLVEMENT

Recruit children to name what the child did to figure out the word. They'll name steps they too can take in figuring out unknown words.

"So readers, turn and talk. What strategies did Danny use that you could use as well when you are reading? And what else could he have tried? As you talk, I'll listen in so we can make a chart of the strategies you come up with."

After children talked in partners for a bit, I signaled for their attention. "Readers, some of you noticed how Danny used his big understandings of the story and his knowledge of icebergs to figure out what the word *hull* meant. Many of you noticed he made a movie in his mind of the story and used that mental movie to help him figure out what *hull* must refer to, and he also drew on his knowledge that this is a disaster story. I've been jotting what you are saying onto a list of strategies readers use to figure out unknown words. What other suggestions do you have to add to our list?" [Fig. XII-2]

After calling on a few children and adding their input to the list, I revealed the chart. "When we encounter tricky words or unclear parts, we roll up our sleeves and get to work. We think of what we know. We consider the general direction of our story. We use parts of the book or stuff in the world to help us. We have lots of ways to figure out words that are unfamiliar to us."

When looking for ways to support a child's vocabulary development, seize on the power of photographs and video tapes. If a child talks about what he sees in a photograph, you can restate what he says, incorporating some of the terminology that you want him to learn and then throwing the conversational ball back to him. If the child who has discussed a photograph while the picture is right in front of him is later asked to talk about that photograph to someone who hasn't seen it, the child will be nudged to become more explicit, embedding more details into his language. All of this is terrifically helpful for his vocabulary development.

The list restates some of the things children had said to each other, but I simply compiled and read off the list. You could do this differently, eliciting from children, but watch the clock! I recorded kids' ideas and then read off my list to keep the minilesson concise, but also so I could make the points as clear as possible.

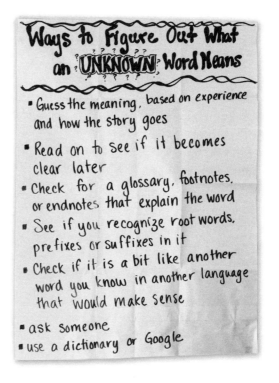

Figure XII-2
This chart is a collection of students' own strategies.

Read a passage that demonstrates that reading on can confirm or alter our word-solving theory. Invite children to discuss the confirmation or alteration of our theory.

"Let's read on, carrying Danny's theory of what *hull* means with us. Let's see if there is another part of the text that mentions what the *hull* is."

> Cousins tried to contact Captain Hazelwood. Even as he did so, a terrible shudder ripped through the ship.
>
> "Rocks!" The rocks were only 50 feet below the surface of the water, but *Exxon Valdez*'s hull went deeper than this. The ship had run aground.

"Turn and talk! Does that confirm or alter our theory of what the word *hull* means?"

After children talked for a minute, I signaled for their attention. "I agree with what you are saying. So far, everything that Danny reads, as he moves on, confirms the mental image he has of the hull. To learn new words, you'll need to carry around your ideas about them even beyond reading time. For example, later on, while watching TV or maybe in some other book or a conversation, that word will come up again, and Danny will develop his sense of what it means even more. That's the way we learn new words!"

The word hull *does not offer the best opportunity to show how all of the strategies for vocabulary building work. If you think looking for prefixes, suffixes, or root words will be helpful, or if your children are multilingual, you would choose a different example vocabulary word for this minilesson, choosing a word that will allow you to show how those strategies can unlock meaning in a word.*

LINK

Remind children that to figure out what new words mean and keep them as part of their vocabulary, they'll need to work hard.

"Remember, always, when you read, it's inevitable that you'll encounter unfamiliar words or tricky phrases. That happens to any kind of reader, whether you're a first grader reading *Biscuit* books or a grown-up scientist reading about nuclear energy. That's the beauty and challenge for readers. We hit hard parts, but when we work at them, we learn new words and ideas. To learn these new words and ideas and ways of naming things, we have to be willing to work hard at figuring out meanings, and we have to hold onto the word by noticing it in other places and books and letting those new sightings add to our understanding of the word. Otherwise, we'll be stuck our whole lives only knowing the words and categories we know right now at this moment!"

CONFERRING AND SMALL-GROUP WORK

Help Children Learn Unknown Words, Either by Pausing Less or by Pausing More

If your minilesson invites your students to be more active word solvers, you'll want to anticipate in advance that a portion of your conferences and small-group work will support word solving, while another portion of your conferences will remind readers to draw on their full repertoire of skills and strategies. It can help to approach the reading workshop having already thought for a moment about what your conferring might be like for your more novice and more advanced word solvers.

Conferring to Support Your More Novice Word Solvers

Pulling alongside Rosa, I found her thumbing through *The Cactus Hotel*. When I asked how her reading was going, I got a small shrug before she pointed to *scab* and *insulated* as two words—both on the same page—that she was trying to "figure out."

"You've pinpointed words that you aren't sure of," I told her. "That's the first step to figuring them out. Good." I paused to let this reassurance sink in. "What's the second step you want to try?" I asked. Rosa shrugged a little. I continued. "For me, I like to feel the tricky word in my mouth, so I pronounce it. Sc-aaab. Scab." I pronounced the first of Rosa's

---

> ### MID-WORKSHOP TEACHING POINT
>
> #### Readers Use New Vocabulary Boldly
>
> "Readers, can I have your eyes and your attention, because I want to teach you something really important?" I waited. "Earlier today, I told you that we can use our sense of what a whole text is about to figure out new words we encounter. I want to say a bit more about that. Here's the thing: When we're reading nonfiction books, we can expect that they will contain words that experts on that topic use to understand and talk about that topic. So if I'm reading a book on butterflies and I come to unfamiliar words like *thorax* or *proboscis*, I know that these are probably the words that butterfly experts use to talk about butterflies. And I know that I not only need to understand the words. I need to use them myself so I can join into the huge, world-wide conversation. If I'm talking to my partner, then, instead of saying something like 'The butterfly uses its nose-thing to get pollen,' I try to say, 'The butterfly uses its proboscis to get pollen.' Using the precise technical word keeps our conversations from getting cluttered up with lots of descriptors and helps us step into the role of being an expert (even when we are apprenticing).
>
> "Right now, look back over your reading—today's reading or a book you read earlier. You have two minutes to Post-it or copy down a few topic-specific words. Go!" After a bit, I said, "So Partner 2, talk to Partner 1 about the subject you have been studying. Don't talk about the new words, but use them as you talk about interesting stuff you have learned. Go!"

---

two words with phonetic deliberation. "It makes the word less scary, right? Kind of like 'Hi word. Now that I've said you out loud, I know you a bit better!' You try with this one." I pointed under *insulated* and let Rosa say it out loud.

"Now since this book, *The Cactus Hotel*, is a story—narrative nonfiction—we know that this one word doesn't count so much because it's *lots* of words that make up meaning. Let's look at the *lots* of words around this word. What is the big meaning, the big story they're telling?"

Note that I pulled Rosa away from examining each single word and brought her into the realm of a retell. I knew that Rosa often had difficulty monitoring for sense. In zooming out and deemphasizing the single word, I sought to anchor Rosa's understanding back into the larger text so that she'd regain the context in which the word was being used.

"'The cactus is not harmed,'" she read.

"Not harmed? Not harmed by what?" I interrupted. Rosa stared at the book and then flipped back a page to inspect the illustration of a woodpecker boring a hole into a cactus.

"Not harmed by this bird," she told me.

"Ah, a woodpecker!" I said, deliberately using the precise word for *bird* given in the text so that Rosa would hear it said out loud. "Ouch!" I added, pointing to the gaping hole the woodpecker had created, and made a pained face.

"'The cactus is not harmed. It forms a tough scab all around the hole to keep itself from drying out,'" read Rosa.

"Okay," I interrupted. Did you find any clues that could give us a sense of what a scab is?"

"The scab protects the plant?" Rosa finally ventured after a minute of thinking.

"The scab protects the cactus," I repeated as I nodded approval. "It's tough and it protects the cactus from drying out, and I guess it is over the hole."

"Like on a cut! A scab," Rosa said, grasping the meaning. "Like a cover over the cut the woodpecker made, right?" Rosa pulled down her sock to show me a tiny scab on her ankle.

"That's right! That is indeed a fine scab." I nodded. "Read on." As Rosa read on for a few minutes, I made her pause and retell what she'd read so that she'd reenter the book's flow of meaning, knowing that she'd have an easier task with the next tricky word if she rode the wave of the story rather than halted at single words.

"The woodpecker gets a weatherproof nest that is shady on hot days and warm and *insulated* on frosty nights," she read. "Warm and insulated. . . ." She looked at me and asked, "Like the cold can't get in?" Because she'd understood what a scab was and picked up the larger meaning of the cactus providing itself protection against the elements, Rosa had the gist of what the sentence suggested. I knew she might be unable to offer a definition of *insulated* if she encountered it in an isolated word list but chose not to create brouhaha around the single word, opting instead to push her attention back into the text and the story. "The scab provides insulation. It doesn't let the frost in. It makes the woodpecker's nest *weatherproof*." I repeated another big word from the text even though Rosa hadn't identified it as challenging. "Windproof," she added knowingly.

"Yes! When you *insulate* something, it becomes windproof and heatproof. It becomes protected from very hot or very cold weather. This little guy must be comfy and cozy in there." I pointed to the woodpecker. I kept sitting next to Rosa as she read the next two pages, offering small

scaffolds that would allow her to retain the gist of the story, hoping that she'd be able to monitor for meaning independently, so that this meaning would help her approximate a sense of the hard words when they appeared.

Note my decision not to allow Rosa's reading to be interrupted by a lengthy explanation of what *insulated* meant in this and other contexts. Instead of seizing the opportunity to incorporate a miniature vocabulary session into the conference by applying what Rosa had learned to a range of other contexts, I kept Rosa close to this story. Rosa often disengages with the book in her hands. On another day, with another reader, I might have extrapolated more word-solving pointers from our shared endeavor, but in this situation, I wanted to give Rosa the confidence that single words need not interrupt the flow of meaning.

Conferring to Support Your More Proficient Word Solvers

Moving on to Fallon, I noted that characteristic total absorption in the text that made her one of the most proficient of my readers. She sat hunched over a book entitled *Black Potatoes*, an account of the Irish Famine of 1845 that seemed to have her complete attention. Indeed, Fallon had no trouble monitoring for sense, and she certainly didn't need to be told not to allow an odd difficult word to hinder her overall comprehension. Nothing short of a tornado would separate Fallon from her book, in fact. I moved to a chair next to Fallon and quietly sat myself down, waiting patiently, and in time, Fallon lifted her head and smiled at me.

"Great book," she said, as she often said about whatever was in her hands. We proceeded to discuss what the book was about before I took a look at a page or two, inquiring about whether there were any words that she might have had to figure out as she read.

I got a shrug and a "Not really." It would have been easy to believe that Fallon deciphered every word she encountered in the text. But having conferred with Fallon in the past, I knew her tendency to breeze past hard words, allowing her grasp of the larger gist of the story to carry her through a read. My teaching, when applied to Fallon, therefore, effectively reversed the teaching point that I'd just offered Rosa. With my struggling readers, I placed greater emphasis on immersion in meaning as a way of decoding, but with more proficient readers for whom immersion and comprehension monitoring weren't a challenge, I sometimes had the opposite advice to offer. To Fallon, therefore, I could say, "Stop and pay attention to new words that appear in your text," and "Use all clues possible to figure out what they mean."

Picking up the book and glancing at the page she'd been reading, I started off randomly: "'Throughout the fall the weather continued to be fickle.' Hmm. This word, *fickle*, what could it mean?" Fallon peered at the page with interest. "Bad?" she ventured.

"The word *bad* could certainly be a good substitute for the word *fickle* in this particular sentence," I nodded. "That's smart. You think of a synonym that works and read on. But let's read on to the next line. 'Some mornings were warm and pleasant but by the afternoon, the skies turned gray and heavy rains fell.' Hmm, so the weather wasn't *all* bad. Sometimes it was good and at other times it was bad. I'm getting a clearer sense of this word *fickle* as something that changes, something that might be good one minute but bad the next."

Then I said, "Fallon, you're a pro at generating a quick synonym or a quick placeholder for a word and reading on. But remember, when you do read forward, don't forget the tricky word you just read, because you'll usually get more clues from the text that will make the meaning of that word clearer. It's the same as developing theories about characters. You make up your mind that the character is, say, mean, but then you read on, knowing that your theory will change."

Fallon nodded, and I added, "And the best thing to do is keep paying attention to the word even after you've put your book down. You have a sense now of what *fickle* means. If you carry this word in your mind and pay attention to wherever you see or hear it being used in the future—and if you use it yourself—all that work will give you an even more accurate sense of what it means. You and the word graduate when you begin writing it yourself. It is so cool to see that!" My aim was to push Fallon from having a passive understanding of the words in her text to using them actively in her own writing. As I left her side, I made a mental note to congratulate her whenever I saw signs of her adopting the advanced vocabulary that characterized the texts she was reading.

TEACHING SHARE

Readers Take the Time to Work with New Words in Various Ways

Tell your students that it takes time to get to know a new word.

Kids, tomorrow we'll be starting some important new work with nonfiction, and before we do that I want to take some time to really pay attention to ways that we can solve tricky words we encounter.

"Have you ever gotten a toy or a gizmo that you didn't know how to use at first? Sometimes I'm not even sure it will be worth the trouble. But if I take the time to work with it for a bit, I usually end up using that new gizmo all the time. Words can be like that. If you take the time to work with them, they can end up being something you wouldn't want to do without."

Tell your students about several methods they might use to learn new words. One method is to use the new words at least twenty times in general conversation or in writing.

"Researchers have studied stuff that kids can do to make words their own. Can I teach you some of the researchers' ideas, and then give you and your partner a minute to see if any of those ways work for you? And if one of these ideas suits you, you could try using it right now. Is that a plan?" The children were game.

"So first, you can make words your own by using them in your talking and writing— like you already did. But you need to use a word about twenty times, so you might make a word card so you can carry a few new words home with you, and when you are having dinner, you can just drop one of those words into your conversation. You can even be a bit silly. You could sit down for dinner and say, I'm going to park my hull right on this chair." And then, if the hamburger smells good, you could say, let's see . . . umm. . . ." I looked to the kids, as if appealing for help.

Grace suggested, "My proboscis tells me this hamburger is gonna be delicious!"

"Perfect," I said. "Using the words like Grace just did is really powerful—and finding a way to make your words portable so you can carry them everywhere is a start. It's like a word wall in your pocket."

COACHING TIPS

Kids' vocabularies should be growing rapidly—at a pace of about one thousand words a year to keep up academically. However, research suggests that only about four hundred of those words can be taught through direct instruction every year, so children must be learning many words on their own by reading and class-room discussion (Beck, McKeown, and Kucan, 2002.)

Tell students that another method for learning new words is to use them in the context of discussing something they care about deeply, and ask them to try it out.

"Here's another pointer, a related one. Apparently, you are especially apt to remember a word if you use the word when you are talking about something you really, really care about—like about a friend or a parent who has made you mad, maybe by not minding their own business or something, or by always hanging around and checking on you. If you use the new word when talking about something that has a lot of emotional power for you, then the word is especially apt to stick. Right now, try it. Take that word—*proboscis*—and pretend you are mad at someone from home. Talk about the person using that word."

Tell students that one more method they might use for learning new words is to pay attention to related words.

After a minute I stopped them. "Can I tell you one more thing that researchers have found? Usually a new word comes all tangled up with other words. Like the hull of a ship is just one part of the ship; it is easier to think about the hull if you think also about the deck, the rudder, the tiller, the centerboard, the bow, and the stern—the works! Sometimes it helps to sketch the subject and label a whole bunch of parts, or to list and categorize words—like 'Parts of a Boat that are Above Water' and 'Parts of the Boat that are Below Water.'"

It's worth noting that the Common Core Standards spotlight the importance of children learning domain-specific words as well as general academic language. It's important for us to help students not only "learn definitions" but also learn to interpret words and phrases, including connotations and figurative meanings.

Research Projects

PART THREE

Becoming Experts on Shared Nonfiction Topics

IN THIS SESSION,

you will teach students that readers can learn a lot about a subject by reading multiple relevant texts on it.

This session marks the start of Part 3 and of the homestretch in this important unit of study. To design culminating sessions of a unit, it is important to fix one's eyes on the ultimate goal. We need, therefore, to ask ourselves, "Before the unit is over, what do we hope to have taught readers? During these final weeks of the unit, what is the most powerful contribution we can make to kids' lives as readers and as people?"

For me, always, during the homestretch of any chunk of teaching, I need to teach toward independence. I need to

GETTING READY

- During minilessons for Part 3, you'll help the class inquire into a whole-class topic. Here, we chose penguins. You could select a different whole-class topic, but the topic of penguins is deeply embedded in the upcoming sessions.

- Assuming your topic is penguins, gather a collection of texts, ideally including *The Life Cycle of an Emperor Penguin* by Bobbie Kalman, *The Penguin* by Beatrice Fontanel, and a few others. Some articles are available on the *Resources for Teaching Reading* CD-ROM, although beautiful books are preferable. Be sure some of the texts on penguins have a clear infrastructure of headings and subheadings.

- Also during this final part of this unit, children will work in small groups comprised of two partnerships (each partnership can work with different levels of texts), and this foursome will study a topic of interest around which you have a collection of accessible texts. Some of the texts will be expository, some narrative, and some will contain headings and subheadings.

- Keep excerpts from *Bugwise* nearby during the teaching component of today's minilesson. If you decide to use a different text, select one that is familiar to children and has a table of contents.

- Each partnership will need a white board and a dry-erase marker (or construction paper and markers) to use during the teaching section.

- Record the title of a chart, "Strategies for Previewing a Collection of Texts on a Subject." You'll construct the rest of this during the teaching section.

- During the latter portion of this minilesson, you'll want to distribute bins containing the text sets you've collected on the topics you have chosen based on the children's interests.

- Prepare a blank chart titled "Penguin Research Group's Plans," which you'll add to and then display during today's active involvement.

remove my scaffolds, release my constraints, and be sure that learners can use what I have taught for their own important purposes, incorporating the new strategies into their own lived lives. And specifically, I need, before this unit ends, to have done what I can to help learners develop the capacity and proclivity to learn about the world. The world's knowledge is expanding at a breathtaking pace: in the four years from 1999 to 2002, alone, the amount of new infor-

> *Children need to learn to learn; they need to learn to initiate research in their own lived lives.*

mation produced in the world approximately equaled the amount produced in the entire previous history of the world (Varian and Lyman, 2003). This means that children need to learn to learn; they need to learn to initiate research in their own lived lives.

True teaching demystifies processes that can seem remote and unattainable. We show kids, for example, that writing does not require a quill pen and magical talent. It is a craft that begins with the simplest willful squiggle, a craft in which we can all participate. Similarly, we show kids that the skilled reader need not be the white-haired professor sitting between stacks of books—that reading well is within the grasp of all of us.

A unit on nonfiction reading makes it necessary for us to demythologize also the act of research. This unit needs to convey to kids that they needn't wait until they are pursuing their doctoral dissertations or working in a science lab before they can engage in research. Researching, like writing and reading, is accessible to us all.

Research itself is little more than formalized curiosity. It is poking and prying with a purpose in mind. Our kids know all about poking and prying; they've been doing little else since they were two and found an earthworm lying sprawled across the sidewalk. The toddler prodding the worm with a stick or catching snowflakes and watching them melt is engaged in a process that is not unlike the work that kids will be doing in this final bend of the road.

In the upcoming session, we help young people learn to formalize their curiosities and manage their learning lives. We invite them to be job captains of their own learning, organizing their work so they reach learning goals that are at least partly of their own choosing. In an ideal world, we will have interviewed children to learn their life passions and then spent tons of money making sure that the classroom library contains collections of accessible texts that reflect the topics that are of special interest to this year's readers. With those resources on hand, we will then have invited each child to construct a learning agenda that is exactly tailored to that child.

However, neither you nor I have thousands of dollars or thousands of hours to spend preparing for this unit of study. Still, we can compromise and make do. As a public school educator, I've always identified with the family in Swiss Family Robinson. Shipwrecked on a deserted tropical island, they salvage what they can from their sinking ship and from their jungle island and build themselves a glorious tree house—and a civilization. In a similar fashion, we are accustomed to assembling our classroom out of wooden spools and discarded carpets found in other people's roadside garbage. Similarly, you can prepare for the final portion of the unit by assembling whatever you can so that your children are given at least a taste of the heady, thrilling work of following the trail of an inquiry. Generally, in the classrooms I know best, teachers construct bins of high-interest topics, gathering approximately a dozen nonfiction texts related to

the topic, half at one reading level and half at another, and then recruit two partnerships (typically each set of partners reading a different level of texts and both partnerships sharing an interest in the topic) to feel as if they've chosen to study the topic around which the texts cluster. The group members often find other texts on the topic to add to the collection.

Even if the upcoming weeks are less than perfect, they can contribute in important ways to a child's learning life. In a large study, Pianta and Belsky (2007) found that American fifth graders are spending 91% of their school day either listening to a teacher talk or working alone; simply giving children the chance to co-construct a shared inquiry represents important progress. Even if the resources for this unit are not perfect, it is important that children are given opportunities to develop the meta-cognitive skills necessary to navigate through a collection of texts, applying deliberately chosen reading strategies to texts that are mind-bogglingly diverse: articles, books, maps, photographs, videos, blogs, charts, collections of data, digital texts, and the like.

Managing a learning project involves working across texts, across time, and, often, across people. When a team of people tackles the job of learning about a subject, the reading process changes because each learner is called upon to teach others and to learn from others, too, integrating their own information with information gleaned by others. In an inquiry such as this, students need to be critical and analytical readers, noting ways in which diverse sources of information build upon and conflict with one another, locating bias, searching for links, and ferreting out implications.

Of course, accomplishing all this requires an entire year, if not an entire K-12 educational experience. This final bend in the road is time enough, however, to give children a felt sense for what nonfiction reading can be like when readers work together with others to construct learning projects. Our goal for this session, then, will be to issue a generous invitation to children. The message will be, "Go to it!" Our teaching will invite children to co-construct learning projects for themselves, working with others to inquire about topics about which they are passionate.

MINILESSON

Becoming Experts on Shared Nonfiction Topics

CONNECTION

Tell your students about the hobbies and areas of expertise of people they know, and suggest that children needn't wait until they are grown up before having passions that help define them.

"Readers, I found out something really cool last night. Did you know that our principal is an expert on bird calls? She can make the call of a loon, the song of a warbler, and the cry of a hawk. And you know Mr. Johnson, our custodian? On weekends, he has a side job making flaming desserts at a fancy restaurant—cakes that are literally on fire when he sets them down in front of the person. He can sing for any kind of occasion, too—songs that go way beyond just 'Happy Birthday to You.' And Mr. Andrews, across the hall—I'm pretty sure you know this already—he is obsessed with tall trees. He is the person in charge of Tall Trees for this whole state, and every summer he drives all over the state checking out the tallest trees. He can climb those trees like a squirrel, scaling up the tree trunk.

"Isn't it amazing that our principal, who looks like just your ordinary principal, is actually an expert on bird calls? Isn't it something to imagine Mr. Andrews leaving his teaching plans behind and scaling up the tallest trees in our state? One person may seem somewhat similar to the next, but actually, seemingly ordinary people are head over heels, totally passionate about all sorts of extraordinary topics. Those topics become part of the people who love them. Your love for a topic, your personal project, helps make you as unique as Mr. Johnson or as our principal.

"I'm telling you this because I think lots of times, kids figure that you have to wait 'til you are grown up to choose a career for yourselves. It might cross your mind—'When I grow up, I hope I can be one of those scientists who invents new kinds of light bulbs'—but most kids feel as if there is not a lot a kid can do toward the goal of becoming an inventor, the conductor of an orchestra, a fashion designer."

COACHING TIPS

If you plan for children to take notes later in the minilesson using white boards, distribute them as children assemble in the meeting area. You could alternatively ask children to record on construction paper or in their reading notebooks. Whatever your choice, manage the paperwork now.

When I was young, it was very important to my parents that each of us kids (and there were nine of us) had hobbies—interests. They supported us in each having pets of our own, and the process of choosing those pets often involved dozens of trips to the library, or drives criss-crossing the country to attend specialty dog shows or Dorset sheep shows. We each belonged to 4-H clubs where we learned to show our particular sort of animal and to present oral reports on it. We played instruments, too, and our parents made sure we took that work very seriously. Years later, I look back with gratitude on the mentoring my parents gave us because I think this helped us to grow up to be people who revel in the pleasure of a personal project. Nonfiction reading takes on new energy when it is part of a personal project. I'm aware, of course, that one bend in the road of one unit of study can't rally every child to be passionately involved in a learning project, but this can be a start.

There is no question that this upcoming work will be richer the more I have been able to first learn the topics kids were already going on about and then provision them with texts to match these topics, or rally them to provision themselves and each other. Consider that as you re-create this unit with your colleagues!

Name your teaching point. Specifically, teach children that people can launch inquiries, previewing a collection of texts and mapping the terrain of a topic to plan the journey toward expertise.

"But I want to teach you that you can choose topics that will become areas of expertise. There's no reason to wait. To embark on a learning project, you gather and preview a collection of texts, mapping out the lay of the land between those texts much as we mapped out the lay of the land within a text. This then can help you plan a learning journey."

TEACHING

Preach about the importance of personal projects, suggesting that when people nourish what would otherwise be fleeting interests, those interests become learning projects. Lay out the plan for their upcoming inquiries.

"Most of us do not only love people; we also love topics. Mr. Johnson loves exotic desserts. Mr. Andrews loves tall trees. You and I can also love topics.

"Okay, love might be too strong a word. But we have embers of love, like those warm coals in a fireplace that can spark into flames. We can blow on our embers of interest and get ourselves to care about a topic.

"For example, I'm realizing that the books I've been reading about dog obedience aren't just things to read. They are part of a personal project. I mean, everything I read about dogs informs what I do with my puppy. I recently read about some monks who train German shepherds, and now I've got Emma signed up to live at the monastery for a month, studying for an advanced degree in dog obedience—and they promise to teach me as well. Do you see that I could call my interest in dog obedience a learning project? [Fig. XIII-1]

"I'm hoping that for the rest of this unit, each of you studies a topic, composing your own learning project about that topic. In our lives, we often embark on private studies (like my study of dog obedience), but it will be more fun if, in this class, we work with a partner or a group on a shared topic. In these bins, I have collections of books on totally cool topics, and later today, we can get started on our learning projects."

Figure XIII-1
This is Emma, as a little puppy. She's growing fast!

It is intentional that I've chosen to spotlight some unusual and precise research topics—exotic desserts, tall trees, dog obedience—as well as an interesting approach to gathering information (tracking down monks who train German shepherds!) to demonstrate for children the wide and varied possibilities available to them in nonfiction research. The point is that there are nonfiction topics everywhere in the world, waiting to be researched.

You might illustrate the way research is part and parcel of your life by showing kids the four web sites that you're looking at to compare prices on where to buy that new camera. Or show them the three magazines you're browsing, each of which details a different way of decorating the bulletin boards for the new year. Whether researchers study cell phones, sharks, or medieval castles, they overview the subject, accrue enough information to compare and contrast and to make wise decisions, find trustworthy sources, and know the best sources upon which to rely. The bigger goal is to reinvent children's notion of research as something they can do for themselves, based on their interests.

Convene a group of four kids, including readers needing support, and suggest they adopt what will be the whole-class inquiry topic. Use this group to demonstrate previewing across several texts.

"I have a topic that I've already investigated enough to know it is a fantastic topic—one we'll all study together during read-aloud—and I'm wondering if I could recruit a few of you to help the whole class to study this topic. I know, Rosa, that you are ready. Would others of you be keen to study penguins? We have some great books and a movie, *The March of the Penguins*."

At this point, a third of the class was on their knees volunteering. I selected four children, including some who struggle with reading. "You'll remember that when we started this unit, I taught you that before nonfiction readers shift into 'go' and read paragraphs of text, we rev up our minds by previewing the title and subtitles, pictures and charts. That way, we can map out the main subtopics a book will cover.

"Today I want to teach you that just as you and I can rev our minds up by previewing *one* text, we can also preview *a collection* of texts. Just as we looked across the table of contents in *Bugwise*, we can also look across a bunch of the texts on a topic and almost construct our own table of contents encompassing all the texts.

"We can notice, for example, that there will be chapters on housebreaking a puppy in each of my dog books. If I want to learn about that, I almost need to reorganize the information so I can say to myself, 'Housebreaking the Puppy' is Chapter 4 of *The Art of Raising a Puppy*, Chapter 7 of *A Handbook on Dog Obedience*, and so forth.

"To learn about a subtopic, we mentally (not physically) scissor the information pertaining to that subtopic—say, housebreaking a puppy—from each of the texts and then combine that information (or our notes on it) into what amounts to almost a little file on that one subtopic.

Notice that the plan for today's workshop is different than usual. Children will not disperse to their seats but will continue working in proximity to each other, in or near the meeting area, for at least the first portion of work time.

There are logistical challenges to this session, and you may decide the easiest way to handle them is to tackle some of the organizational work away from the minilesson. For example, off stage, earlier in the day or even on a previous day, you may have already convened small groups comprised of several partnerships, doing the complex social engineering involved in bringing together partnerships and accessible, interesting texts.

I mentioned the movie to lure these youngsters to agree to the topic. I didn't want to just tell kids they would be studying penguins. Sometimes I have to do some fancy footwork to give kids choices while also channeling them in particular directions.

I suggest this group study the topic that the whole class will learn about during minilessons because a couple of the students are strugglers, and I know that if the whole class and I spend some time on their topic, this will be a way for us to provide shoulders for them to stand upon. I know that the less proficient readers in this group will not be able to read some of the particularly rich texts on the topic, so the fact that I'll be reading texts aloud will give them access to conceptually rich information, providing them with a heady context for the texts they'll be able to read with independence.

This minilesson is just one of many instances in which learners return to a strategy they learned earlier. Here, they return to the strategy of previewing. Of course, this previewing extends the work children did earlier in the year. An uninformed person, glancing at the units of study curriculum as a whole, might think that a strategy is taught just once, but in fact, units of study are carefully designed so that children return to strategies they learned earlier, using those strategies in progressively more challenging situations.

You may decide that it is not useful to try talking abstractly about the process you'll soon demonstrate. Kids may need to see you do the work, and only then hear about it. On the other hand, for more sophisticated learners, this is a way to situate the work you will soon do, making the demonstration more transferable.

"Earlier, as you arrived in the meeting area, I gave you or your partner a white board and a marker pen. Will you be researchers and record notes about the process that the penguin group and I use as we get started previewing our texts? (One of you can record, and the other can whisper stuff to add.) Notice that we will preview to map out the terrain (the structure) of our topic, and then we will use the new table of contents, one that synthesizes our entire text set, to plot a path we can follow in our research."

Convening Rosa, Gabe, Tyrell, and David at the front of the meeting area around a basket of penguin books, I said, "So, we have these texts on penguins." As I distributed books, I said, "This one is called *The Penguin*," speaking as if to the small group, though aware that the entire class needed to listen in. "This other has a more specific title: *The Life Cycle of an Emperor Penguin*. I'm not sure why that one kind of penguin—the emperor penguin—gets all the attention, are you?" I mused aloud to the members of my little study group, not expecting a reply at that time.

"Let's see if the two books sort of go over the same topics, shall we?" I said to the members of the small group and opened the books to facilitate this work. "Hmm." The children in the research group and I looked at the books for an instant. Murmuring to myself, I said (speaking loud enough for the whole class to hear), "My expectation is that because these are books on a kind of animal, they'll contain the usual chapters about the animal's body, its home, its food, its enemies, its life cycle. (Generally, a reader can think about how a sort of subject is usually handled and then check to see if a particular text follows or diverts from that pattern.) Let's see if our books tend to follow the subtopics we imagined." I jotted the topics around the outer area of a big sheet of chart paper that would later become a flow chart or map of the penguins. The children in the small group pointed to and mentioned parts of the texts that fit the expectations, and when possible, we recorded relevant page numbers alongside the subtopics.

Your teaching will be revisiting prediction and previewing strategies that you have already taught. Children will use those strategies with new sorts of texts and across texts. Strategy learning takes time and requires repeated demonstrations and repeated opportunities to practice with support. This is especially the case when the goal is for learners to use the strategies with such automaticity that the learner can eventually focus not on his or her ways of seeing but, rather, on that which is being seen. Some researchers suggest teaching six-week units of study on a single strategy, for example, six weeks on prediction and another six weeks on envisionment. The units of study in this series assume that no one reading strategy can really stand on its own two legs for long. So these units are not designed to maintain a spotlight on any one reading strategy for extended chunks of time but, instead, to spiral back to a skill again and again across time, providing kids with repeated instruction and extensive opportunities for practice around a small handful of essential comprehension skills. Obviously those skills become more complex over time. For example, the prediction children do in this session will take readers' abilities to predict to new levels.

Let me caution you right from the start that although, of course, you could select a different topic for the work you do with your children—there is nothing sacrosanct about penguins—you might regret making such a choice. Penguins do weave through many of the remaining sessions of the unit. Penguins are actually enthralling creatures, too. My suggestion is that if this is your first time teaching this unit, you might actually take on this topic and even secure the two paperback books I've mentioned.

The array of subtopics that you record will resurface later in this minilesson. Jot quickly because you are modeling note-taking (not making a long-lasting chart). When completed, this flow chart could serve as a table of contents for the collection of books in your text set, with the book titles (use abbreviations) and page numbers cited alongside each subtopic.

Holding up *The Life Cycle of an Emperor Penguin*, Rosa said, "This book mostly has those chapters." She turned to the table of contents and read, 'A Penguin Body,' 'Hunters and Hunted,' 'Homes,' 'Mating,' 'Baby Penguins.' Tossing *The Penguin* up in the air and catching it, Tyrell chimed in, "Yeah, mine has most of those same sections, and stuff on chicks, too."

Speaking to the members of the inquiry group in such a way that everyone could overhear, I said, "Later you can fill in the page numbers so that if you want to learn about a particular subtopic, you'll know where to find that subtopic. For now, let's see if there are subtopics other than those we anticipated." I began looking.

Stepping out of role, I said in an aside to the class, "You should be taking notes on your white boards, recording the questions we ask, the processes we use. Did you record that we thought about what the subtopics are apt to be in a text about this topic and then looked to see if our books followed those expectations? Did you note that now we are looking to see if some subtopics are surprising to us?"

Gabe pointed to a chapter on cold weather, and I said, "You are right. This book has a chapter on the cold climate in which the penguins live, and lots of animal books don't talk about the weather, do they? I guess that goes with this particular animal. Let's see if the other penguin book has a chapter on the cold. Oh, look! It does!"

I then said to the class, "Gabe has shown us that there are chapters in both the books on cold climate, so we should definitely add that subtopic and those pages to our organizational plan."

I said, "Let's see if there are ways this book is different from that one."

Rosa pointed out that her book had a chapter called, 'Journey on the Ice,' and Tyrell's didn't have the same. I nodded, fascinated by this observation, but then added, "You gotta really check because sometimes the same information will be under different titles. Do you see that Tyrell's book has a chapter called 'Moving on Land.' That doesn't say 'journey,' but I bet it tells about the penguins' same journey, whatever that is. Those journey/moving chapters sort of remind me of the chapters on migration, though I don't think penguins migrate." In an aside, I added, "When I'm previewing books to create almost a single table of contents across the books, I definitely draw on what I already know about the topic," and then I added 'Journey' to what was becoming a solar system of subtopics pertaining to these two books on penguins.

It is hard to overemphasize the importance of this sort of demonstration. Perkins, a researcher from Harvard who has studied creative thinking, writes, "Imagine learning to dance when the dancers around you are all invisible. Imagine learning a sport when the players who already know the game can't be seen. Bizarre as this may sound, something close to it happens all the time in one very important area of learning: learning to think. Thinking is pretty much invisible. To be sure, sometimes people explain the thought behind a particular conclusion, but often they do not. Mostly thinking happens under the hood with the marvelous engine of our mind." (Perkins 2003, p. 1)

I actually know quite a lot about penguins and know what the journey is that the books reference, but my goal was to model the sort of mind work that I expected readers would be doing with their topics, and this wasn't the right occasion to launch into a long explanation of this creature's habits. I'm showing how readers can preview a collection of texts; modeling that I am a know-it-all is definitely not the correct path to take.

Pause to let children record your process for previewing a text-set. While they do this, solicit help from a couple of nearby children to construct your own version of the notes children will have taken by now.

Speaking to the class, I said, "Researchers, you have just one more minute to be sure you have recorded the questions we asked, the processes we followed." As some children continued taking notes, I asked a few nearby children to tell me what they'd recorded on their white boards. As they told me what they'd jotted, I wrote notes on chart paper for the whole class to see, completing a chart that I'd already titled but had left blank.

Strategies for Previewing a Collection of Texts on a Subject

- *Think about subtopics you expect. Which are present across the texts? Which aren't? Note subtopics you didn't expect that are here. Are they in all the texts?*

- *Make a list of main topics and the chapters in each book that address that subtopic, making a table of contents that applies across the texts.*

ACTIVE INVOLVEMENT

Distribute new texts on the class topic (penguins) to clusters of children, asking them to preview the texts in ways that add to the cross-text table of contents.

I distributed my other penguin books and articles, and as I did this, I said, "Your study groups will work with more than two texts, so let me distribute some other texts on penguins. I want you and the kids around you to preview the text I distribute to you, using the strategies you know for doing this (I gestured to the chart on which I'd just listed those strategies), integrating information from this new text in with the other two books." I held up the two books we'd already previewed.

Notice that I did not engage the whole class in reciting what they'd written, but instead, I gave the class continued time to work, and as they worked, I took notes based on input from a few children. Also notice that my notes aren't worded in ways that exactly match the children's wording. My goal is to create a chart that will be as clear as possible for the whole class, drawing on kids' contributions but tweaking them when necessary. Of course, it is also great to solicit input from children and to coauthor a chart together.

I'll eventually add the following bullet points onto this chart:

- *Think, "How will we organize our learning?" and decide on a plan for who will read what and for how readers will record and share what has been learned.*

- *Before you start to read, remember to think, "What sort of text is this? How do I vary my reading strategies to match the kind of text I am reading?"*

You'll want to decide whether to make this chart at all and whether to make it ahead of time. You'll notice that the current teaching has focused on bullets one and two. The last two bullets will be mentioned only in passing, but they are important. Probably you will want to keep those pointers alive in readers' minds, so eventually you will probably chart them.

The CD-ROM contains a score of expository texts that you can print out and use in your teaching. You may have already done so. Some of those texts are on penguins. Even if children have already read them, they can be recycled into this activity.

Children needn't read the texts you distribute closely, and they certainly won't have time to do so. It is fine if you don't have enough texts for children to review them in pairs. Four children can huddle around a penguin text. And remember that some of the texts you distribute might address larger topics—say, ocean animals, requiring children to find how penguins fit into the topic.

While children huddled, previewing the texts, I showed the penguin research group that the large piece of chart paper on which I'd jotted subtopics could actually become the start to a map of their research terrain. We wrote "Penguins" at the center of the chart paper, looking like the sun at the center of the solar system, with this large heading surrounded by revolving subtopics. I asked the children in the study group to add any subtopics necessary so the list was more complete and even to add a few page numbers and initials of book titles beside some of the subtopics. [Fig. XIII-2]

Meanwhile, I brought a bin of books on another topic (extreme weather) to Kobe, Malik, Emma, and Izzy and talked this group into an interest in studying this topic—one I knew some of them were predisposed to like anyway. I left the bin of books with them, so while many clusters of readers looked over books related to the whole-class inquiry, these four began to dig into their own topic. Now eight children were well launched into their learning projects. Four groups to go!

Reconvene members of the class, showing how the flow chart representation of penguins that the subgroup created.

"Readers, can I have your attention?" I said and waited until silence settled over the room. Pointing to the flow chart, I said, "You'll see that the Penguin Research Group has mapped subtopics pertaining to their topic. They know that when they actually settle down to read, they'll learn a bunch on some of these subtopics. What other subtopics did you find in your penguin books that could get added to their map?"

Tyrell suggested love songs in a silly voice before collapsing in giggles. I motioned to make a new subheading. Then I paused and said, "I'm wondering if maybe this goes with something that's already up here." My team helped me realize that love songs could be a subset of the subtopic mating, so I then began listing subordinate topics under that heading. Other subtopics got added to the chart—new clothes, for example (even though I suspected it actually pertained to penguin bodies), and victims (though I expected this pertained to enemies). In the interest of saving time, I said to the class, "If you have other subtopics to add, will you let this group know later?

You might elect to create a table of contents rather than a flow chart. Either way, your point will be to synthesize across the texts. The chart can be totally incomplete for now.

Figure XIII-2
This style of chart—with topic and subtopics—can help students plan their research.

Note that I'm leaving a number of items that I am pretty sure will turn out in the end to be incorrect. It will be important to show children the messiness involved in mapping the terrain of a topic, and I'm looking forward to the children coming, on their own, to the conclusion that actually new clothes is an extension of bodies, and so forth. The point is not only to create a map of the topic, penguins, but also to use this one case in point as a way to teach children transferable skills.

LINK

Explain that you have collections of books on high-interest topics. Recruit partners or foursomes to be excited about specific text sets and distribute the bins of books, asking children to preview them and to devise a learning plan, starting with easy books.

"I have a couple of collections of books on topics that I know many of you are interested in, and I'm wondering if, before you disperse, we could do a bit of business. I was wondering if Aly, Kadija, and Sarah—the three of you have interest in immigration and might want to read up on it, 'cause this bin is amazing on that topic." Predictably, the girls squealed with pleasure as I passed the bin to them. "And Jane, Danny, and Brandon, I am wondering if you'd like to build on some reading work Jane did earlier in our narrative bend when she read about the effort to build libraries in Pakistan." Again I distributed a bin.

"So readers, after you preview a collection of texts, after making a Table of Contents, it's helpful to think, 'What will we read first? How will we organize ourselves across the group to learn a whole lot together about this topic?'"

Turning to the members of the Penguin Research Group, I said, while the rest of the class listened, "How do you all think you should organize yourselves to get started learning about this topic, penguins?"

Then I added, "I'm going to give you one pointer. Usually it helps to start by reading easy books on a topic first because those books often give a quick overview of the whole topic. Those books function almost like the picture on the box of the jigsaw puzzle does, giving us a big picture of the whole topic, at the start, before you begin the slower work of piecing one little bit together with another." Turning to the class, I said to the larger group, "I want all of you to do the work the penguin group has been doing. Make a table of contents or a flow chart showing the subtopics across books and plan which texts you'll real first and whether you'll read them aloud or whether two of you will read one particular text and two will read another, or what your plan will be."

Guthrie and Henderson (2004) recently did a meta-analysis of twenty-two experimental or quasi-experimental studies of reading motivation and achievement, and they found the factors most strongly linked to success included access to interesting texts that children could read, choice over what to read, who to read with, where to read, and the possibility of student collaboration. I'm trying to help students feel as if they have had a say in these topics, and that has required some behind-the-scenes engineering.

When distributing sets of books to children, it is important to consider text difficulty. I deliberately made most of the research groups heterogeneous, and the texts in their set either matched the levels they could read or were easier than the texts they could read. I do not hold with the idea that children will be fascinated by looking over books they can't read. To me, if a book is too hard, it is not apt to be fascinating. When possible, I took a second to talk up a book or two.

In her influential new book, Powerful Learning, *Linda Darling Hammond cited research from the National Academy of Sciences summary of how children learn (Donovan and Bransford, 2005), stating that one of the three crucial principles of learning is the notion that "students learn more effectively if they understand how they learn and how to manage their own learning." Referring to this as a "metacognitive approach," they said, "Through modeling and coaching, teachers can teach students how to use a range of learning strategies. . . . Successful teachers provide carefully designed 'scaffolds' to help students take each step in the learning journey" (p. 5).*

CONFERRING AND SMALL-GROUP WORK

Coach Small Groups to Map Their Texts and to Make Learning Plans

At the start of *Building a Reading Life*, I likened a reading workshop teacher to the circus man who gets plates spinning at the ends of sticks and then moves quickly among those spinning plates, using a light touch to keep the plates spinning. That circus man will be busy during any reading workshop and will be especially busy when the job is literally to set all the plates in motion. That's your job today. It is made all the more challenging by the fact that you will want your students to feel as if they're making the decisions, launching their own momentum. This, of course, slows things down.

When working with small groups, it will help to keep the image of that circus man in mind. Imagine yourself pulling alongside each of your small groups two or three times within forty minutes of reading (not always, but now, at the start of this work). To do that, you absolutely can't settle down with one group and make yourself comfortable! Some teachers find that it helps to kneel uncomfortably or to crouch awkwardly alongside tables of kids because the sheer discomfort keeps us from overstaying with that one group! I personally think that solution is beyond the call of duty, but the point remains: if we're going to keep the plates spinning, we need to move quickly from one small group to another. In general, it helps to listen to the members of a group for a moment, then to talk into what the group is doing to get them started in a direction that feels productive, and then—rather than staying to coach into whatever you mobilize—to move on to another group, planning to circle back to the original group in ten or fifteen minutes. If the groups are working in corners of the meeting area, you can move clockwise, from one small group to the next, the next, the next, circling back to each group more than once.

MID-WORKSHOP TEACHING POINT

Readers Preview Different Texts Differently

"Researchers, by now most of you have previewed your pile of books, or at least a few of them, making a flow chart of some of the subtopics you'll probably learn about, and already you have been teaching me stuff as you do this work. I thought I was going to be the teacher, but you all are making incredible discoveries.

"Some of you mentioned to me that when you go to preview your collection of texts, it's not as easy for you as it was with penguins because some of your all-about texts don't have subheadings, and some are even harder to preview because they are narrative nonfiction texts.

"That is so smart to realize that readers preview texts differently. We talked before about how it helps to look over a text and to ask, 'What kind of text is this?' because if it is an all-about text, we read it differently than if it is a narrative. You are so smart to remind me that readers not only read texts differently based on their structure, but we also preview them differently!

Here's a little tip. "If you want to preview a text that does not have headings, you and your group mates can dip into the start, the middle, and the end, reading just little snippets to ascertain what it seems to be mostly about. And it is true that your sense of subtopics that will be woven into narratives will be more approximate. That's simply the case. The discoveries you are making are brilliant! Okay, you can get back to work."

Launch Inquiry Groups and Channel Them to Create Diagrams that Preview and Overview Their Text Sets

Because I'd launched a few inquiry groups within the minilesson and had not yet launched others, as I moved among the partnerships sitting together on the carpet, my first order of business was to convene a third and fourth foursome of readers. I collected four children and told that group (and then another) that the evening before, I'd been looking over the books in our class library and realized that we had a terrific collection of books on such and such topic, a topic that I was pretty sure those particular children would love. Were they game? Because if not, I had another collection they might prefer on such and such. In one instance, because I definitely wanted the group to rally around castles, I made the alternative as unappealing as possible!

In this way, I launched a group on sharks and one on medieval times and, more specifically, on castles and weapons. For no reason save for the fact that I couldn't handle everyone's needs at once, I sent another six readers to browse among other possible bins of topic-centered books, suggesting each of the readers come up with a list of first-, second-, and third-choice topics. After I'd launched the shark and castle inquiry groups, I glanced over children's choices and engineered a few other groups based on them. My goal was efficiency and student investment.

Once the groups were formed, and each group was sitting around a small collection of texts on their topic, I tended to say something like this to each group: "You'll want to make a map of your subject like the penguin group has done, putting the subtopics that you find across all your books onto your chart paper and then capturing where each subtopic can be found, with the chapter number or page numbers recorded."

Make Sure Readers Move from Previewing to Actual Reading

Of course, to use the Penguin Research Group as a touchstone for that day's classroom, I needed to make sure the members of that group progressed from making a flow chart toward reading some of the easiest texts in their bin. I turned to the Penguin Research Group, Rosa, David, Gabe, and Tyrell, and said, "You could put this book where all of you can see it and read it in unison (like we do during shared reading of a big book), or one person can read aloud and then stop and call 'turn and talk.' Either way, be sure you remember to preview the book, predicting what it will probably tell you. Then as you read, when your mind is brimful, stop to talk about what you are learning and thinking. If you want, you can make a few key notes on your chart paper or in your reader's notebooks—just jotting key words and phrases." As that group got started, I brought another two groups to see what they were doing, acknowledging that the other groups might work similarly or differently.

Once groups of children had previewed their books to create a flow chart of subtopics and had read and talked about their easiest texts, I outlined various ways of proceeding, making a point to leave decisions up to the group members. "Perhaps you'll decide that each group member will research a different subtopic," I said, "reading about that one subtopic from a bunch of books. Or perhaps the whole group will want to read up on one shared subtopic, with each of you (or each partnership) reading a different book on that topic and then all of you comparing notes."

Then I said, "My bigger point is that either way, when a group of people sets out to do a shared inquiry, the important thing is that the group first previews or looks over the resources on hand, mapping out the terrain (I gestured to the chart paper diagram of the subtopics we expected to learn related to penguins), and then the group talks about how it will get started on the work."

With my help, the Penguin Research Group had by this time recorded their work plan on chart paper, so I posted the plan on the easel. *[Fig. XIII-3]*

> **Penguin Group's Plan**
> - Shared reading of easiest book, with Stop and talks
> - Each person reads about penguin's body from different books
> - Main idea, supports
> - People teach each other
> - The Group makes shared notes

Figure XIII-3
When you read the research suggesting children need scaffolds, you may imagine something fancy. You needn't. This written record of the group's plan is a teacher-made scaffold. Another time, you'll expect children to record their own plans.

Charting the Penguin Research Group's plans onto large chart paper acted as a scaffold for this particular group but also showcased a research process that I knew would be helpful to other children in the class. While meeting with the penguin group I said, "Researchers, your plan is posted up here. It is like a mentor text for the rest of the class. I hope you don't mind that you are acting as teachers to your classmates."

Anticipate the Predictable Problems Children Will Encounter When Trying to Work Collaboratively within Small Inquiry Groups

Some groups of children seemed to struggle terribly over the collaborative work that these groups required. The temptation may be to break the foursomes into partnerships and allow them to work in those smaller social arrangements. I did that exact thing as a short-term solution for this first day. But in general, it is clear to me that children will absolutely need to learn to collaborate in a productive fashion with each other. There are few advantages to allowing them to circumvent these challenges.

Now, and during the upcoming unit on historical fiction, you will definitely want to convey to children that reading time is for reading. It is absolutely not possible for children to waste precious reading time with endless quarrels. They need to resolve their tensions and move on to reading, even if they must settle for some purely arbitrary way to solve the problem. If three readers are all tugging at the same book with none of them showing the grace enough to say, "Why don't you read it now and I'll read it when you are done," and if they can't come to a reasonable resolution, then they may need to draw straws to settle the matter. What is not possible is for them to fritter away reading time. Nor is it possible for

the group to come racing to you for arbitration on every little debate. "You are going to need to figure out a solution, and you have two minutes to do so," you can say, "even if you decide to just proceed in alphabetical order."

Sometimes it won't be quarrels that threaten to chase away all the time for reading. Sometimes, instead, children simply make the procedural work of this project into such a big deal that after twenty minutes, they're still simply making a flow chart representing the subheadings in their books. When I saw this situation in the making, I shepherded kids along to reading, reminding them that in this unit, as always, they need to read an enormous volume of books.

Frankly, it's a bit of a euphemism to describe the work you do today as conferring. Your focus will be on getting one and then another small group going and then bringing other groups to see the work that you helped the first group launch.

TEACHING SHARE

Readers Share What We Are Learning and Thinking

Remind students to use what they know about big ideas and supportive details when they share their learning with their groups.

"Readers, eyes up here. When you made plans, how many of you made the wise decision to start by reading easy texts that overview your topic?" I made a thumbs up gesture to signal that I'd like them to let me know with this gesture, and most signaled that yes, that was what they'd done. "Wise decision.

"Can I ask you something else? Do you remember that earlier in our nonfiction work, as we read, we collected the main ideas (I showed my hand) and the supportive details? (I gestured to my fingers.) You all are going to be teaching each other what you learn, and growing a huge project about your topic, so you will probably want to return to the work of learning about big ideas and supportive information. And I continue to notice that zillions of young readers have a hard time really thinking, 'What are the big ideas here, the ideas that pull everything together?' Sometimes you can find those ideas if you read bolds and introductory commentary really closely. Sometimes the authors never come right out and say the big ideas. Instead, they try to seduce you into thinking only about details by piling more and more details into your minds. Make sure you take the time, with your group, to give attention to what the big ideas are that are said, or suggested, in your texts." *[Fig. XIII-4]*

Tell children to record their thinking in writing and remind them of several ways to do so.

"You can decide whether you will be taking notes in your reader's notebook or on Post-its or on your flow chart. Either way, you probably will want to outline those all-important main ideas (I showed my hand) as well as some of the supports. (I touched one finger and then another to illustrate the concept of bullet points.) You may, however, invent some other system for getting your arms around your topic. You are definitely the authors of your learning lives right now, and my job will be to observe and admire the way you organize your learning."

COACHING TIPS

Figure XIII-4
Talk about a *graphic* organizer!

Those of you who teach third grade will want to remind your students that often there is more than one main idea in a text. Sometimes an author posits one main idea in an obvious fashion and meanwhile also gestures toward others. It will take some astuteness on the part of students to derive these other big ideas. Be ready to help children push themselves and each other to uncover these.

After readers worked for seven or eight minutes, I closed the workshop by saying, "Readers, we have just a few minutes left. You and your group need to decide what to do with these last minutes. It may be that you haven't yet mapped out a flow chart that shows the subtopics you're expecting to study—in which case, you may want to help each other do that. Or you may want to return to the subtopics you have read about and jot some main ideas and specific details on your flow chart or in your reading notebooks. Then again, one of you may want to teach the others about whatever you've read. If you do that, be sure you organize your lessons into main ideas and supporting details, and remember to use gestures and your pointing finger and illustrations to teach well. I'll circulate to admire the learning work you are doing together." [Fig. XIII-5]

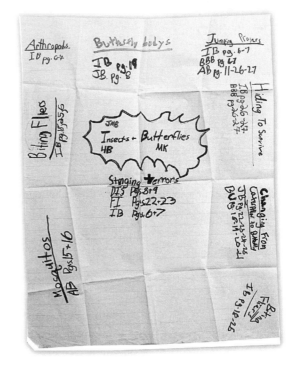

Figure XIII-5
These researchers have mapped the terrain of their topic, and now different readers will tackle different subtopics.

Pursuing Collaborative Inquiries with Commitment

IN THIS SESSION,

you'll teach children that strong readers pitch in to collaborative reading work with enthusiasm and commitment.

ou've launched the members of your class on shared learning adventures. You've invited them to climb aboard Ms. Frizzle's bus and to travel together on shared inquiries into topics that you hope will interest them. You no doubt can think of a score of little teaching points that you could teach at this stage. Children will need help note-taking, comparing and contrasting texts, assimilating the academic vocabulary of their topic, talking and thinking in response to what they read, and moving deliberately from one section of a text to another. But all of that must wait. There is just one thing that matters above all, and it is the hardest thing to teach. It's engagement. It's passion.

There is probably not one among us who does not agree that there is little that matters more than engagement.

We've all known the joy of teaching children who are engaged, who are invested, and we've known the struggle of teaching children who are apathetic, who are disengaged. My worry is that sometimes we act as if disengagement is acceptable, as if that's the norm. We note that kids seem disengaged and shrug, saying, "What are you going to do? Kids will be kids."

Principals sometimes do the same with teachers. All too often, principals set teachers up to teach a tedious curriculum, and then when we seem apathetic about the content of our teaching, they say, "That's teachers for you." But they're wrong—because if they had asked us for our input, invited us to work together to make dreams come true, and provided us with images of possibility from which we could make choices and alongside which we could be inventive,

GETTING READY

- Children will need their reading and note-taking materials with them in the meeting area to begin the work of developing plans for their research.

- Research groups will need to sit together in the meeting area throughout the upcoming sessions so they can share texts and responses to texts.

- Be ready to observe and record transcripts of children's research groups.

- Bring out "Ways Nonfiction Readers Read with Power" checklist from earlier sessions.

- While children are teaching each other in today's share, it will be helpful to make note of work you can compliment at the start of tomorrow's minilesson.

they would see that there is not a teacher among us who does not want to work with heart and soul on endeavors we deem significant—and kids are no different.

This session returns to a theme that has woven its way throughout these units of study. "Your reading life is yours," the session says to kids. "You are the author of your own reading life." The session says, "The choice is yours. You can be a curmudgeon—or you can go for the gold." It's not a new message, but each time you convey this message, you put a different spin on it, and hopefully, kids will emerge from the year understanding that it is, in fact, true. Our lives are ours to fashion.

Maybe, if we say this often enough to the kids, we'll even hear the message ourselves.

> *There is just one thing that matters above all, and it is the hardest thing to teach. It's engagement. It's passion.*

MINILESSON

Pursuing Collaborative Inquiries with Commitment

CONNECTION

Explain to readers that they have a choice in whether they invest themselves in their reading projects or treat the projects as a curmudgeon would.

"Readers, I want to talk with you about something that is as important as any topic we will address this year. I'm not quite sure how to put it into words. I was in bed last night, tossing and turning, trying to figure out a way to say what I need to say.

"Readers, it is this: You have a choice. You can invest yourself heart and soul in the learning project you and your group began yesterday, taking the project on like this is the opportunity of a lifetime. Or you can be that curmudgeon who says (I leaned back in my chair, assuming a slouchy, bored-looking posture), 'Oh, geez. We gotta read more books? And this time we're supposed to stick with one topic?'

We're once again coming back to this idea of being a curmudgeon. And of course it is questionable whether one can create engagement in our students by harping on the topic. But if you look closely at the minilessons in these units, and especially in this unit, you should see that we are not only talking about engagement, we are working hard to foster it. Kids are given choice. Minilessons are increasingly interactive. Learning is social and collaborative. Keep watching and you'll see that the final stretch of this unit even ropes in humor as a way to create engagement. The message to us, as teachers, and to kids must be that engagement matters. More specifically, a personal investment in learning matters. Heifetz and Linsky (2002) suggest that "the person with the problem is the problem, and is the solution"

"The other day I read an article in the *New York Times Book Review* about a collection of letters written by a Nobel laureate theoretical physicist, Richard Feynman. In one of those letters, written to a kid who had asked for advice, Feynman wrote, 'Work hard to find something that fascinates you. When you find it you will know your life-work. A man may be digging a ditch for someone else, or because he is forced to . . . but another man, working even harder, may not be recognized as different by the bystander—but he may be digging for treasure. So dig for treasure.'

I originally included this quote in the preface to this session, not the minilesson. That is, I originally thought of it as appropriate for teachers, not kids. And I do understand that it is high level for kids. But just as we read poems aloud that are far beyond our grasp, let alone our kids' grasp, knowing that those poems will move and touch us all and will ignite something in us, so, too, I think we can sometimes share inspirational quotes that we know are a bit beyond kids' reach. I do not perseverate over this quote, and the minilesson does not require that kids totally understand it. I hope they'll sense that it is deeply important to me, as it is, and I hope some of its magic will rub off on the kids.

Name your teaching point. Specifically, teach children that we have a choice in how we read, and that we can decide to read as if we are digging for treasure or we can read because we feel forced to do so.

"When you are reading—whether it is about penguins or hurricanes, insects or medieval times, or anything else—you can dig because you've been forced to do so, or you can dig because you're digging for treasure! Someone watching nearby might not be able to discern the difference, but there's a world of difference between the two. So, readers, dig for treasure. Read for treasure."

TEACHING

Tell an anecdote that suggests that human beings can decide, mind over matter, how we will feel about something. We're not passive victims of our feelings, including the feeling of being interested in the subjects we're studying.

"How do you do that? How do you turn your mind on, your curiosity on, your energy on? I mean, the human psyche, the mind and spirit, is not controlled by an on-off switch that operates like a light switch. What if the truth is that you don't find any of these subjects all that interesting?" I see some readers nodding in agreement as I ask these questions.

"These questions bring to mind a book that I read by a man named Steven Covey. The book has been on the best-seller list for years. Your parents have probably read his books. Millions of people turn to them because he helps people figure out how to live their lives. Anyhow, in one of those books, he tells about how a man came to him and said, 'I'm married to this woman, and I am finding I don't really love her that much anymore. I mean—I want to stay married to her and all, but I just don't love her, not like I used to. What should I do?'

"And Steven Covey said, 'You want my advice?'

"'Oh, yes,' the man said.

"'Well here it is: Love her.'

"'That's just it,' the man said. 'I don't love her. Not like I should. What should I do?'

You might even find it helpful to write the Richard Feynman quote on chart paper and hang the quote in a prominent place in your classroom. The concept of today's minilesson is one that you have been stressing to your readers all year, and displaying such a positive, life-affirming quote in your classroom community may serve as a physical reminder of the choices that readers can make all day, all year.

I find it helps to put into words what children are feeling. So when I say, "How do you turn your mind on? I mean, we can't just say, 'I'm going to be interested,' as if interest is controlled by an on-off switch," I'm hoping the kids will nod in agreement—and then I will proceed to address (and hopefully counter) this feeling.

This little sermon constitutes the entire teaching section of this minilesson. You should note that this is a bit different than usual.

"'Well, starting today, start loving her,' Covey said. He went on to tell the man that absolutely, people can choose to care about someone. That man could begin spending time thinking about all the ways he does appreciate his wife. He could begin telling others about his appreciation for her and acting more appreciative of her.

"You might think it odd that I am giving you all advice on how husbands and wives, mothers and fathers, can stay in love with each other, but the truth is that Steven Covey's advice relates not only to the relationships that any one of us has with other people but also to the relationships we have with the subjects that we study. We can decide to be curmudgeons, or we can decide to be learners. And in a way, we actually can decide to turn on our minds, our psyches, our curiosity, rather like one can turn on a light switch. We can decide, 'I'm not just glancing at this book. I'm digging for treasure.' Remember the quote from educator Paulo Freire that I've shared with you before? 'Reading is not walking on words, it's grasping the soul of them.' You can grasp the soul of words about penguins or hurricanes or insects, or you can decide not to do that. The choice is up to you."

Dr. Covey, the author of The 7 Habits of Highly Effective People, *teaches people how to rewire a mental map that blames others or the situation into a more productive, proactive mental map. He says, "Anytime we think the problem is 'out there,' that thought is the problem." The notion that our thoughts control our lives is one that children benefit from being told. We are always talking about choice when it comes to the workshop model, and today we take the concept of choice one step further by presenting not only choices for learning projects, but choices for how we even think about our work.*

ACTIVE INVOLVEMENT

Suggest that students need to keep energy high not only for themselves but also because one person's zeal (or apathy) will be contagious, affecting others. Channel them to discuss within their group ways that group members can keep energy high.

"It's not totally true, though, when I say, 'The choice is up to you.' When you work with a small group of your peers, the truth is that the others in your group influence you—and you influence them. One reason that it matters so much that you invest yourself in this work is that research has shown that if you don't invest yourself, if you decide to be a curmudgeon, you'll turn your whole group into curmudgeons.

Teachers, notice how today's discussion of curmudgeons goes beyond the idea that readers hurt their own lives by being curmudgeons and becomes an argument for how negativity and low energy permeate other people's work as well. Whereas we began these units by rallying readers to push themselves to be excited and engaged for their own benefit, we are now urging readers to be excited and engaged for the sake of others. The content, then, of today's session mirrors the idea that children are moving beyond learning how to author their own reading life and toward learning that reading can be a social activity.

"I'm serious about that. The other day, on National Public Radio, I listened to a man named Will Felps give a talk about small groups. The talk was called 'One Bad Apple,' and basically, he shared his findings on small-group work. To study how groups of people operate, he had an undercover actor join different small groups, and in some of the groups the man acted like he was so exhausted he could barely do anything. They videotaped the exhausted man interacting with the groups, and in every group, shortly after the actor who was acting exhausted joined the group, every group member's head would be sagging, and they would all be sighing wearily. Then the man went undercover as a different bad apple, joining a different small group. He became the sort of person who complains about everything, who whines and moans. Can you picture the scene? They put him into all these different small groups where people were working energetically together, and you guessed it. After this bad apple joined a group, right there on the videotape, you'd see the other people in his group become as negative as that man had been! The point of all this research was this: bad apples spoil the bunch.

"So right now, before you go any farther, will you and your research colleagues talk a little bit about ways you can make sure your energy for this work stays as high as possible? Talk about the sorts of things you could imagine doing together as you research your topic—things that will make your energy go up, not down. Generate ideas for how to make this a really terrific way for you to spend time together."

The room was filled with hubbub. [Fig. XIV-1]

LINK

Invite children to make a plan within their inquiry group for how the group and the individuals in it will keep energy and investment high.

"While you all were talking, I heard some really smart ideas for how you will keep your engagement and energy levels high. When I point my baton at you, please share your suggestions."

I pointed my pretend baton at Jack, who said, "We thought we could say things to each other like 'I'm so excited!' and 'Wow! Cool!' so that we get each other up for things."

Then I waved the baton at Sam, who laid out his group's proposals in detail. "We thought people could do extra, not just reading the books in our bin but find websites

I highly recommend you search for this podcast. My colleagues and I shared it with a group of several hundred principals that lead the Teachers College Reading and Writing Project's focus schools, and it sparked lots of laughter and lots of insights, too. Your colleagues across your school (and your children) would benefit from listening to this together and talking about the implications.

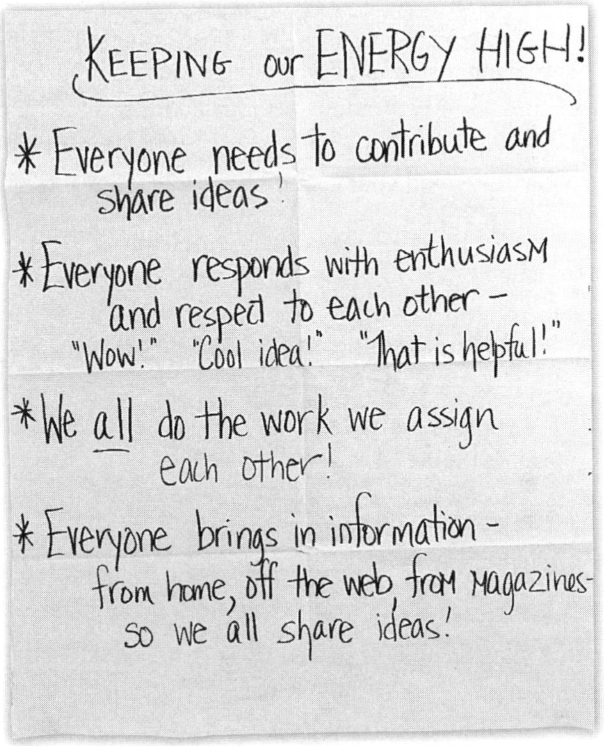

Figure XIV-1
You won't be apt to make a chart like this during the minilesson, but if you record children's ideas, you can make this at the end of the day.

like *National Geographic Kids* and *TIME For Kids*. We can look for information at home, too, not just at school."

Finally, I gestured toward Kadija, who added, "We said we gotta show each other we want to do this, not like (she slouched) and not talk so no one can hear. We should sit where we can hear."

"Those are terrific suggestions for keeping your attention piqued, your energy pumping! Before you go, take a sec to plan your reading work for today. As a group, plan what you'll each read today. Will you swap books so that you read the book your partner read yesterday? Will you and your group mates each return to the book you were reading yesterday and this time tackle a couple of new subtopics? No matter what, I'm sure you'll want to rev up your minds by looking over the text before you start reading. And don't forget to use our chart, 'Nonfiction Readers Read with Power,' checklist to remind you of stuff you can be doing." *[Figs. XIV-2a and XIV-2b]*

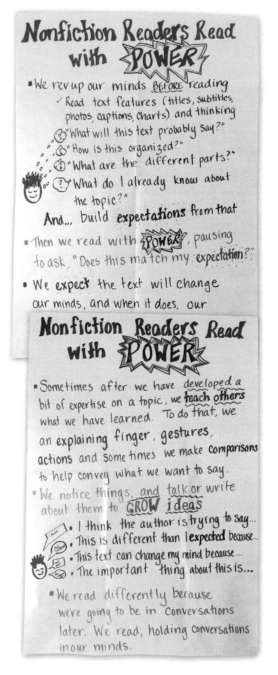

Figure XIV-2b
This is an extension of the chart on the right.

Figure XIV-2a
Revisiting charts from previous sessions reminds students to apply previous knowledge.

CONFERRING AND SMALL-GROUP WORK

Support Readers in Collaborating to Build Ideas

If your children aren't yet settled into their inquiry groups, provisioned with appropriate books, and if they have not yet begun reading those books, then you'll have your hands full. And if the kids find it very difficult to stop squabbling and settle into reading, then you'll feel as if you wish you had rollerblades. You'll be busy, but the upside is that at least you won't have any trouble knowing how to confer. As long as your kids' needs are dire and in your face, you will at least feel needed. It will be harder to confer once the groups are off and running, and it's that work this section will support.

When Conferring with Inquiry Groups, You Need to Clarify Your Role—and the Children's Role

Once the groups are under way, you'll want to draw your chair up to one group after another and take in the show. The work they'll be doing will be different from anything they've done until now, and you need to take it in. You need this, but so do they. They need to see you listening intently to their conversations, poring over their notes, and observing their decisions. You have invited your children to author reading lives, and it is critical that they see that you are spellbound by their decisions.

> ### MID-WORKSHOP TEACHING POINT
>
> #### Readers Note the Structure of a Text and Adjust Accordingly
>
> "Remember, as you read, that just as a fisherman needs to choose hooks that will work for particular fish in particular waters, you'll need to choose reading strategies that will help you draw from the particular texts you are reading. Look at the text you have been reading today and think, 'Is this mostly a narrative? A true story?' Remember, it could be a narrative of how a group of people, or a group of sharks, did something. If it is a narrative, it will be organized by time: first, then next. There will be a main character—a person, a cactus, a group of people. Thumbs up if the text you are reading is mostly a narrative."
>
> The children signaled their replies, and I said, "Those of you who are reading narratives, you are probably developing theories about your characters—about the he, she, it, or they around which this true story revolves. And you are probably thinking about ways your characters—your penguins, your people, your whales—are meeting the challenges of their lives.
>
> "How many of you are reading texts that are organized more by categories, in an all-about way, perhaps with subheadings or with spaces in which you, the reader, can sort of supply your own headings?" Many thumbs went up. "If you are reading expository texts, you're probably gathering main ideas and supports." As I said this, I showed my whole hand and my fingers.
>
> "How many of you aren't sure how your text is structured?" A few tentative thumbs showed up this time. "It is wise of you to realize that although many nonfiction texts can get divided into those two piles, there are lots of texts that are sort of in between. Many of these are what
>
> *continued on next page*

I pulled my chair alongside the Extreme Weather Research Group. Presumably out of politeness, they stopped their conversation and turned to tell me what they'd been doing and to show me the Post-its and the simple boxes and bullets one of them had made in preparation for their conversation.

I signaled for the group members to ignore me and then added, "Anytime I draw close and you are working, you need to keep working because I'm dying to study what you do." I drew out my clipboard and began recording this transcript of their conversation. The inquiry groups of today will soon give way to the book clubs of tomorrow, so now is a good time for youngsters to be reminded that they never need to stop work just because I've drawn near.

Listen, Letting the Group Members Find Their Ways of Talking Together Before You Coach

Returning to the conversation, Malik picked up his Post-it and read, "Tornadoes and hurricanes are really alike because they are both whirlwinds, so they both do the same amount of damage." He shot me a sideways glance, and I grinned quickly in support, but then looked back to the rest of the group to channel Malik to do the same.

Kobe jumped right in and said with a puckish grin, "Yeah, they rip off roofs and they send people into the sky, ahhhh!" He pantomimed someone flying. Soon the group began referencing pictures and talking about what they would have done had they been the people in some of the pictures. For a minute, it looked like a giant wind had turned all the members of the group upside down, as they all spun about, pretending to grasp for a footing.

It was tempting to put the kibosh on their moment of playacting, but I reined myself in and continued recording the conversation. As I did, I thought, "Who doesn't look at the photographs of tidal waves and imagine ourselves being swept off to sea, alongside cars and trees, telephone poles and each other? Haven't we been saying all along that readers will ideally feel as if they are in the shoes of the character, experiencing all that the character is experiencing? Then, too, isn't engagement important enough that it's worth a moment of playful chaos?" I find I can coach myself as well as the kids when I confer.

Perhaps conscious of my presence, Emma, sitting stock straight in her seat, spoke over the pantomime, asking a very teacherly question. "But how does it form? How does a tornado or hurricane form?" Emma was always a strong voice during book talks, but I wasn't accustomed to her taking the reins so firmly in hand. I was pleased to see her assume this leadership role in this group's conversation and wondered briefly if this would turn out to be one of the advantages of the heterogeneous grouping.

I wondered, too, if Emma was going to proceed to answer her own question but didn't find out because Malik interrupted to squeal, "Oh! Oh! Oh! I can answer that," and he whipped through the pages of the *Magic Tree House Research Guide: Twisters and Other Terrible Storms* until he got to the chapter called "Rain and Storms." The kids watched as he studied a page or two, searching for his answer. "It's the mixture of water

---

continued from previous page

MID-WORKSHOP TEACHING POINT

people call hybrids. Part of the book will be a narrative, and part all-about, or expository. I bet you already know how to read books like that. It takes changing your fishing hooks, doesn't it?

"So my first reminder is to notice the kind of text you are reading and to adjust your reading strategies accordingly." Then I turned the corner in the mid-workshop teaching point and said, "My second reminder pertains to some work you should probably do right now. Remember that when your mind is brimful, this is a good time to jot or talk, and that you want to do whichever you choose with intensity and energy, so that it makes a difference. I'm hoping I can nudge you to do some jotting now because we'll use those jottings later."

---

and cold," he began and then flipped the page to look for more information. Looking up after a moment, he said, "Well, it begins as just rain for hurricanes, this says. For tornadoes, I'm not sure. You got that answer?" he asked Emma. Watching, I couldn't help but note that without support from me, these youngsters were doing the compare and contrast work that is highlighted in the Common Core Standards.

Emma shook her head, no, and said, "I haven't read that part yet. But I'm thinking how a hurricane or tsunami is created in the middle of the sea and it starts to get bumpy and then it creates one."

Izzy returned to the topic of tornadoes and said, "Twisters sometimes suck things up if they have enough power." She used her hands to gesture as if she was a twister. Without elaborating any more, she changed the subject back to hurricanes. "And the hurricanes get created by water vapor. A lot of things get created by the water vapor, actually."

Kobe, who'd been frowning slightly, deep in thought, finally said, "Well, it's like water creates a lot of things, and water is so important for us to live. We drink water, but water can also be bad like the hurricane, and it comes down on us." He pointed to a gruesome picture and added, "We would get killed by all of those. There's a lot of things on this earth that can be our enemy."

Earlier, Kobe had worried about the hurricanes and twisters ripping off roofs of houses and imagined he was one of the people in the photos. He was clearly connecting to this topic in a human-interest, empathetic way.

Decide How You Can—and Can't—Intervene Toward the Goal of Lifting the Level of Work Not Only Today But Also Tomorrow

Listening, it occurred to me that Kobe had just said an idea that I thought was quite beautiful—that water, which we need, can also hurt us. I

---

wanted to stop the conversation right there, to star what Kobe had said and to ask the group to think long and hard about his insightful comment. I wanted to add on my own thoughts, pointing out that actually it is not just water but all things that are not inherently good or bad, but can be either.

I resisted my instinct to jump in and sermonize at that point, cautioning myself that even if I entered the conversation to say something that was very wise (and it wasn't all that clear that my two cents was the penultimate), it was really beside the point that I could generate a wonderful thought. I am, after all, the adult. One would hope I could outperform the kids!

Remember that our job in a conference (and this is the same whether we are conferring with an inquiry group, a club, a small group, or an individual) is to teach the reader in such a way that not only today's conversation and today's reading gets better, but also tomorrow's. Our job is to interact today in ways that lift the level of tomorrow and tomorrow's tomorrow

As I sat, weighing whether I should say something or not, Emma proceeded to say, "Now that I think about it, I realize that actually hurricanes and twisters and tornadoes all create something that's twisting up. Twisters bring houses up, hurricanes bring waves up."

Another child or two added on for just a bit, and I continued to record what they said. The talk, however, seemed to de-escalate a bit, almost as if the twister of ideas had passed. At this point, I decided to enter into the conversation, as I am apt to do, to compliment and to teach. I knew that my presence would be needed within another minute or two in the other groups. So I dove in.

Compliment and Teach, Just As You'd Do in a Conference

"I absolutely love the way your thinking has been almost like a twister. As your ideas have gone round and round, you've picked stuff up—bringing in a comparison of different kinds of storms, thinking about the role of water across all these forms of extreme weather. I think the subject is so huge and important that all of you are pitching in your best thinking, and that's why your ideas keep going up and up and up."

Then I said, "Can I give you one tip about a way to make your talk even more powerful?" The kids nodded, their chests puffed a bit already in pleasure at my support.

"This might seem like it is off topic, but it is not. Have you ever heard of the device that some people carry around when they are searching for precious metals? Like on a beach? People walk around like this (I held my imaginary metal detector in front of me, pretending to steer it back and forth). All of a sudden it will start beeping like mad when it detects a precious metal like gold or silver. And that's the spot that the person will dig into to find the precious metal—the gold coins or the silver necklace.

"I'm asking you about this because when you talk with a bunch of people or when you think by yourself about a book, it is really important to imagine that you're holding one of those metal detectors out in front of you so that you have a way to detect the gold in your ideas and in your conversations. When someone shares an idea that is golden, your imaginary device starts beeping like crazy. That tells you that this is a place to stop and dig in. We need to listen really carefully to what each other says and what we say, and to what we think, too, so that we can say, 'Right there! That's it! Hold that thought.' And then we need to go back to the golden part and try to mine it, to follow the good parts to more and more and more good stuff.

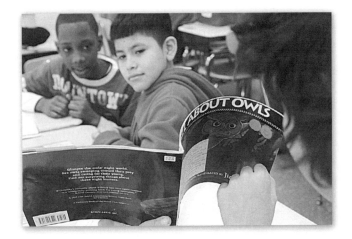

TEACHING SHARE

Readers Consolidate What We Know As We Teach Others

Talk up the value of teaching others as a way to keep our own ideas alive. Then send one representative from each inquiry group to another group to teach their content.

"Readers, eyes up here," I said. "I want to tell you one of the quotations that has meant the most to me in my whole life. I waited until I had the group's full attention. "A great psychologist, Erik Erikson, once said, 'Human beings are so constituted as to need to teach because ideas are kept alive by being shared, truths by being professed.' For me it is true that when I teach a subject, then I end up learning that subject. So I'm going to give you and your team five minutes to lesson-plan, and then I'm going to send some of you to teach another research group about your subject.

"As you plan your teaching, please remember that learners will be interested in whatever interests you. If a big idea feels important to you, you can share it in a way that makes it important to someone else. If a detail matters to you, you can share that detail in such a way that it will intrigue someone else. Remember, too, that learners almost always find it helpful to learn information that has been organized. Instead of just pouring a bunch of details out before your learners, it helps to present main ideas and supportive details or categories of information.

"In a minute or two, I'm going to disperse you to other groups and ask you to do some teaching, so quickly, right now, lesson-plan together. What will you teach if you are your group's ambassador? What will be your main ideas? Your supports? What will you point to in your text? Act out? What comparisons will you make to help people imagine your topic?"

After five minutes in which the room hummed with energy as children prepared for their teaching, I said, "I'm going to move among the groups, tapping one person on the shoulder, and that person will be your ambassador, traveling as a teacher to another group."

I started by tapping Jack on the shoulder, and he eagerly jumped up from his spot on the rug, traveling quickly to the group of learners sitting across the room. As I moved to other groups, tapping others to serve as teachers, Jack meanwhile began his teaching by saying, "Our group is researching sharks, and all the books we've read have talked about how sharks are really violent." Then Jack read from his group mate's notebook, "Sharks are really dangerous animals who will attack you and rip you to shreds if you're not careful."

COACHING TIPS

Actually, there are lots of ways to structure information, and if I could do so I would tuck a quick lecture on this topic right into the midst of this teaching share. We can structure information according to a compare–and-contrast structure, a cause–and-effect structure, a descriptive structure (which might progress from head to toe, right to left, outer to inner, etc.), or a narrative structure, among others. I simply do not have time to explain this right now, so I am opting for a second-best placeholder option and talking simply about big ideas and supportive points. Most of those structures can, in fact, fit into this more general one. That is, if I was to teach you in a compare-and-contrast way, I could still have big ideas—A is similar to B in many ways; A is also different than B in several ways—and bullets.

This teaching share hearkens back to Session IV, and you will want to encourage children to use some of the tips and strategies for teaching each other that were taught in that minilesson. Simply moving that chart to a prominent spot is one way to help. As you coach into what children do, encourage them to include gestures, to sketch diagrams, and to vary intonation to engage learners into the teaching.

Notice that first everyone prepares for the role of teaching ambassador, and only later do I select one child from each group.

At this point, I intervened to direct Jack's attention to the chart that reminded him of methods teachers use to teach, and as I left, he was listing smaller points across his fingers. Touching his finger, Jack said, "Basically, we realized first that sharks will attack you if you are bleeding. . . ."

I left the Shark Research Group and moved on to others. Jasmine was telling her students, "I learned that some butterflies migrate south every year as the weather gets cold, just like birds do. I was really surprised about that, 'cause it is weird. You see flocks of birds in the fall flying south, but you don't see flocks of butterflies."

Then she added, "I almost forgot—the coolest thing! Butterflies go to the same places every fall. Like monarch butterflies migrate to Mexico, and even to the exact same towns— the same tree, even—that their mothers and fathers came from."

I approached the next group and immediately noticed Brandon's compassion for the people in Korphe. The kids listening in were clearly captivated. I could tell that Brandon had them under his spell. "One big idea I had is that the people of Korphe appreciate everything that Greg Mortenson did and are grateful for everything they have. We need to care about what's happening in Pakistan and Afghanistan." *[Fig. XIV-4]*

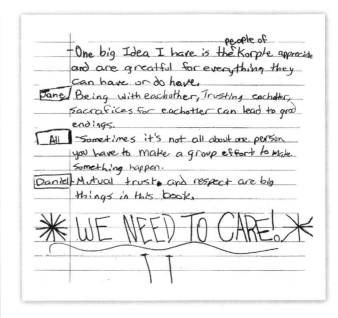

Figure XIV-4
This group has read *Listen to the Wind* and articles based on *Three Cups of Tea*.

Using the Lingo of Experts

Pause for a moment and reflect on the specialized vocabulary that you have learned while working within these units of study. It's probably become second nature for you to talk about the connection, teaching point, teaching share, active involvement, and link components in minilessons. If you weren't already accustomed to channeling kids to "turn and talk," you're accustomed to this now. Hopefully you have far clearer understanding of reading skills you no doubt knew about long ago: terms such as prediction, envisionment, and using text structures to support comprehension. I suspect that the term curmudgeon has become part of your everyday life as well. Certainly you and I now share a very precise understanding of what it can mean to research, compliment, and teach within a reading conference or a strategy lesson. Although those are not new words, they've taken on specialized meanings. I hope that even the very concept of a "unit of study" has taken on new meaning for you.

The work you have done to assimilate the specialized lingo of this approach to teaching is not inconsequential. In fact, learning new ways with words has allowed you to become an insider in a community of practice. Our shared vocabulary is not only a tool for talking; it is also a tool for thinking. You can approach a minilesson thinking about your teaching point, and you can do this in part because you have a term for the particular moment when you try to crystallize what it is you want kids to learn. The term allows you to grip onto this aspect of your teaching, to turn it around in your mind. The term even allows you to disagree with the whole concept of a teaching point, and other terms support the same sorts of thinking. There is, then, a thin line between vocabulary development and conceptual development—or should I say, between acquiring new vocabulary and learning new concepts.

As children study penguins, weather, medieval times, or whatever else they investigate, they will profit from your

GETTING READY

- Be prepared to begin the minilesson by sharing anecdotal observations you gathered yesterday about students' engagement in their reading work, or use the anecdote in this text, explaining that this example is from another classroom.

- Have chart paper and markers handy for jotting notes.

- Prepare a list of technical vocabulary related to the whole-class research project to unveil in the active involvement.

support as they acquire ways with words that are integral to their subjects. Be sure that your emphasis is not so much on children learning the words of their topic as on them learning the concepts of their topic (the language will follow the concepts). Your goal is not for children to score well on a multiple choice vocabulary quiz. Instead, it is for them to have command enough of their new subjects that they can grow ideas, solve problems, understand, and communicate.

> *Our shared vocabulary is not only a tool for talking; it is also a tool for thinking.*

In her book *Powerful Learning,* Linda Darling-Hammond points out that if we were teaching kids the difference between veins and arteries and our goal was simply for them to be able to parrot the correct definitions of the terms, then it might be reasonable to help children remember how to describe what an artery is simply through the use of a mnemonic technique such as the sentence "Art was thick around the middle, so he wore pants with an elastic waistband." By remembering that sentence, kids can remember that arteries are thick and elastic. If, on the other hand, our goal is vocabulary not as an end in itself but as a tool for

developing conceptual knowledge, then children need to learn why arteries have those defining characteristics. Darling-Hammond explains, "For example, arteries carry blood from the heart, blood that is pumped in spurts. This helps explain why they need to be elastic (to handle the spurts). In contrast, veins carry blood back to the heart and hence need less elasticity due to lessening of the spurts." When vocabulary is learned as part of a deep immersion in a subject matter, then concepts are often learned first. First children learn that the heart is a pump, that it pumps blood away from it and through the tubes and pipes of the body. Only later do children attach new terms—artery, circulatory system, blood pressure—to the topic they're studying, and at that point, artery is just one term in a web of related terms that also include veins, cardiovascular system, sonograms, heart chambers, ventricles, and the like. A reader is apt to become acquainted with many of these terms, all at once, and then if the reader is encouraged to do so, he or she might begin to approximate what it means to think and talk and imagine using those terms.

This part of the learning process will necessarily involve approximation as the learner role-plays the way into being an insider. The learner will, for a time, refer to the penguins' preen gland as their thingamagig (just as I refer to almost anything technical with similar imprecision). Eventually they'll progress to the place where they use and confuse words. That's what language learners do: use and confuse, at first. That's what all of us do when trying to use a second language to communicate, let alone to think, to understand. As teachers, our goal needs to be to encourage approximation, to welcome role playing, and to join wholeheartedly into grand and, yes, technical conversations.

MINILESSON

Using the Lingo of Experts

CONNECTION

COACHING TIPS

Celebrate the work that children did yesterday as they took on the role of teachers. Emphasize that readers taught each other by forwarding big ideas and then providing supportive details.

"Yesterday I loved listening to you teaching each other your areas of expertise, and I saw how you remembered to use gestures and actions, your pointing finger, and your explaining voice to communicate with each other.

"You were teaching each other not just cool little facts but also the big ideas that surround those facts. In the course Rosa taught to another research group, I thought at first that she was going to share a whole bunch of random, cool facts about the penguin. Rosa started by explaining that each penguin has its very own call. When a male penguin makes his particular call, Rosa said, the female who mated that male a whole year earlier recognizes her mate's call, and then, even in a colony of 300,000 birds, the mates find each other. That's definitely a cool detail, but here is the really important thing: Rosa didn't just tell this one cool fact. She also talked about the big thing that this fact showed. She made the one little fact much more important because she said, 'This goes with the big idea that penguins are very loyal to each other.' That wasn't one of the main ideas *in her book*. It was a big idea that Rosa grew all on her own!

"After Rosa explained her big idea that penguins are loyal to each other and told us about finding their mates through their calls, she told us more examples of them being loyal. After they lay an egg, for example, she told us the male penguin will brood that egg for as long as two months, sitting right there on it, not eating a thing, losing as much as half his body weight, waiting until the female comes home to take her turn. Only after passing the egg to the female does the male go off on his own fishing trip. That's loyalty!

"Rosa even made a box for her big idea and put examples under the box, specific things she taught us about the idea." I drew a quick outline to show what she had done.

I could have asked Rosa to tell her classmates about her work and to show it to them, and she would presumably have profited from the chance to do that. I didn't make that choice because, as I told her story, I popped out the parts of it that I wanted the other children to glean. You'll notice that I am working to counter the natural instinct of kids to simply record cool details. I know that they'll do this anyhow and that cool facts and weird details will become the talk of the town, but I am trying to bring out the concepts and ideas that situate those ideas. My goal is not so much that children take notes in boxes-and-bullets style as that they organize their learning and their teaching and that they read expecting to learn overarching concepts.

> **Penguins loyal**
>
> * Call for each other
>
> * Brood eggs no matter what

"Do you see how Rosa explained that big concept that penguins are loyal creatures (I pointed to this part of the informal outline), and she backed that up with details (I pointed to the subordinate bullets in the outline)?

"My new point for today is this. As I thought about Rosa's teaching, I realized that there was more than one thing that Rosa did that made her teaching strong, and we can learn from all she did. Yes, she organized her thinking so she brought out her own big ideas and gave us detailed examples of those ideas. But she also did something else. She incorporated actual technical vocabulary about the lives of penguins. She didn't say, 'Penguins live in a place with 300,000 other penguins.' No. Instead, she reached for precise words and said, 'Penguins live in a *colony* of 300,000 other penguins.' She didn't say penguins sit on the eggs. She said the penguins *brood* their eggs. That means sit on them! This wording gave her teaching added credibility and precision and power. She not only knew what she was talking about, but she sounded like she knew too, and she was able to communicate precisely!"

Name your teaching point. Teach children that part of becoming an expert on a topic is becoming at home with the specialized lingo of that topic.

"There is just one main tip that I want to give you all to help you go from good to great. My tip is this: when you become an expert on a topic, it is important to begin using the technical vocabulary of that subject. Even if you're really just beginning to learn about a subject, you can accelerate your learning curve by 'talking the talk.'

Teaching

Teach the concept of technical language, inviting each child to brainstorm the words he or she knows pertaining to an area of expertise. Provide examples of technical language for the whole-class inquiry topic and teach ways to record the terms.

Using anecdotes about the children gives legitimacy to their work as readers and researchers within the reading workshop and within the classroom community. When you use kids' stories, you are also showing how you pay attention to them. Their work matters. They matter. And that added accountability only stands to bolster their engagement.

Helping your students learn the meaning of the domain-specific words that they encounter in texts is an important part of the Common Core Standards. The goal is not only that your students learn a specific set of words but also that they learn how to learn academic language through reading. Although you'll want to support them in learning the lingo of their topic, support them also in learning the more general, academic words that direct thinking. Terms and phrases such as "advantages and disadvantages," "analyze the factors that contribute to," or "compare and contrast the reasons for" will have particular payoff. Consider using some of those kinds of phrases throughout your minilessons in place of the more general injunction to "turn and talk."

"Any subject matter has its own set of technical terms. For example, teachers have lots of our own technical terms. We assess your reading using running records. We call the class together for minilessons. We ask you to turn and talk. These aren't words that just anyone uses. No, these words are technical terms that teachers use to talk about our subject. Now, think of a subject that you know well. For some of you, it's a video game, a kind of music, a sport. Think of one such subject right now." As they thought, I voiced over, "You may be thinking about your religion, your hobby, your role as a big sister."

After many of them seemed to have settled on a topic they knew well, I said, "Now, list across your fingers at least five specialized words that you know because of your expertise on that topic."

When I knelt beside Jessica I found that, as expected, she was thinking of knitting words, some of which I recognized but none of which I understood. Stretching her fingers out in an exaggerated way to keep count, Jessica said, "Purl, casting on, bind off, gauge."

As children thought to themselves, I upped the ante. "Right now, can you think of a sentence or two you could say about your subject that contains so many specialized words that other people won't have the faintest idea what in the world you are saying?"

Again I gave children a moment to think and then said, "If you thought of a sentence or two, try saying it to the people around you and see if they can grasp your meaning." As they did this, I listened in.

Tyrell said to David and Gabe, "At the skate park, this dude bailed on the halfpipe when he carved a turn."

Behind me, I heard Brianna say, "I was watching a World Cup qualifier match and the striker on Brazil nutmegged a fullback from the other team."

Convening the group, Sam shared his sentence with the class, "In the third period, I split the D and dumped the puck for my teammate who could have had a hat trick, but the ref called him offside."

Academic vocabulary will be a special concern when you are working with your English language learners. The most important thing to say about this is that you mustn't detour around academic vocabulary. Newman's research shows that high-challenge work is more engaging. All students, regardless of background, achieve at higher levels when they participate in intellectually challenging work—but some will need scaffolds. Opportunities to talk in low-risk groupings such as partnerships and small inquiry groups are critical, as are opportunities to talk with photographs and objects at hand. It is easier to talk about the preen gland of the penguin if a photograph of a penguin is in front of you. But it is also important for students to learn to rely on language alone, so the challenge to travel to another group of students and teach them about a topic, now without a prop, is also important.

Then I said, "As the saying goes, that's Greek to me," and the class joined in to register whether they understood Sam or not. "Readers, whatever the subject, if it belongs to you, then you know terms related to that subject. You know the secret code of that subject."

Encourage readers to 'talk the talk' of their research topics. Using your whole-class inquiry as a case in point, encourage youngsters to incorporate technical language into their talking and thinking about their research subjects.

"I can tell that some of you are enjoying strutting about as experts, using the lingo that experts use and that doesn't mean much to the rest of us. And that's my point. What you are doing is what insiders in any subject matter do. So my suggestion is this: as you develop expertise in a subject, it helps to 'talk the talk.' If you are learning about penguins, then don't say that some penguins have yellow top hats. It's the macaroni penguin that is crested, with feathers sticking out of the top of its head. And all those penguins stay warm not because they have a layer of fat under their skin. It's called blubber. It wouldn't be polite to say that *I* have a layer of blubber under my skin, thank you very much, but talking that way about penguins is not only polite, it reveals your expertise. And once you are accustomed to using the word blubber, then you can explain that the way the male and the female penguin incubate their egg, despite the freezing temperatures, is they tuck the egg inside the brood pouch, which is made of a thick layer of blubber."

Tell learners that they'll want to devise a system for recording technical language. Perhaps key terms are incorporated into research notes or collected on a word card or a word keychain.

"If we're going to start gathering all these technical terms and using them in smart ways, then we'll need to invent some system for recording the terms. Perhaps you'll record key words under the subheadings on the map of your subtopics. You'll want to capture what the term means—perhaps illustrating each term with a picture or using each term in a sentence. Or perhaps you'll make a word card and keep it out on your desk or fill a keychain full of words.

"But here is my big point. The way to become familiar with the words is to begin using them, even if you don't use them perfectly correctly. Some people believe it helps to

You'll notice that there is a thin line between this teaching section and the active involvement. I'm trying to get readers to realize that they already know what it's like to use specialized vocabulary, which will make it easier for me to teach them to use the specialized vocabulary they are learning in their nonfiction texts.

Remember that penguins are not only the class topic. They are also the topic that one small group is researching. You should be able to see how the class teaching does a lot to give that one group a leg up in their research. There are lots of ways to support strugglers. The overlap between the class work and this one small group's work provides scaffolds that function as training wheels. And think how much more attentive those children will be in the minilesson because their topic is the topic of discussion!

There are studies that show that children's language learning depends not only on their exposure to vocabulary, but also their engagement with the vocabulary. Peer-to-peer talk and small-group conversations in which children use vocabulary they are just coming to know increases the amount of active involvement with the new words, and research suggests this pays off (Hart and Risley, 1995). Beck and McKeown claim that "researchers who observed teacher-student read aloud interaction identified talk surrounding reading as the most valuable aspect for enhancing children's language development" (2006).

personalize the terms by figuring out how they relate to your own life, as when I asked you to please not talk about my blubber. I could have added that I do not think my husband would like the idea that it is his job to incubate an egg by sitting for two months with the egg held delicately in a brood pouch! Do you see how taking the terms into our own life, personalizing them, is a somewhat silly way to grasp what they mean, but it makes the words memorable? The most important way to learn the technical terms of a topic, though, is to talk and think about the subject, using those terms, relating them to your knowledge of the world."

ACTIVE INVOLVEMENT

Recruit research teams to develop a word bank of technical terms related to their topic.

"Right now, I want you and your research mates to huddle together and see if you can come up with two or three words for a word bank of technical terms related to your subject. You can absolutely glance at one of your books. You just have one minute to do this, though. Go!"

After children worked for a bit, I voiced over, saying, "You and your group mates need to decide how you want to record and store your technical terms. Will you record them on your flow chart? On a word card? In your reading notebooks? And then you can start making that word bank right now, really quickly." [Figs. XV-1, XV-2, XV-3, and XV-4]

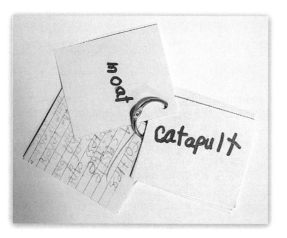

I watched Lily scribble words into a new word bank as the others called out terms they remembered. Jasmine had already written thorax and antennae and now said, "Abdomen," and then began dictating the definition, saying, "Doesn't that mean their stomach region? It's like our stomach, but harder and longer."

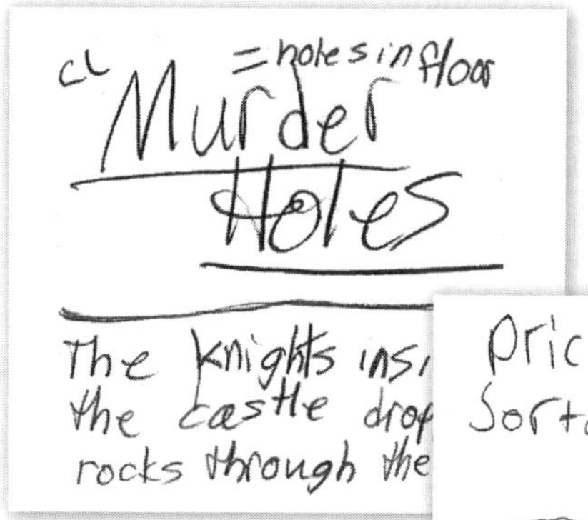

Figure XV-4
Some students make word banks and clip them together on key rings.

Figure XV-1
Cumulonimbus clouds are tall and dense and often indicate rain to come.

As always, you need to be the sheepdog your children, barking and herding so this moves along briskly. Even if children only come up with one word, they can progress from the find-the-word phase to the thinking-about-how-to-record-the-word phase.

Figure XV-2
This is a term that almost begs for dramatic reenactment!

Figure XV-3
We wouldn't normally think of prickley as an academic domain-specific term, but it's fun when kids catch us by surprise.

Channel members of inquiry groups to use the technical vocabulary they are developing as they chat about their subjects, stressing that approximation is crucial.

Not waiting for children to finish the job, I again voiced over. "I know you are not done, but let's move to the really important thing, and that is using those words. Talk about your subject together and tuck the terms you've just collected into your regular conversation about your subject. You'll probably feel as if you are pretending to be a real expert on your topic. That's how we learn."

I crouched down next to the immigration group and heard Kadija say, "I think it must have been really frightening to be an immigrant traveling in steerage. Especially if you were a little kid."

"Totally!" Aly said. "It was tough being a poor immigrant. If you were wealthy, you could travel first or second class and you got to America quickly. And you didn't usually have to go through an inspection. But, like, if you were poor, you had to pass all these exams, like the trachoma exam. And the next minute, you could be sent back home."

I gave this group a thumbs up and then convened the class and said, "Readers, you're all off to a great start! You're gathering the precise words on your topic and, more importantly, discussing your topic using those terms. Let's try it with penguin words, only just for fun, use penguin terminology to talk with each other about today's lunch." As I said this, I revealed a list of academic vocabulary related to our whole-class inquiry.

In any active involvement, you're aiming to get children to try their hands at something. This is not the time to make perfect word banks or record every single word you know about a topic. At this point in the unit, readers will probably be able to rattle off a handful of vocabulary words at least, and once you see that children have done so, bring them back together for the link. This work is ongoing and shouldn't take more than a minute or two during the minilesson.

Word Bank for Penguin Topic

habitats	brood
colonies	brood pouch
rookeries	down
blubber	fledgling
countershading	tobogganing
camouflage	predators
molts	carnivores
incubated	

I listened in as the children talked and overheard an animated Fallon say, "Those burgers today were disgusting because they were full of blubber!"

"Well, actually, I loved my burger. I guess, uh, uh, I'm a real carnivore!" Sam replied.

"I agree, Sam," Kwami chimed in. "I loved it! That burger went right down my throat!"

Fallon put her hands on her hips and said, "Kwami, down means the feathers on a penguin's body, not down your throat!"

Kwami laughed. "Okay, okay." He looked over the chart. "Then I'm a predator because I'd hunt animals myself to get meat!"

LINK

Remind children to continue developing word banks as they read. Before they leave the meeting area, ask them to plan how they will spend share time.

"In a minute, researchers, you are going to get started reading, collecting the lingo of your topics and trying to take on that lingo as you think and write about your topic. Before you get started, talk for a minute about your plans for today.

"I'm not going to tell you what to do during today's share time, so decide now what you'll do so you can read toward your planned way of sharing. For example, maybe each of you has been studying a different subtopic today, going between several books on that one subtopic. If you have been doing that, your group might decide to end reading time by each teaching each other (making sure to use gestures, a teaching finger, and the lingo of your subtopic). Alternatively, perhaps your whole group will research one particular subtopic or study with one big question in mind. For example, you might all compare and contrast different sorts of storms, thinking how they are similar and different from each other. You might research whether global warming may account for some of the extreme weather that we've experienced in recent years, and you might use the end of the workshop as a time for a whole-group conversation about your focus topic.

"So groups, after you have talked about how you will read and how you will use today's share time, get started. Go!"

You'll notice that this minilesson overflows with activities. They're all such fun that I couldn't resist putting them here, but you'll only be able to involve your students in all this work if you really nip at their heels, never waiting for anyone to complete an activity, allowing just a moment for each portion of each activity. You might suggest kids draw with fingers on the rug, only, to illustrate a vocabulary word, as a way to move things along. More likely, you'll bypass some parts of this minilesson.

Notice the repeated offering of choice. During this unit, and across the year, we have presented children with a menu of options for how to best spend their time as readers. Providing children with ways in which they can share the information they gather helps readers manage their reading time and be accountable for their work.

CONFERRING AND SMALL-GROUP WORK

Coach Readers Into Being Proactive, Anticipating Questions and Choosing Stances

You will probably find that it's hard to keep up with (let alone keep ahead of) your inquiry groups. The class will probably feel like it's buzzing with energy and as if everything is a bit out of hand. With your kids inquiring about half a dozen topics, you won't be able to keep a handle on all the information they're learning. And because you have emphasized that the inquiry groups can make choices, it won't be easy to scan the room and see how each of the groups has fared in, say, an effort to add technical vocabulary to their conversations and their notes. The fact that groups are encouraged to make choices will make supervision harder.

I think it is important to understand that in life, there are always benefits and costs to any decision. If your principal decides that instead of convening the entire faculty into a meeting that he or she runs with a firm hand, teachers will instead meet in interest-based study groups, then your principal will feel very much as you feel. On the days when you and your colleagues don't convene in the school library for a full-faculty meeting but instead gather in small groups, meeting in classrooms up and down the halls of the school, the principal will no doubt feel a bit out of control. How can he or she know whether people start on time? Stay on task? Work diligently? Stand back from neg-

ativity? There is, of course, a lot the principal can do to understand and support distributed small-group work, but the truth is that yes, indeed, there will have been a trade-off. The work will be less controlled, less managed, and less supervised. But it will probably also be more productive, more energetic, more grounded in classrooms, and more fun.

So if you feel that things are a bit out of hand, remind yourself that it is not a mistake that you feel this way. That is the plan. You have made conscious, deliberate trade-offs and done so for good reason.

The flip side of this is that absolutely, there are things you can do to help yourself stay more abreast of what your children are doing, and one of those is that you can spend more time outside of the reading workshop studying your children's work and even meeting with members of some of the inquiry groups. At the end of any one day's reading workshop, you can say to the members of a group or two, "I didn't get a chance to talk with you today, but I am dying to see what you have been thinking. Could you leave your group's inquiry bin with me so I can spend some time during lunch poring over the work you have been doing?"

MID-WORKSHOP TEACHING POINT

Readers Create Ideas to Bring to the Conversation

"Researchers, earlier you made plans for your group's share time at the end of today's workshop. That sharing will happen in just fifteen more minutes. In a minute I'm going to ask you to think about what you'll bring to that share, but first I want to tell you a little story.

"The other day, I went to a potluck dinner. The whole idea of a potluck is that everyone brings something to eat, and all the goodies are combined on a giant banquet table. I entirely forgot about the dinner until just before it started, and the only store open was the one connected to the gas station. All I could find at the store were napkins. When I pulled my car up at the person's house, others who parked behind me were getting out of their cars, and each person seemed to be carrying one of those big casserole dishes, holding the dish with hot pads, walking really quickly as if to say, 'This is heavy, excuse me, me.' (I imitated the way a person walks, carrying a steaming hot casserole or a giant platter loaded with an absolutely perfect turkey.) And I only had a little plastic bag with napkins at the bottom of it. (I adapted my role play to this.) I was so embarrassed by those napkins. I walked in, just imagining people during dinner eyeing the lavish feast and saying, 'Which of these dishes did you bring?' and trying to picture how I'd have the gall to point to the little stack of napkins at the end of the table. I'm telling you this because your inquiry group is like a potluck feast—and you want to be sure you aren't the one coming with a little plastic bag containing a package of napkins!"

Teach Readers to Anticipate the Questions Others Will Ask About a Topic and to Read Call-Out Boxes and Diagrams in Preparation for Those Questions

Although I'd worked with the members of this Extreme Weather Group just the preceding day, and we generally aspire to distribute our teaching time equally among our readers (spending more time with strugglers), there are instances when one group of children begins to follow a line of work that we hope might serve as a model for the rest of the class, and in those instances we sometimes decide to work with that group for a sequence of days. This was one such occasion.

The members of the Extreme Weather Group had only been reading for fifteen minutes when I approached them. I'd expected that Izzy and Emma would be continuing to read about the science behind extreme weather and that Malik and Kobe would be reading about hurricanes themselves, but in fact, Malik, too, was now reading about the atmosphere. Kobe, on the other hand, had collected a score of small Post-its about hurricanes and was continuing with that topic.

I first pulled Kobe away from the group and admired the sheer volume of thinking he'd done the night before. "I notice Malik has gone on to researching other subtopics, so your group is going to rely on you alone for information about hurricanes," I said, hoping to raise the stakes for him. Kobe nodded and explained that he had already found parts of three different books on the topic, so he was pretty sure he'd have a lot of stuff to teach. I then helped him make sure his learning was organized in preparation for the teaching that he'd soon be doing and encouraged him to ask the questions that he was pretty sure the others would ask, drawing from information in the call-out boxes, diagrams, and pictures as well as in the text to help him be ready for the questions he anticipated his group mates would soon pose.

Teach Readers to Shift Their Ways of Talking, Reading, and Writing When the Content Becomes Dense and Complex

Kobe, however, didn't have long to do this work because I then suggested that the rest of the inquiry group talk about their research right then, rather than waiting for the end of reading time, so I could listen in for a bit. Kobe joined that conversation.

I signaled "hood off" to Malik, who obligingly popped his head out of his hoodie and began. "I'm reading about the sky. I learned that the atmosphere . . . without it, we wouldn't be living. We'd be floating up into space. Which I thought was pretty cool. Me and Izzy were just saying how it would be really fun to have a day without atmosphere, where you just float around!" He grinned conspiratorially at Kobe, who seemed quite taken by the idea.

Kobe jumped onto Malik's idea, saying, "That would be awesome! Only we'd get stuck on the ceiling if we were inside. But oh, the school would float up too!"

I knew this imaginative pair would be off and running with this theme, so I steered the conversation for a moment. "So Izzy, you were reading about atmosphere too? What can you add to what Malik learned?"

"Umm . . . Well, without the atmosphere we wouldn't be living on the planet, and the atmosphere is very important for us." She stopped as if finished, but I gestured to suggest she continue. "The atmosphere is sort of like when the cold air pushes down. . . ." Izzy's voice trailed off for a second as she paused, glanced at her word bank, and then restated the sentence to incorporate a word-bank word. "When cold air pressures down on the hot air, the hot air goes up, so if we didn't have the atmosphere the hot air would push down on us, and we would go up. So we would die because we wouldn't have any oxygen to breathe, and the pressure would be too much." Again she looked at her word bank and added, "Even the barometer would say so." She added, "I also thought that was so cool because you just take the atmosphere for granted! You can't see it, so you don't think about it."

Malik hadn't seemed to really hear Izzy's complex and somewhat convoluted exposition, or if he had, he understood it better than I did, so he pressed on to a new aspect of the topic. "Well, I'm also wondering if without the atmosphere, we would have rain or tsunamis or twisters? I mean, with no atmosphere to trap it, everything would just float out into space."

I tapped the word gravity on his word card, and he restated his idea to include that word. I did not want to take the group off course by making an especially big deal of the need to use technical vocabulary, but I also didn't want to leave the minilesson behind totally.

"Well, we would have rain. It's just that it wouldn't rain down to earth. It would rain into space, and it would just float around in space," Emma said.

At this point, I jumped in. "Holy moly. My head is spinning over all you are saying. I thought you would be talking about big storms—hurricanes and tornadoes and stuff, but you have tackled the science behind all that, the hardest and most complex topics of all. Atmosphere, air pressure, gravity, barometers—these are gigantically complex words and concepts, especially in relationship to how this all affects extreme weather. I am proud of you for going for the hard stuff."

Then I added, "Earlier, when I talked about you having a choice to make—you can be interested or you can be curmudgeons—I'm now realizing that all of us have another choice. We can tackle the confusing stuff, the hard science, of our topic, or we can stick to the human interest, more lightweight parts. Readers decide not only whether we're going to be interested or not, but also whether we are going to be ambitious or not. It is like you guys have decided to ski the black diamond trails. (Those are the ones with cliffs on them that are almost life threatening.) Congratulations."

Then, shifting to the teaching component of my small-group work, I said, "I also want to give you a tip. When you get to complex topics such as these, you need to shift how you read and talk. The words in your books may not be hard, but really truly understanding the ideas will definitely be hard. You need to think to yourself, 'Whoa! This is hard!' and then do the extra work necessary to truly understand these complicated ideas. It is like when a car goes up a really steep hill, the motor needs to shift into low gear because it is traveling steep terrain. When you are working on dense concepts like you've been tackling, your talking and thinking needs to shift into a different gear."

Finally I added, "I'm going to move on to another group, but see if you can think of some special reading strategies you could use to make sure that everyone in your group totally grasps the concepts you are talking about. You might decide to make diagrams and put them at the center of your conversation or to read a section of text super slowly—perhaps with one person reading a bit aloud and then everyone talking and thinking really hard about that passage. You might decide to ask each other tons of questions or to try using your teaching voice and finger and gestures not only to teach but to understand. After you figure out what you can do to understand this complex stuff, get started doing that, and I'll come back to see if I can help."

As I moved on to work with another inquiry group, I recorded notes on the conference I'd just conducted. I was aware that I'd celebrated the fact that the youngsters were tackling the hard science of their topic and extolled the group members to "shift into a different gear" when handling such complex topics and that I really hadn't done a lot yet to help them know what that might entail. Later, as I reflected on the group, I made notes about the work I could do with them in the future.

First, I noted that another time, I might listen to their conversation with the intention of saying back to them what they said, only cloaking their language in more academic vocabulary. The young child comes home from the park and says, "Daddy push. I touch tree." The parent takes the child's intended meaning and bits of the child's own language, and restates what the child has said in more adult syntax. "Did Daddy push you high? Did he push you so high that you touched the tree? Did your toe touch the leaves on the tree? Wow! Daddy pushed you so high that you touched the leaves on the tree! That's terrific. Go tell Miles about what you did in the park." We expect when the child repeats the news, that this time he'll incorporate a bit more of our adult syntax.

Pauline Gibbons, author of *English Language Learners, Academic Literacy, and Thinking: Learning in the Challenge Zone*, says that "students need opportunities to interact in contexts that require the use of more 'literate talk.' These kinds of conversations provide a bridge between their everyday talk and the more explicit talk associated with academic literacy." She demonstrates, for example, how a teacher might listen to the language of a student talking about magnets and then restate what the children say to each other much as a parent restates what the toddler says. The adult's version of the child's message can incorporate terms that refer to concepts such as magnetic force and magnetic attraction.

I also noted that another time, I could help children step into the roles of coaches, coaching each other to use technical vocabulary words, just as I'd coached them to do. That is, when one child said to another, "The drops of water go up into the sky," the listener could point to the technical term, evaporation, as a signal, nudging the speaker to restate the sentence, this time incorporating the new bit of vocabulary.

Nudge Readers from a Passive Recognition of Technical Words into Active Usage of Them

I next moved in on a discussion that the shark group was having about two of their books. When I pulled alongside their group, the readers were chattering excitedly over their find. One book stated that sharks were covered in scales, while the other book was open to a page with illustrated close-ups that revealed small sharp teeth covering a shark's skin.

It was clear that Isaac was leading the discussion. "'Cause look, those are definitely like teeth, all over, and they are really sharp. Like even if a diver brushes against the side of a shark's body, he could get badly injured because these cut badly," he was telling the other two. "I know the other book said scales, but these are definitely not scales. Look at them!" He pointed proudly to the illustrations he'd found.

Sam was skeptical. "Well, maybe they are scales and it's just that they're shaped like teeth. 'Cause the book is probably not wrong, totally wrong. Unless some sharks have scales and some have teeth on their bodies."

Glancing at one of the open books between them, I saw the heading "Dermal Denticles" over the illustration. I kept listening for a minute or two longer, waiting to see if Isaac would use the word denticles instead of teeth-like things.' When he referred once more to the denticles as 'teeth-thingies," I intervened. "That's an interesting looking word," I said, pointing to denticle. "What does it mean?"

"I think it means teeth, 'cause that's what's here, plus dent is like dentist." I made a mental note. Isaac had some grasp of the word even though he was avoiding using it while talking. "These things—denticles," Isaac said, his normally confident voice faltering hesitantly for a split second, "are like sharp teeth, and they cover the whole body." The split-second hesitation was enough to tell me that this was the first time Isaac had actually articulated the word.

Earlier in my teaching, I have taught readers to insert synonyms in place of difficult words, but recently, I watched a reader paraphrase a text that said, "Owls are raptors . . . they have lethal talons . . . they are nocturnal," so that to the reader, the text said only, "Owls are eat dead stuff . . . they have sharp claws that kill . . . they hunt at night." Watching that, I began to think about what was being lost when children strip texts of technical vocabulary. I vowed to do more to encourage them to use unfamiliar words in their talking and writing, so those words become their own. During conferring, you and I can nudge readers from a passive recognition of technical words into active use of them.

"You know, when you use a word like denticle while talking about sharks, it sends a powerful message to the listener," I told Isaac. "Just by hearing that word from your mouth, your listener knows that you know your sharks." I tend to compliment whatever I want to see more of, so I persisted with the praise, tucking my teaching under it. "Technical words like these reflect true expertise, and I'm proud of you for using them. It's like, if I hear two people describing the same illness, I suspect the one who calls it 'heart disease' is probably a layman and the one who calls it 'ventricular hypertrophy' is probably the expert.

"Sometimes, though," I continued, "the reason that we don't use a technical word while talking isn't because we don't know the word, or we aren't sure how it's pronounced since we've only read it and never heard it. We need to be brave!" The fact that Isaac had avoided the word and then faltered while saying it suggested to me that he was self-conscious about whether he'd be able to correctly say the unfamiliar word out loud. I picked up a book from a nearby shelf—one on owls. Flipping through it, I stopped at a complicated-looking word, said it to myself quietly a couple of times, and then pointed it out to the members of the Shark Research Group. "If I was aiming at being an expert on owls, I wouldn't say that owls squeeze their prey to death. I'd try to use raptor lingo. I'd say that owls asphyxiate their prey. The word asphyxiate looks so hard to pronounce, so I had to break it down into its separate syllables and practice a couple of times—as-phyx-i-ate. Using the technical language of experts means getting our mouths around words that aren't really everyday usage for most people."

I left the Shark Research Group, recorded notes on the conference, and moved on.

TEACHING SHARE

Readers Collaborate and Construct New Meanings

Celebrate the engagement you see in the room and help readers realize that engaged *nonfiction* reading often feels different than engaged *fiction* reading.

"Readers, at the start of this unit, you each made yourself into a statue of a great nonfiction reader. Some of you sat upright in front of a computer screen or held the newspaper up to your nose or read a brochure or flicked through the pages of an atlas. Back then, at the start of the unit, your images all involved one person reading one text. Right now, think about a moment that has happened in this classroom lately that, to you, captures what this sort of nonfiction reading looks and feels like." I gave children a moment to conjure up an image, and meanwhile I did this as well.

"I'm wondering whether, for some of you, the moment you have in mind involves not just one lone reader, with his or her nose in the text. Give me a thumbs up if your image involves more than one reader, if your picture of nonfiction reading includes collaboration with other readers." Many so indicated.

"And give me a thumbs up if your image of great nonfiction reading involves not just one text at a time but work across texts." Again, many readers so indicated.

Send kids off to work in their groups, allowing them to decide how they'll partake of what each other has brought to the "potluck supper" of their group.

"Let's take the remaining minutes of our reading workshop for the sort of reading work that doesn't look at all like nose-in-the-book reading! Get with your inquiry group and decide how you're going to partake of what each has brought to the potluck feast, to the study group, and get started."

Watch for the ways your teaching can have resonance, for ways you can revisit previous minilessons, carrying the content forward. Some minilessons will especially strike a chord with children—and those will be the ones you harken back to especially. It is not a small thing to teach children that what they've learned earlier becomes part and parcel of what they do now.

If you wanted to do so, you could re-create a statue of nonfiction reading, this time making it more like a frieze involving three or four readers working alongside and in interaction with each other. I decided not to do this here because I'm trying to give youngsters as much time as possible to talk, read, and write—all tall orders.

Writing to Think About Nonfiction

I want kids to know the experience I have, over and over again, whenever I embark on a new inquiry. Perhaps I'm studying content area literacy, perhaps differentiation. Whatever the topic, I live like a magnet on that topic, collecting from everywhere. I wear my obsession on my sleeve. Everyone I know hears about my inquiry, and informants emerge from all corners of my life. With the help of those informants, I gather books, articles, new experts, artifacts, and resources. I feel overwhelmed. I build shelves, files, and categories. I read the easiest texts first, trying to give myself a broad overview of the terrain. Then I sort the stuff on my shelves; I remake categories. I try to figure out the different approaches, perspectives, and views that I encounter. I dig for assumptions and probe for implications. I come to sense points of view and biases and to locate myself within the cacophony of voices.

I find that I'm feeling strongly, that I have my own point of view and some tentative theories. I chart a course for myself, and I'm off. I read, I record, I cumulate, I talk, I question, and I read some more. The map changes under my feet. I read, write, compare, question, and teach. I consolidate what I know and what I do not know. I plan, search, read, theorize, test, draft, teach, and revise. In short, I learn. This is the process that I want kids to experience from the inside.

Almost forty years ago, in what is now a classic book, *The Process of Education*, Jerome Bruner wrote, "The foundations of any subject may be taught to anybody in some form. There is nothing more central to a discipline than its way of

GETTING READY

- Today's session incorporates a long passage from Gerald Durrell's book, *The Whispering Land*. You will use the passage in today's connection to help readers grow big ideas about a nonfiction text. If you choose to demonstrate with another text, select a narrative nonfiction passage that will be highly engaging for your readers.

- Children will need to bring their reading materials, particularly their reader's notebooks, to the meeting area. During the connection you will ask readers to jot their ideas in response to the read-aloud.

thinking. There is nothing more important in its teaching than to provide the child with the earliest opportunity to learn that way of thinking—the forms of connection, the attitudes, hopes, jokes, and frustrations that go with it. In a word, the best introduction to a subject is the subject itself."

Now, forty years after Jerome Bruner challenged us to see education as nothing short of inviting children to function as full participants in the culture and work of a discipline, edu-

> *Reading is thinking, and the most powerful tool that human beings have for thinking is the pen. So go to it.*

cators are beginning to listen to him. From all corners, we hear that the only way in which our children will possibly be ready for the challenges of the twenty-first century is if we do nothing less. Describing this new mission, Michael Fullan, Peter Hill, and Carmen Crevola, in their book *Breakthrough*, say, "The new mission . . . is about learning to learn, about becoming independent thinkers and learners. It is about problem-solving, teamwork, knowledge of the world, adaptability."

Education not only needs to involve socializing children to function as full participants within the culture and structure of a discipline, it also needs to help readers ratchet up the ambitiousness of their thinking, so we help them progress toward higher levels of proficiency. A proficiency in content area literacy requires people to read with attentiveness not only to facts, but also to perspectives, thinking, "What is it that this author wants me to believe—to feel?" and weighing the assumptions that inform such a perspective.

This session reminds children that neither readers nor learners are mere duplicating machines, that both learning and reading involve growing ideas, talking, and thinking in response to texts and constructing meaning. The session stands on the shoulders of earlier work, but whereas earlier we suggested children Post-it in response to texts and taught them to look across Post-its to grow hunches and theories that relate not just to a specific instance but to trends and patterns, this session emphasizes that a person's initial theories need to change, becoming more specific, more precisely true, and more provocative as the person follows the path of an idea.

This session, then, invites readers and learners to push past the boundaries of Post-its and theory charts to write and think in ways that are more exploratory and expansive than any response they've been asked to provide until now. You essentially say, "Reading is thinking, and the most powerful tool that human beings have for thinking is the pen. So go to it."

Some children will dig deep and soar high. Some will look at you a bit blankly and say, "Huh? What should I do?" Perhaps some children can work in tandem with a partner so that a "more knowing other" can provide the scaffolding that Vygotsky describes as so critical. After all, all of us can do some things now, with support, that we can later do on our own.

Remember, too, that the teaching you have already done earlier in the year can be a resource. Today simply adds another tool and another way of thinking to the repertoire that you've made available to the class. The important thing is that learners are not mere duplicating machines, but instead, learners grow ideas in response to all they take in. They collect, connect, sort, yes . . . and they also find themselves developing their own points of view, their own tentative theories. The pen helps them to do this. This session invites young people into nothing less.

MINILESSON

Writing to Think About Nonfiction

CONNECTION

Set children up for a very long connection. Tell them you will be reading a true story about the class's inquiry topic and ask them to listen for the character's traits, motivations, and struggles and for the big ideas the story conveys.

"Readers, it's not always easy to have our own thoughts as we read. We read, we listen, and we are carried along on someone else's thinking. Then there is silence, and it takes courage to speak into that silence, to replace the other person's words with our own. But good readers are not only listeners. We talk back. We think in response.

"Today I want to read you snippets of a story. It is a true story, written for adults by a famous naturalist, recounting his visit to a penguin colony. I want you to listen, and as you often do when you listen to stories, try to be there in the world of the story, aiming to understand the main characters. In this instance, they are penguins. Try to understand these characters' traits—their motivations, their struggles—and try above all to let the story mean something big and important to you. The author, Gerald Durrell, is not only giving you information; he is trying to convey big ideas to you.

"Remember, the author of *Firehouse*, David Halberstam, told us that behind any great story, there is an idea. Behind the story of *Firehouse*, there was the idea that on that terrible day when the World Trade Center towers came down, the men in the firehouse fought till the end for each other and paid tribute to their deeply woven relationships by doing everything they could to rescue others even if it meant risking their own lives. As you listen to this excerpt from *The Whispering Land*, know that I am going to ask you, 'What are some of the ideas this generates for you? What does the text make you think?'"

A word of warning. The connection alone spans pages and pages, involving a very long read-aloud. This minilesson will not follow the usual template.

It seems timely to mention again a quote from Tomas Alex Tizon, a journalist for The Seattle Times, *who once tried to explain why human beings need stories. He said,*

"Thank God for stories—Stories give shape to experience and allow us to go through life unblind. Without them, everything that happens would float around, undifferentiated. None of it would mean anything. Once you have a version of what happened, all the good stuff about being human comes into play. You can laugh, feel awe, commit a passionate act, get pissed, want to change things."

Notice that I do a fair amount of setup work before launching into what will be a very long read-aloud. You will always want to help readers know if there is a specific angle with which you want them to listen to a text or an anecdote, but this is especially important in an instance like this when the text is an extremely long one.

A Sea of Headwaiters

Ahead of us the low brown scrub petered out, and in its place was a great desert of sun-cracked sand. This was separated from the sea beyond by a crescent-shaped ridge of white sand dunes . . . It was in this desert area, protected from the sea wind by the encircling arm of the dunes, that the penguins had created their city. As far as the eye could see, on every side, the ground was pockmarked with nesting burrows, some a mere half-hearted scrape in the sand, some several feet deep. These craters made the place look like a small section of the moon's surface . . . In among these craters waddled the biggest collection of penguins I had ever seen, like a sea of pygmy headwaiters, shuffling solemnly to and fro . . . The distant sand dunes were freckled with the tiny plodding figures of penguins, either climbing the steep slope or sliding down them.

Early in the morning, one of the parent birds (either male or female) would set out towards the sea, leaving its mate in charge of the nestlings. In order to get to the sea the bird had to cover about a mile and a half of the most grueling and difficult terrain imaginable. First they had to pick their way through the vast patchwork of nesting burrows . . . [then] they were faced by the desert area, where the sand was caked and split by the sun . . . so hot that it was painful to touch, and yet the penguins would plod dutifully across it, pausing frequently for a rest, as though in a trance . . . But, when they reached the other side of the desert they were faced with another obstacle, the sand dunes. These towered over the diminutive figures of the birds like a snow-white chain of Himalayan mountains . . . [When they finally reached the far side of the dunes] there was the sea, blue, glittering, lisping seductively on the shore, and to get to it they had to drag their tired bodies over the stony beach, where the pebbles scrunched and wobbled under their feet, throwing them off balance. But at last it was over . . . and they plunged into the cool water.

"After fishing, they'd head home, and I'll move forward to describe their homecoming."

Once the parent bird reached the edge of the colony, it had to run the gauntlet of several thousand youngsters before it reached its own nest-burrow and babies. All these youngsters were convinced that, by launching themselves at the adult bird in a sort of tackle, they could get it to regurgitate the food it was carrying. So the adult had to avoid the attacks

Since this passage you are reading is quite long, you will want to read in a dramatic tone, illustrating some of the ideas by acting them out or gesturing. For example, while reading the line, "In among these craters waddled the biggest collection of penguins I had ever seen, like a sea of pygmy headwaiters, shuffling solemnly to and fro," you could sway side to side in your chair, as the penguins are described as doing. However, I caution you against overdoing this or acting parts out as if they are silly, because you'll want children listening for the big ideas, the larger concepts that weave throughout this account. Just make the tiniest gestures to convey a hint of the content.

Another day, you could return to this text, as you do to so many of your read-alouds, to study it with particular lenses. For example, when helping children learn how to talk about the ideas they grow as they learn about a subject, you may want to point out that many nonfiction writers relay on metaphor or comparisons to convey their meanings. This passage likens the landscape to the moon's surface, the penguins to a sea of pygmy headwaiters, the sand dunes to a snow-white chain of Himalayan mountains. Durrell also illustrates how authors choose perspectives from which to write. He writes in such a way that we assume the perspective of a penguin—no small feat!

I'm skipping past a chunk of the text and using that one line to signal to children that I am doing this. I'm aware this is very long, and it is written for adult readers. It is sophisticated. But it is also, I think, beautiful writing, and I want to give kids access to it. Imagine how powerful this is for the penguin inquiry group, too!

of these fat, furry youngsters by dodging to and fro like a skilful centre-forward on a football field. Generally the parent would end up at its nest-borrow . . . It would squat down at the entrance to the burrow and stare at its feet pensively, making motions like someone trying to stifle an acute attack of hiccups.

On seeing this, the youngsters would work themselves into a frenzy of delighted anticipation, uttering their wild, wheezing cries, flapping their wings frantically, pressing themselves close to the parent bird's body, and stretching up their beaks and clattering them against the adult's. This would go on for perhaps thirty seconds, when the parent would suddenly—with an expression of relief—regurgitate vigorously, plunging its beak so deeply into the gaping mouths of the youngsters you felt sure it would never be able to pull its head out again.

The babies, satisfied and apparently not stabbed from stem to stern by the delivery of the first course, would squat on their plump behinds and meditate . . . All would be quiet for five minutes or so, and then suddenly the parent would start its strange hiccupping motions again and pandemonium would break out immediately.

Leaning back in my chair, exhaling a big breath, I said, "Whew! What excitement!" Children nodded in agreement with their eyes open wide.

Invite readers to jot their big ideas that came to mind as you read the previous passage.

"Right now, while your ideas are swirling around your mind, write down the big ideas that you have about this passage."

As soon as the children began jotting, I voiced over with, "Get past simply jotting 'Ugh' in response to the story of the parent penguin regurgitating. Take your mind firmly in hand and say to your own mind, 'You can do better than that. Think big thoughts. Think about what this whole story is trying to say.'" I gave them a minute to write, and then after a bit, voiced over again. "The author took the time to research this and write it all beautifully; what was he hoping to communicate?"

Children wrote in their notebooks. The room was filled with the scratch of pens. I voiced over their work, saying, "Readers, I rarely take the time to read a whole long text during one of our minilessons, and this is perhaps the longest writing we've done inside of a minilesson this year. This should signal to you that this is important work. Keep working." [Figs. XVI-1 and XVI-2]

Although you will probably not be able to highlight this point just now, the passage that you will read can function as a gigantic mentor text for the learning projects that you've launched in your class. The author of this text, Gerald Durrell, epitomizes what it can mean to be enthralled by a topic. Instead of merely conducting research by reading a few books, Durrell's research takes him to the farthest corners of the world, where he observes, with rapt attention, the daily life of a penguin colony. One could say, he reads penguins.

Information sparks ideas. Sometimes, collecting information can stop thinking—overwhelming the brain, for example, making the "inbox" too full for the system to work. But often, information becomes grist for the mill, and it is almost impossible to not think in response to choice facts.

You'll notice that this connection is longer than others. I've not only read a story; I've also asked children to write their ideas. I could have moved much of the children's writing to the active involvement section, but I wanted children to generate ideas quickly now, so they would have an opportunity to elaborate on them later in the minilesson.

Name your teaching point. Tell children that nonfiction readers and researchers don't just collect facts. We also think.

"Today I want to teach you that reading involves not just listening, taking in information and ideas. Reading also involves talking back, replacing the author's words with our own. And here is the secret: readers can write before we know what we think or what we have to say. We can write as a way to figure out what we have to say. When we write, we often start with one thought, one feeling, and then we hold that thought, that feeling, in our hands, and we put it on the paper. And then we follow that thought to another, and another, until we are following a path of thoughtfulness."

TEACHING

Tell of a youngster who used writing to follow a path of thoughtfulness. The writing could be about a topic unrelated to nonfiction reading. Your point is to show that by writing, a person blazes a trail of thought. Debrief after sharing the text.

"A fifth-grader named Max wrote about the clubhouse that had been behind his childhood home, the home that was sold. He had driven past the old house and seen that the people had taken the clubhouse down. He could have just written that—the facts. But Max knows that writing can be a way to figure out what he feels and thinks so he used writing to go out on the thin ice of new thoughts. As his pen raced down the page, he wrote his way along what many people call 'a journey of thought.'

"Let me read you his writing. You could listen and think, 'What does that have to do with nonfiction reading or with penguins or castles or hurricanes?' My point is that you and I can use writing to take us on a similar journey to figure out what we are thinking about our topic. The process is the same whether one is thinking about tree houses or about penguins. So listen to Max's writing, and then you're going to have time to go back to the writing you just did about penguins, to reread it and rethink it, or to rethink an idea you have about your research topic."

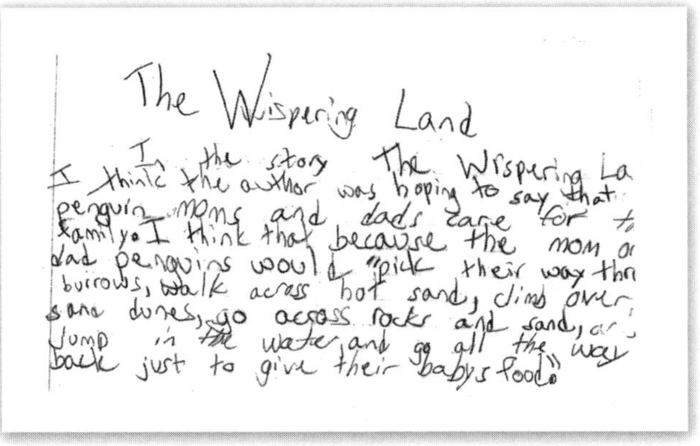

Figure XVI-1
This reader has internalized the structure of making and then supporting a claim.

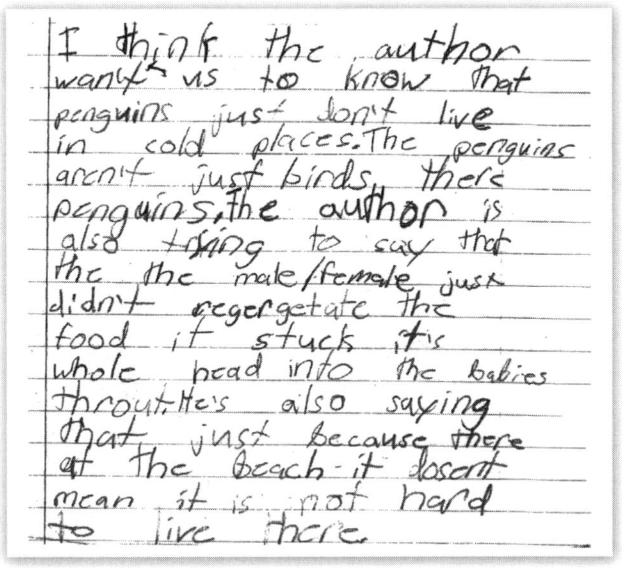

Figure XVI-2
Who was it who said, "We need to let thoughts run like tap water, so that after a time they become clear?"

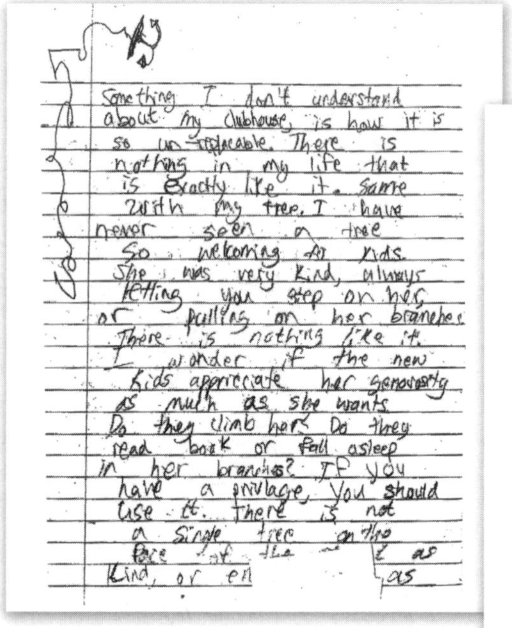

Figure XVI-3a
Page 1, Max's journey of thought.

Figure XVI-3b
Page 2, Max's journey of thought.

Figure XVI-3c
Page 3, Max's journey of thought.

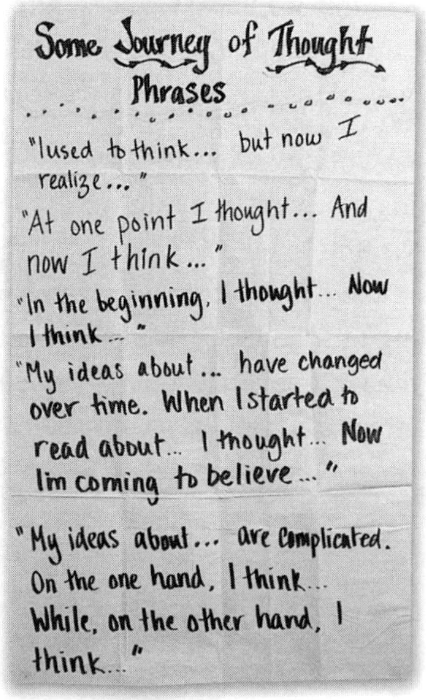

Figure XVI-4
What a gold mine this chart is! Teach your students to use phrases like these to push their thinking.

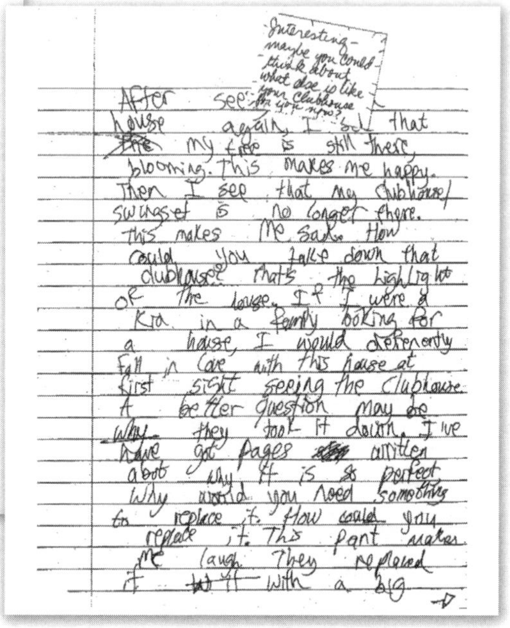

Debrief, pointing out what the child did that you hope readers do often, including using some phrases that support a journey of thought.

"Do you see that Max started off wondering how the new family could possibly have taken down the clubhouse? Then he went to a new, related subject: How come they'd replaced the clubhouse with a black net? All the things that he did in that clubhouse can't begin to be done in a net. Listing those things led Max to a dawning insight: Although the kids that live in his old home don't have his childhood clubhouse, he still has it because he has memories of it. [Figs. XVI-3a, XVI-3b, and XVI-3c]

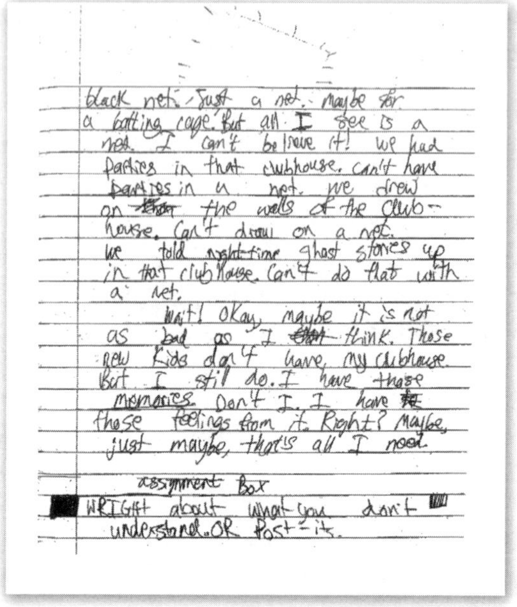

"In a second, you're going to either reread what you wrote about the passage I read today, or rethink an idea about your research topic. Either way you'll try to push your thinking to dawning new insights. When a person wants to do this sort of writing, it can help to borrow some phrases that sort of get you going [Figs. XVI-4]. Those phrases are like training wheels. They get you started, but then as you write, you write faster and faster, and that creates its own momentum, helping you go forward, on and on, to ideas you didn't even expect to have."

Writing to Grow Ideas

- *Write a thought. Try to use precise words to capture that thought. Often it takes a sentence or two to capture a thought, not just a few words.*
- *Sometimes it helps to write, "In other words . . ." and to try saying the same thought differently, reaching for the precisely true words. Then you can say, "That is . . ." and try again to say the thought.*
- *Once you've recorded a thought, it helps to think more about that thought. Usually an idea comes to the tip of your pen if you keep your pen moving.*
- *Pause to reread. If a line seems especially important, true, or new, copy that line onto the top of a clean white sheet of paper and write to grow that idea, using all the ideas described above.*

Active Involvement

Ask children to try taking a journey of thought like the one you've used as an example—this time using their own topics as starting points and using the thought prompts as needed.

"So readers, right now, think back to an idea you've had about penguins or about your study topic and see if you can write as Max has done, in a way that gets you thinking one set of ideas, and then, as you write on and on down the page, you'll come to a new set of ideas. I'm going to be quiet so you can write, write, write."

Children scrawled and I gave them a few extra minutes to write, because they all seemed engaged. I peered over some kids' shoulders to see what they'd come up with. Grace and David had both returned to their penguin jottings from the start of the minilesson and pushed themselves to write about surprising ideas. *[Figs. XVI-5 and XVI-6]* Aly had written a couple questions. *[Fig. XVI-7]*

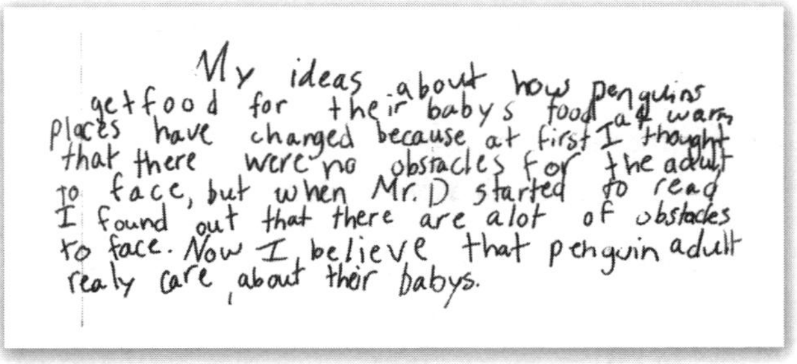
My ideas about how penguins get food for their babys food at warm places have changed because at first I thought that there were no obstacles for the adult to face, but when Mr. D started to read I found out that there are alot of obstacles to face. Now I believe that penguin adult realy care about their babys.

Figure XVI-5
Notice how David uses contrasting ideas to pop out his new insight.

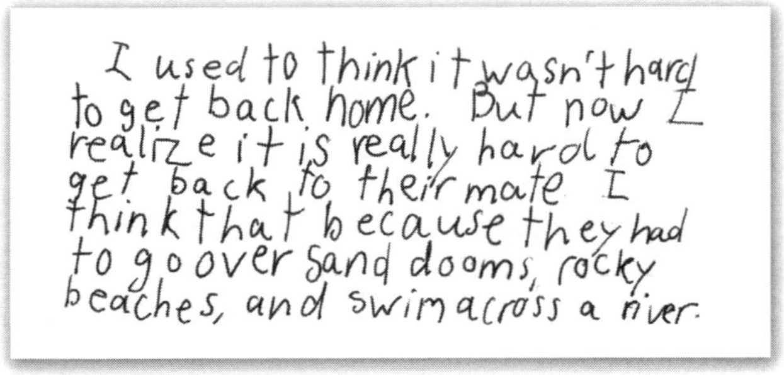
I used to think it wasn't hard to get back home. But now I realize it is really hard to get back to their mate. I think that because they had to go over sand dooms, rocky beaches, and swim across a river.

Figure XVI-6
"I used to think . . . but now I realize. . . ." prompt can help students put a journey of thought onto the page.

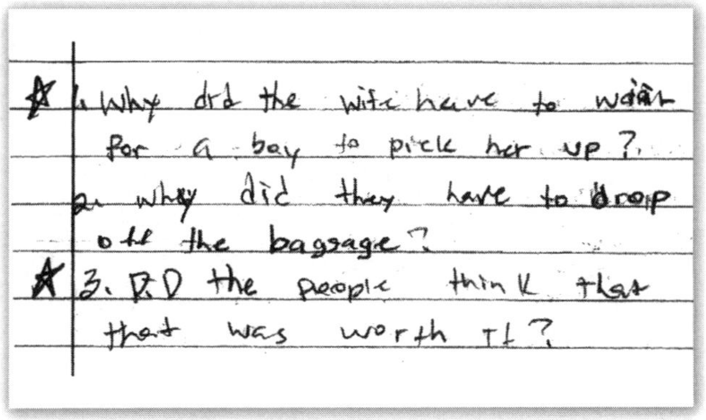
★ 1. Why did the wife have to wait for a boy to pick her up?
2. why did they have to drop off the baggage?
★ 3. DID the people think that that was worth it?

Figure XVI-7
Aly had chosen a few questions from her list and mused about them.

José had written several reactions to his reading. *[Fig. XVI-8]*

Invite children to think and talk about how techniques they've used as writers will help develop their ideas as readers.

"I want you and your partner to look at the writing that one of you did and talk about how these techniques could help you be better nonfiction readers and thinkers. Talk about whether you think you'll do some of this writing as you continue your inquiry, or do you think that for now, Post-its and theory charts are working fine for you? Because one of the important things for learners to know is that just as text structures matter to readers, they also matter to writers, and you all can choose the structure for your notes and your thoughts, knowing that different structures are suited to different sorts of thinking."

Link

Help children recall that nonfiction readers don't just comb for facts, but rather, we seek to be wiser about the world. Channel children to take out their own research materials and begin writing about their ideas.

"Researchers, I hope you will always remember that we don't do research just to become fact-combers. Instead, we take a bit of information, a bit of the world, and we hold it up to the light. We think about it. We think about it one way and then another way. We talk about it, we Post-it about it, we chart about it, and we write long about it. Doing this work helps us become wiser about the world, because we want to do all the good stuff that human beings do: to laugh, to feel awe, to grow an insight, to realize a pattern, to resolve to change things. We research not only to collect, but also to think. And the best tool human beings have for thinking is the pen.

"So before you leave the meeting area, I want you and the members of your group to talk about this: When and how will you take what you have seen or learned or noticed as you collect information on your research topics and make sure this stuff gets through to you, make sure that it makes you think, and rethink, and follow a pathway of thinking?"

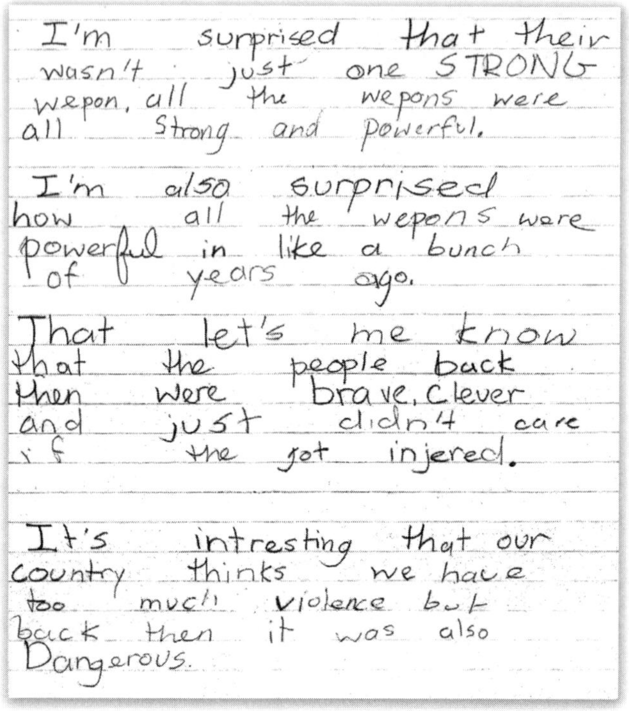
I'm surprised that their wasn't just one STRONG wepon, all the wepons were all Strong and powerful.

I'm also surprised how all the wepons were powerful in like a bunch of years ago.

That let's me know that the people back then were brave, clever and just didn't care if the got injered.

It's intresting that our country thinks we have too much violence but back then it was also Dangerous.

Figure XVI-8
José is wise to attend to realizations that surprise him, because these represent dawning new ideas.

It is always important for you to think about ways in which you can differentiate your teaching so that you provide extra scaffolds to children who need support. Today's lesson will set children up to read with an angle, gleaning the information that is applicable to the big ideas they are growing as they read, and to use graphic organizers to help organize their research. Some children will find this challenging. At the headwaters of this work, you may pair a few children together so that one child does more of the actual writing, the other helps with the thinking, and the two can work as a productive heterogeneous partnership.

CONFERRING AND SMALL-GROUP WORK

Help Kids Write Not Only to Record but Also to Think

Sometimes We Confer First with One Reader from a Group and Then Use that One Reader's Work as a Mentor Text for the Other Group Members

It was reading (rather than talking) time when I decided to work with the members of the immigration research group.

I'd overheard Kadija and Sarah talking about Ellis Island as they came in one morning, and Aly was practically glued nose-first into her book. It can be tempting with obviously engaged and interested students like these three to just let them be. They were certainly learning and on task and taking in the work. But it is important to push all of our students to make their best work stronger, and I always keep in mind that attempting to break new trails for learners is a form of staff-development and curriculum development for myself, helping me to imagine new minilessons, bends-in-the-road, and units of study.

I knew one option was to ask the group to stop reading and to talk with me, but I was loathe to interrupt Sarah and Kadija's reading when they had just opened their books and

settled into them. I figured I'd start by conferring with just Aly and see where that led me. My thought was that I'd probably be able to help her do some more writing-to-think work, because I knew that she had been fired up over an idea she'd landed on earlier.

When I pulled my chair alongside Aly, she had already read a few books and filled a few pages with notes. "Can you walk me through your thinking?" I asked.

"Well," she said, "I've got the process down that they came through."

"They?" I asked, although I was fairly sure she was referring to immigrants to America.

"Yeah, see it says 'What was the process that the immigrants came through?' she read from her paper. As she did this, I scanned the page and saw that she'd recorded a long list of the steps immigrants took when arriving at Ellis Island. *[Fig. XVI-9]*

"Has making this list been helpful?" I asked.

Aly nodded. "Yeah, 'cause now I have it all in my mind."

Aly's comment made sense to me. I often write as a way to organize information so that I can feel as if I've

---

MID-WORKSHOP TEACHING POINT

Researchers Go from Collecting to Growing Ideas

"Researchers, can I stop you?" I waited until all eyes were on me. "In our writing workshop, many of you have learned that writing starts with collecting stuff—entries, scraps. Our former poet laureate, Donald Hall, titles his autobiography, *String Too Short to be Saved*. He talks about how, as a writer, he cherishes collecting scraps and bits—strings too short to be saved—because he knows that at a later time, he can look back over stuff, and that stuff may spark ideas. Many of us think of our writer's notebook as a place where we collect strings too short to be saved. We reread all we've collected and see bits that somehow go together and mean something, and then we write ourselves a poem, a memoir, a story.

"The research workshop is not all that different from the writing workshop. You've been collecting information and observations and ideas about your subject—collecting in your minds, in jotted notes, in the map of your subject. To actually make something of all you are learning, you need to go from collecting to growing ideas. I am pretty sure that in the writing you have done today, you have some seed ideas that you could grow into something bigger. Share what you have written with your research mates and see if you have some seed ideas you want to develop, individually or as a group.

"Once researchers have a seed idea or two, then we usually return to reading—to our research. Only we read differently because we are not only collecting; we are also reacting, feeling, thinking."

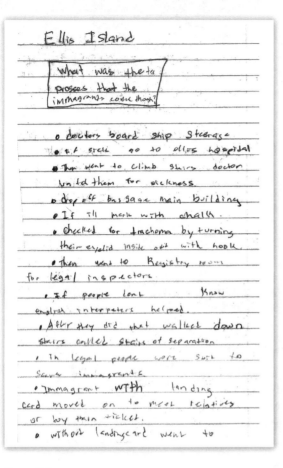

Figure XVI-9
This is Aly's effort to get her mind around the process the
immigrants went through at Ellis Island.

got some control over it. Also, what she had done did require some skills. She had synthesized large swaths of expository text into one clear list.

I also noticed something else, however. Earlier in the year, when Aly was reading fiction, she would often write about what she'd read in the tiniest of detail, but then she almost always added some really insightful thoughts at the end of her details. She had not added her own thoughts at the end of her list about the immigrants' entry into the United States. It seemed to me that if I encouraged her to record insights after she made her list, this might extend her work to a rather obvious next step. Then again, perhaps Aly was just on the brink of doing that and didn't even

need a nudge from me. Now that I had a hypothesis, I needed to do a bit more research.

"Are you thinking of writing other stuff, or what?" I asked.

"I think that's all that I know about how they came," Aly answered. "But I could look at the book and have more."

Aly's response confirmed my impression that she was pretty focused on simply collecting the factual information from the book, rather than using that information to develop her own ideas about it as she'd done when reading fiction.

Help Readers Think About the Structure Not Only of the Texts They Read but Also of the Notes They Make

"How are you liking this research project?" I asked, taking a tack that I thought might reveal some of the thinking she was already doing in response to the books she was reading.

"Good, 'cause it really makes you feel like you lived then. I mean, it isn't chapter books, but it almost is because you imagine it's you, going down the stairs of separation and all." She talked a bit more about empathizing with the immigrants.

"When you say, 'It isn't chapter books,' I pressed, what do you mean?"

"Oops. I mean it isn't narrative. It isn't a story. Like this book," she said, gesturing to the book she'd been reading. "This has little stories in it, but the whole thing is all-about, with subheads and all. But when I read it, I almost make it a story in my mind, 'cause I imagine that I am there."

At this point, I felt sure I had enough sense of Aly's work to be helpful. "Aly, I have a suggestion for you, but first I have to tell you that I am floored by what you just said. You just realized something that is so huge I can't believe it is coming out of the mouth of a nine-year-old! You are totally right that it is not only texts that can be written as all-about books or as stories. Readers' minds can organize information either way! And you are saying that you have taken this all-about book that has categories of information, and you are reading it as if it is fiction, as if it is a narrative, because you, the reader, are supplying the main character who is going through all the information—the facts. That is so cool.

"Although I was not going to teach this to kids your age, I can tell you that the same thing could be done in reverse. You could take a story—like, say, historic fiction, about immigration—"

Aly interrupted to say, "Like *Letters from Rifka?*"

I nodded, "Absolutely. You could take *Letters from Rifka* and read it in a way that had your notes looking almost like a report, with categories of information!"

Support Readers' Efforts to Assimilate and Use Technical Vocabulary

I added, "Let's talk more in a minute about your discovery that you can read expository texts almost as if they are fiction, because I first want to tell you one other talent you have that you may not even realize. A moment ago, when you said that you could picture yourself going down those 'stairs of separation,' I have to tell you that I love the way you effortlessly pick up so many of the terms that come with your topic. You know how some people cherish the olden-day quality of, say, an antique wooden table, while other people just think that any plastic modern table would be as good? It's like you appreciate the olden-day quality of the words, and you don't just throw those beautiful old words away. In your list of the steps immigrants had to take and your discussion about how you empathize with the immigrants, you use so many of those olden-day terms—the stairs of separation, the steerage, the registry, the landing cards. It makes your list of facts feel like literature, or like history. I hope this is not just that you love Ellis Island words but that instead, it's that you love the lingo of any topic. It is a special gift."

Aly smiled and nodded, rubbing one purple nail-polished fingernail.

Channel Readers to Write Not Only to Collect Information but Also to Grow Ideas

"I have a suggestion. I agree that it is helpful to collect what you see in the book, to run your hands through the contents and even the words of the book as you've done, but you never want to let yourself believe that what's written in the book is all that you know. Because there's stuff in the book and then there's stuff in your mind—the stuff you think and feel and wonder as you read. And more of your writing time needs to be spent pushing yourself to write about the stuff in your mind. You have gotten so good at growing ideas when you read fiction and need to still do that with nonfiction." I checked to see if Aly was still with me, and she was nodding in affirmation.

I pressed on. "Would you reread your list, maybe a couple times, and then write what you are thinking?" As Aly did a bit of writing, I checked in with other readers and then returned five minutes later. *[Fig. XVI-10]*

I complimented Aly on realizing that one way to develop ideas was to choose a question or two to actually pursue—to ponder. I then reminded her of what she'd said earlier about how she was reading even this expository text, in the shoes of a character. "I bet you can imagine what people are thinking and feeling because of the way you are reading this," I said and suggested she could, if she wanted to do so, write as if she was one of the characters going through this process, perhaps even being that wife (see her first question) who had to wait for a boy to pick her up.

Aly didn't take up my nudge to write in the perspective of an arriving immigrant, but she did draw on her emotional response to the text to write her thoughts.

[Figs. XVI-11 and XVI-12a]

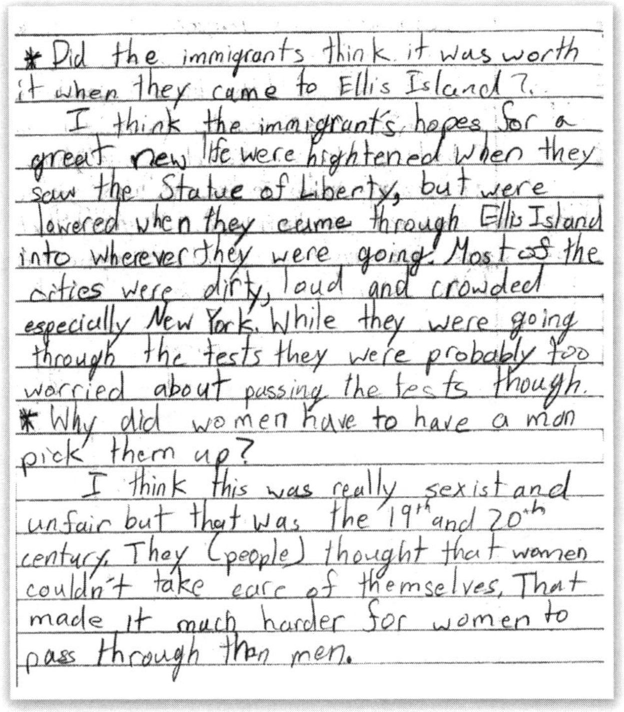

*Did the immigrants think it was worth it when they came to Ellis Island?
I think the immigrant's hopes for a great new life were hightened when they saw the Statue of Liberty, but were lowered when they came through Ellis Island into wherever they were going. Most of the cities were dirty, loud and crowded especially New York. While they were going through the tests they were probably too worried about passing the tests though.
*Why did women have to have a man pick them up?
I think this was really sexist and unfair but that was the 19th and 20th century. They (people) thought that women couldn't take care of themselves. That made it much harder for women to pass through than men.

Figure XVI-10

Figure XVI-11

> I think because they though that the girl would not find A Job so the boy could let her go or keep her. I think it is very mean to do that. A girl can get A Job evenif it is a girl. A girl can get A sewing Job. It is very mean for A girl to wait for a boy to come and claim her or she has to go back, that is very sexist. It is very unfair that it is good there is No rule about it now.

Figure XVI-12a

> Did the Immagrant think that it was worth it to go though all that worth?
>
> I would think that it would be worth it because it my old home was under war and then I would come here. then I can get A better education and get A better Job even IF I am a girl even IF I dont get pick Up I will try to sneek out of ellis island with A couple of boys and pretend I am with them or I would Just lye to the soldiers to tell them that my uncle Is sick and cant pick me up.

I nodded when I saw the start of Aly's work and pointed out to her the difference between the mere list and the list that then gave way to this sort of reflection. "After this, Aly, be sure that you remember that readers write not just to hold onto what others have said, but also to hold onto what we have to say, and that sometimes takes sitting with your pen in hand, just waiting for words to come. But they'll come."

Using the Conference with One Child as the Teaching Content for Small-Group Instruction

Instead of holding the same exact conference again with Sarah and Kadija, who I guessed would also benefit from this work, I decided to recruit Aly to help me teach them what she'd just done, using her own work as an example. She was, of course, delighted to be in the teacher role and to share what she'd written with her friends. I interrupted Kadija and Sarah, who were reading and jotting notes in their notebooks, and pulled them over. Aly showed them the work she had done—from the initial factual Post-it through to the "writing long" she'd done in response to her own questions. She talked them through the work, and I listened, ready to clarify if need be. When she was done, I invited all three of them to imagine how they might use writing to continue pushing their thinking as Aly had done. I left the girls talking, and when I circled back I noticed that each girl had made a list of questions (some borrowed from each other) and had decided on a few from each list to which they would write in response.

Kadija, a first-generation immigrant (from South Africa) herself, had written this: [Fig. XVI-12b]

> In the 20th century people were not as aware of what woman could do. They did not think that woman would be able to get Jobs and they thought woman would have no money and will live homless, and America did not want more people on the streats. The people wanted to be sure they will live a life with progress.

Figure XVI-12b
Kadija's writing-to-think.

I was particularly happy to see that Sarah was excited to share her ideas with her group mates. She generally tended to hang in the background a bit and to go along with what others said in spite of her own insightful ideas.

I complimented them all on how well they'd used writing to deepen their thinking and pointed out that writing long can help a person think new ideas. I asked them to make a plan for their next steps and to keep in mind that from this day on, they would each use writing to help them learn.

At the end of the workshop the girls decided to continue to write from their questions for homework, and then to read, carrying questions in their mind, seeing if they could find evidence to support or revise their thinking. They planned on having a "big conversation" the next day.

TEACHING SHARE

Researchers Find Our Own Angle on What We've Read

Draw a parallel for your students between the writing work they are doing as readers and the writing work they do in writing workshop. Then ask them to read through their jottings and find a seed idea for a line of thinking they may pursue as they research.

"Readers, by now I'm sure it's no surprise to you that there are many parallels between the work we do in writing workshop and the work we do in reading workshop. Jotting your ideas as you read is similar to the work we do at the beginning of a unit of study in writing, when we collect lots of entries in a particular genre. Your jottings reflect the variety of new things you're learning. For instance, the penguin group has jottings that cover facts about everything from where penguins live and how they've adapted to predators and other dangers penguins face to the unique way they take care of their children. That's a lot to be thinking about and holding onto. It's sometimes hard to do deep thinking about such a range of information.

"When archaeologists are digging for bones and other artifacts, they know that if they move around a site, always just brushing off the top layer of dust, they're not likely to find much. It's only when they stay in one spot, digging deeper into the ground, that they uncover the really exciting items—objects covered by decades, centuries even, of earth, sometimes objects that they had no idea they would find. That's what it's like when you canvas your entries in your reading notebooks. You're rereading, taking stock, to pick one spot in which to start digging.

"So, just like we do in the writing workshop, we now have to select one idea—a seed idea, as we call it in writing—and think and write about our topic by focusing on that one idea. So, perhaps Gabe is reading over his jottings and decides that the idea that is most interesting to him is that penguins have all sorts of physical adaptations that allow them to survive in the icy environment in Antarctica. And maybe Tyrell is rereading his jottings, and he decides that his seed idea, the way he'll be considering his topic, will have something to do with how penguins eat. Each of you will select an idea that inspires your passions, that gets your mind going. This idea will also give you a sort of lens to look through as you continue reading. You'll be thinking about how a text connects to your seed idea, and that idea will be the thread through most of your jottings.

COACHING TIPS FROM LUCY CALKINS

"Right now, open your notebooks and take a few moments to reread your jottings. Some of you might already have an inkling about what idea you'll select. Maybe without even realizing, you've already been seeking information about that idea, writing about it, and talking about it with your inquiry partners. Star or underline that idea in your notebook. I'll give you a few moments to do that, and if you pick quickly, you can copy that idea on the next page of your notebook and generate a little bit of writing based on that idea." [Figs. XVI-13 and XVI-14]

I looked over some students' shoulders as they bent over their notebooks, most intent on rereading. "Remember," I said, "it will probably help you if the idea you pick is not a little tidbit but, instead, an idea that you're confident will have a depth of information."

I saw that Kobe, in the Extreme Weather Group, was in a few seconds writing about his idea. "Some people follow dangerous storms, like tornadoes, as a job or hobby." Meanwhile others, in other groups, were doing similiar work [Figs. XVI-13 and XVI-14], Izzy boxed out the idea "Some storms are so severe that they cause major damage to places and the people who live there" and started writing about that. [Fig. XVI-15]

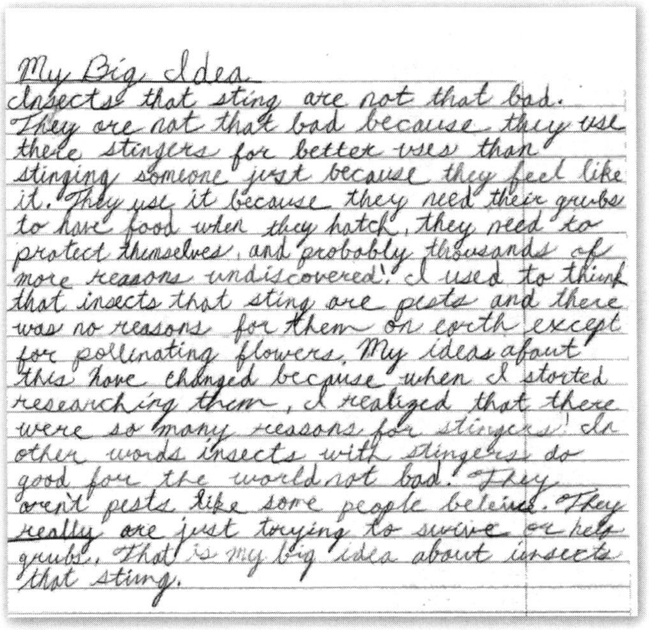

My Big Idea.
Insects that sting are not that bad. They are not that bad because they use their stingers for better uses than stinging someone just because they feel like it. They use it because they need their grubs to have food when they hatch, they need to protect themselves, and probably thousands of more reasons undiscovered! I used to think that insects that sting are pests and there was no reasons for them on earth except for pollinating flowers. My ideas about this have changed because when I started researching them, I realized that there were so many reasons for stingers! In other words insects with stingers do good for the world not bad! They aren't pests like some people believe. They really are just trying to survive or help grubs. That is my big idea about insects that sting.

Figure XVI-13
Jasmine begins some thinking and writing in this interval of time, and returns to it later. Note her effortless incorporation of phrases such as "My ideas have changed. . . . "

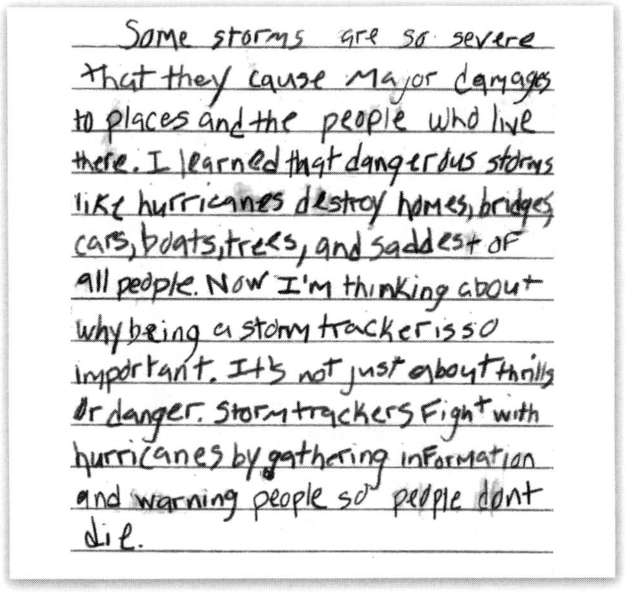

Some storms are so severe that they cause major damage to places and the people who live there. I learned that dangerous storms like hurricanes destroy homes, bridges cars, boats, trees, and saddest of all people. Now I'm thinking about why being a storm tracker is so important. It's not just about thrills or danger. Storm trackers fight with hurricanes by gathering information and warning people so people dont die.

Figure XVI-15
Kobe didn't hesitate before selecting and writing about this seed idea.

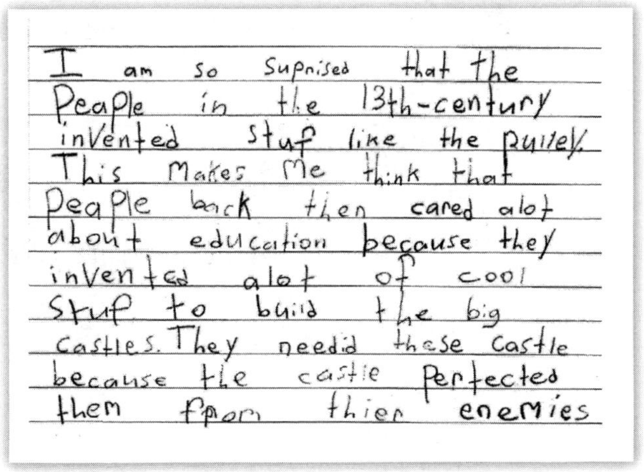

I am so suprised that the people in the 13th-century invented stuf like the pulley. This makes me think that people back then cared alot about education because they invented alot of cool stuf to build the big castles. They needd these castle because the castle perfected them from thier enemies

Figure XVI-14
The progression from a detail to a generalization is impressive. Young people read to learn to shift up and down the ladder of abstraction.

SESSION XVII

IN THIS SESSION,
you'll teach students to notice that authors write from different perspectives, provoking varying responses in readers.

Reading Critically: What is the Author Making Us Feel, and How?

ne of the greatest teaching points of nonfiction reading was delivered by a fictional spider who was a master of literacy in her own right. As E. B. White's Charlotte spun words into her web, she stated, "People are very gullible. They'll believe anything they see in print." Charlotte, like all great writers, knew how to pick words with care and to use her literacy to persuade and convince.

As we help our students roll up their sleeves and do the work that nonfiction readers the world over do, it becomes increasingly urgent to address what Charlotte referred to as the "gullibility" of readers. As ambitious teachers of literacy, we want our students to know a kind of literacy that means far more than the ability to decode texts, comprehend a story line, and follow a sequence of events through a mental movie. We hope that our kids' literacies will enable

them to look at a text with an expert eye and see how the text was put together, why trouble was taken to put it together in a certain way, and who benefits from its publication. We want our youngsters to grow up able not only to read words but also to read intentions—and implications—behind words.

In this unit so far, we've helped readers to read intertextually and encouraged them to adopt an insider's lingo on a topic. We've stressed the importance of responding to reading and especially of picking up a pencil to record and to follow the ideas that occur to them about the topic. This minilesson and the few that follow will feel slightly different from the work we've been doing thus far. From deep immersion we now shift to a deconstructive stance, adopting a certain distance from a text to study it critically. The upcoming sessions lay the foundation for this work, taking

GETTING READY

- For the connection, select two books on the same nonfiction topic that approach this topic from completely different—even opposing—stances. Make sure cover illustrations, titles, or photos inside clearly emphasize this difference.

- Children will need to bring their bins of books to the meeting area for the active involvement.

- Create a chart, "Strategies for Dealing with Conflicting Information in Nonfiction Texts," to add to in the active involvement.

- Have chart paper handy as you confer with students.

- Create a chart to unveil in the mid-workshop teaching point: "Readers Ask Critical Questions About a Text"

advantage of children's inquiry stance on a single topic to help them read with enough depth that they'll be able to consider how each text reports from its own angle.

In doing this, we're subtly picking up a thread from the previous unit and weaving it into this genre's teaching. "Characters—like people—are not just one way," we noted earlier, looking at protagonists of fiction. In the lessons that follow, we'll be saying much the same thing about topics of

> *We want our youngsters to grow up able not only to read words but also to read intentions—and implications—behind words.*

nonfiction. Sharks, penguins, and castles are not just one way! An apple will look different to the artist searching for hues of ochre than it would to a preoccupied pie-maker. All texts, even those that report "facts," are deliberate human constructions, and they position the reader. Reading can, in the end, impart the wisdom that there is no absolute truth—there are only reports on this truth—and that a report, no matter how well meaning, cannot claim total freedom from bias.

Perhaps this is what literacy boils down to—a reading of the texts on paper as well as texts that codify human behavior and life in all its richness and diversity. In the sessions that follow, we begin this exciting work of taking texts apart like a researcher and a critic might. This leg of the journey, even as it culminates the work on nonfiction reading, will open up possibilities for lifelong observation and inquiry in our kids' lives. We hope, in the end, to have children who read in a way that might meet with E. B. White's Charlotte's approval. We hope our children look at the words in a web and glance, not just at the pig, but also up at the spider, wondering not merely at the meaning, but also at the origins, source, motivation, angle, and implications of the words they've been served.

MINILESSON

Reading Critically: What is the Author Making Us Feel, and How?

CONNECTION

Tell the story of a time when you watched a still-life art class, noticing that each artist saw the items—a pear and an apple—from a different perspective.

"About two weeks ago, I walked into an art class in the high school. The students were busy at their easels doing what is called a still-life sketch. This means they put something—for these students it was a few pieces of fruit and a bottle—on a podium in the center of the room, and everyone sat around those objects and sketched what they saw. So there were about twenty artists, sitting around the same pear, the same red apple, and the same green bottle in the same room at the same time, quietly sketching.

"But here's the strange thing. As I tiptoed around the room, eyeing every artist's easel, I expected to see the same thing! After all, everyone was drawing the same old apple, pear, and bottle. But since people couldn't sit in the exact same spot, everyone had a different angle that they drew from, so here's the thing: It was like they saw different sides of the same thing.

"Readers, it wasn't just that. Their sketching style, the shadows they noted, even the size and scale of each person's sketch, was different. One artist had shaded brown, orange and green into the red of his apple—colors I hadn't even noticed in that apple,

COACHING TIPS

If you appreciate this minilesson and would like to do more of this sort of teaching, be sure you turn to Constructing Curriculum: Alternate Units of Study. *There are several alternate units that develop the theme of this session with great detail. There is also a session in Volume 2 of Unit 4,* Tackling Complex Texts *that spotlights perspective and it's a favorite.*

If you tell this story well, children's minds will be racing ahead of you, predicting what you have yet to say. Notice that I'm using the skills of narrative writing to unfold this event in a step-by-step sequential fashion. I even tell the internal as well as the external story and use exact dialogue, employing the qualities of good writing we teach in writing workshop.

You may decide to make your point using visuals. Choose two different photographs of a topic—tigers, Roman baths, the President's inauguration.

quite frankly. Another artist had managed to make that ordinary green bottle look a bit spooky, like there were spirits hiding in there, waiting to be released or something—the mood of each picture was different.

"I thought at once of you. Walking around those artists, looking at how they each saw and drew the same subject so differently reminded me of how I've been walking around conferring with you all, noting that many of you are holding books on the same topic but how each of your books addresses the topic so differently. Lily might be holding a book about insects and say something like, 'Wow, those dung beetles are *nasty*! I can't believe they bury their eggs in a ball of dung.'" I held up a picture of the dung beetle in action. *[Fig. XVII-1]*

"And Jasmine might be holding another book about insects and say, 'Gosh, those dung beetles are really *smart*! They bury their eggs in a place where they know no one would go. That's so clever because many animals eat beetle babies.'"

State your teaching point. Specifically, tell children that the more we read, the more readers of nonfiction realize that one nonfiction book is but one version of the truth.

"Today, I want to teach you that every writer's version of the truth is colored by his or her own understanding or experience or access to information or motivation. Just like every artist in a still-life class can't possibly be sitting in exactly the same spot, seeing the same angles, the same shadows, so too, every author writing about the Civil War won't report from the same stance."

Teaching

Contrast the different ways in which several books approach a common topic.

"Readers, I've been helping my son plan his mountain trekking trip through Nepal. We went to the library the other day to look at some books about mountains in that general region of the world, and we found a bunch on Mount Everest.

"Look at this first one entitled *Everest: Summit of Achievement*. 'Hmm,' we thought as we plucked this out of the bookshelf. 'For some people, Everest is more than a mountain—it is a goal.' And here's another entitled *The Top of the World: Climbing Mount Everest*. Miles doesn't plan to climb Everest, but these books made the mountains of Nepal seem more exciting.

Figure XVII-1
This beetle has buried her eggs in a bit of dung. One reader may think this nasty, another smart.

There are endless possible variations to this anecdote. Over the years, many teachers have found it effective to show their classes four different front-page photographs of the President at the oath-taking ceremony. The photographs spoke for themselves: taken seconds apart by different photographers stationed at varying vantage points, the photographs capture a single historic moment, each with a different zoom, angle, and point of focus. The President's hand on the Bible is prominent in one, while the beaming silhouette of the First Lady's profile frames another. Placed next to each other, the photographs—and their accompanying headlines—clearly showed kids that each photographer has used his or her own lens to perceive and re-create the same historical moment.

If you can hold up three or four book title wordings and cover illustrations that depict completely different stances on a common nonfiction topic, that'd be great. Of course, your topic need not be Mount Everest!

"But readers, then we plucked another book out, and its title didn't suggest excitement, *Everest: Mountain without Mercy*. Suddenly the mountain began looking cruel rather than exciting. Then we found another, *High Crimes: The Fate of Everest in an Age of Greed*. Readers, here's another word that made me shudder—crimes! This book suggests that the people who climb mountains like Everest are a bigger menace than the mountain—that there are thieves, drug dealers, and murderers in the basecamps."

"It's the same old mountain, but each nonfiction writer sees it through his or her own eyes. Everest might be majestic and exciting and merciless and downright dangerous at the same time, depending on whose book we are reading. And this is true of any nonfiction topic. Different nonfiction sources will provide us with different angles."

Suggest to kids that part of becoming an expert on a single topic requires us to evaluate sources asking, "Which source do I trust more, and why?"

"So readers, sometimes different sources might even tell us completely opposite things about the same topic. As nonfiction readers read more and more on a single topic, we compare and contrast different texts and evaluate them. We ask ourselves: 'Of all these nonfiction resources, which do I trust more than the others? Which nonfiction resource, or resources, is most apt for my needs or rings true and seems the more credible, more trustworthy?'"

Demonstrate that readers scour their reading materials for information about the authorship and the dates and motives of publication to ascertain if this book or reading material has a convincing claim to authority on the subject.

"Readers, what Miles did next really taught me something, not just about Everest but about reading. He listened to my horrified reaction to the criminal underworld mentioned in the book *High Crimes: The Fate of Everest in an Age of Greed* and said, 'Not necessarily! It isn't necessary that everyone who climbs Everest meets exactly the same characters that this climber met. Perhaps this is a report of one troubled expedition alone. Or maybe they had a really bad guide.' Do you see what he did, readers? He cast doubt! He basically told me that I don't have to take everything I read as absolute truth!

In this demonstration, I've played up the title semantics, showing how word selection is crucial in communicating not just a stance but a feeling—setting the stage for an upcoming lesson in which readers will delve deeper into this work—exploring the ways in which nonfiction books position the reader to feel a certain way about a topic. You might just as well decide to focus less on the titles and more on the cover illustrations, depending on your particular book set.

It's not only part of the research for a person to evaluate the perspectives and assumptions underlying a particular resource. This is also a skill that is essential to the standards.

This is work that you or I do when we choose which news station we trust more than another or which teaching guide we'd rather consult over another. And, of course, what we learn is radically different if we turn on Fox News or MSNBC, or if we turn to a basal series or Units of Study for Teaching Reading.

In the 21st century, when the Internet brings information to us more easily, it becomes particularly important to teach readers to be critical consumers. All that glitters is not gold.

"Then he looked at the blurb and flipped the book open and scanned through some of the pages and said, 'By the way, this guy climbed Everest back in 2004. A lot could have changed since then.' So he chose not to trust this one book on Everest too completely. Instead, he picked up this book, *Everest: Eighty Years of Triumph and Tragedy*, and said, 'This seems more like it would give me a more balanced picture.'

"Readers, my son chose which source to trust. What's more, his choice had to do with his own reasons for wanting to read about Everest. He wanted a generic picture rather than one man's account. And he looked critically at all the choices before he chose which one to go by. This is the work that strong nonfiction readers do. When we find contradictory information in our books, we choose the sources that seem most apt and trustworthy to us."

As I said this, I made the accompanying motions to drive home my point—displaying the blurb, flipping open the book, and making a show of skimming before discarding the book to pick up another.

ACTIVE INVOLVEMENT

Suggest that readers research one aspect of their topic, scanning two different sources on that aspect, noting how the different sources approach the topic from different angles.

"Readers, let's give this a try with the research that you are conducting. I know each one of you has a specific focus for your research. Just for now, I want your group to take on one shared subtopic. Choose something specific that you know has been written about in several texts. For example, the castle group could pick something like 'uses of the great hall.' The extreme weather group could pick something like 'causes of hurricanes,' and the butterflies and insects group could pick something like 'why butterflies migrate.' It doesn't really matter which subtopic you pick, it's just for today so please quickly select a focus and then take a few minutes to compare sources on that topic.

"First find the parts of your texts that deal with that topic. You can use the tables of contents you made earlier. For example, I know the immigration group decided to research check-in procedures at Ellis Island. So Aly, Kadija, and Sarah could notice how different texts show different things about the check-in procedure. See if you can figure out how each source is angled differently."

In this active involvement I am more directive than ususal. I ask students to narrow their research so they can compare sources on that subtopic. Ultimately, my goal is to scaffold them toward more independence by helping them to know how to handle conflicting information as it arises. For now, though, I'm steering them toward places where I hope they'll find conflicts, so I can show them ways to handle those conflicts.

As the students, still sitting in the meeting area, began talking and working in their groups to come up with an angle for their topics, I crouched alongside one group and then another, helping them narrow or broaden their focus as needed.

Convene the class and tell about one group's discovery that their different texts approached the topic differently.

"I overheard some pretty sophisticated work coming from your groups and asked Kobe to tell all of us what his group discovered."

Kobe said, "Well, Emma and I were reading about Hurricane Katrina and how people got out of New Orleans. Emma had an article from *TIME For Kids* telling about how the city's plan to get cars out worked pretty well. It said that most people with cars just drove out. But my article said that lots of people got stuck getting out and especially the poor people. So the information wasn't the same."

I added in, "What's amazing is, you were reading about an event that happened fairly recently, not long ago in history. There are zillions of people who were actually there. It's not like you're reading about the ancient Egyptians and there's no one alive to tell us exactly what things were like. And still the information you are reading seems different."

Tell the class that the group described above will need to decide which sources are trustworthy by researching the perspective from which the text was written. Others need to do this as well.

Then I said to the class, "Readers, Kobe and his group have a decision to make about the conflicting information in their Hurricane Katrina articles—and all of you have the same decisions to make when your sources conflict with each other." I unveiled the start of a chart, one that included only one bullet for now.

"One thing the Extreme Weather Group can do is they can research the sources of the conflicting information. Maybe one source is more reliable than the other. Maybe one of the sources was someone who was actually there, trying to drive out of the city when the hurricane was hitting. Maybe the other source works for the mayor of New Orleans and doesn't want any blame, so he is saying things worked smoothly during the disaster."

You'll find as you move among your groups that sources differ from one another in varying ways. Often, the emphases sources place on information will be different, or the ways information is conveyed will be different. In this session, some groups found pieces of information in their books that directly contradicted each other. For another group, the way their topic was presented varied across sources. For another, it was the amount of information given, with one source going more in-depth than the others.

Of course, the different reports on Hurricane Katrina harken back to the image conveyed at the start of the minilesson. Twenty people sitting around the same pear, apple, and green bottle will each see the items differently.

Strategies for Dealing with Conflicting Information in Nonfiction Texts

- *Decide which source seems more believable or which angle feels better to you.*

Then I said, "The immigration group read different stories about arriving at Ellis Island, but they came to a different conclusion. They decided both stories were true, and each filled in holes in the other story. I'll add that way of dealing with conflicting sources to our chart.

LINK

Tell your students about a time during a previous year when students thought they'd found an error in their readings because information was contradictory. Tell them that by researching the sources, they determined one source was more reliable.

"Readers, last year, in the middle of the reading workshop, a group of kids who were studying the ancient Mayans ran up to me saying, frantically, 'There's a problem! We found a mistake!' They had two different sources of information on the sacred ball game Mayans played, and one book said that the losing team of the ball game would be killed by the winning team as a sacrifice to the gods, while a second said that it was the captain of the winning team who would be killed and this was because winning a ball game was like being given a direct ticket to heaven.

"The kids checked their sources. The text that claimed that the losers were killed was a book that had been written by an archeologist who was actually Mayan in decent and who had spent her whole life studying the ancient Mayans, whereas the source that said the winning teams' captain was killed was really a text on interpreting dreams, a text that just mentioned the Mayans in passing. It wasn't therefore as trustworthy. In the end, my students learned not only about Mayans, but also about research. As you read lots of texts on the same focused topic, I hope you see that different perspectives on a topic will see and report different things. I hope you see that it is fascinating to try to figure out why one person's vision of a topic is different from another's. And, of course, the most powerful thing of all is to realize that we each see from our own perspective."

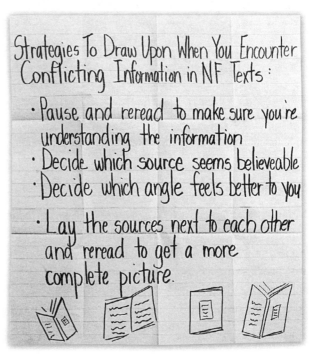

Strategies To Draw Upon When You Encounter Conflicting Information in NF Texts:
- Pause and reread to make sure you're understanding the information
- Decide which source seems believeable
- Decide which angle feels better to you
- Lay the sources next to each other and reread to get a more complete picture.

CONFERRING AND SMALL-GROUP WORK

Deepen Students' Engagement with Conflicting Sources

Teach that Conflicting Information Might Actually Present Different Experiences

You might urge readers to note where two texts provide conflicting information and urge students to research further or to pick the source that appears more trustworthy. The fact, however, is that in nonfiction literature published by renowned companies for children, rarely will students encounter information that stands in polar opposition to the information in another text. It is more likely that various texts will provide different nuances or angles rather than outright opposing differences. What students might perceive to be conflicting information might not turn out to be quite so contradictory. Often texts report more than one truth or more than one experience.

When I pulled alongside Sarah, she was reading *Shutting Out the Sky: Life in the Tenements of New York 1880–1924*. After a bit of research, talking with her about what she was working on, I realized that she had found some information in this text that conflicted with what she had read in previous texts—as well as earlier in this one—but wasn't sure what to do with it.

> ## MID-WORKSHOP TEACHING POINT
>
> ### Readers Ponder the Agendas that Have Shaped Texts
>
> "Readers, can I stop you? I was just working with the Shark Group, and they've noticed something interesting. Jack had shared that his book, *Shark Attack!*, left him with the impression that sharks are brutal, vicious eaters of humans. The title, the cover photo, and all the images within the book suggest this. But then Isaac pointed out that the book he'd been reading, *Chomp! A Book About Sharks*, depicts sharks as almost gentle creatures, hunted by people who want to sell their fins and hang their jaws for display above their fireplaces. His book suggests that sharks are being driven to extinction!"
>
> I turned to Isaac and Jack and said, "Can you tell us about your different books?"
>
> Jack stood and showed the class the escalating violence in his book. One picture had the word chomp written alongside it, and many featured rows upon rows of razor-sharp teeth.
>
> Isaac, in contrast, showed a book in which the sharks' mouths were closed, not open, and the fish were swimming gracefully through the water.
>
> Thanking the boys, I turned to the rest of the class. "Isn't that fascinating, readers? Even the covers of these books make us think something completely different about sharks. But here's what's really worth noting: Jack and Isaac have asked a very important question: Why did one
>
> *continued on next page*

"I'm pretty sure this book is saying different things about immigrants' experience in America," Sarah said. "Something must be wrong. It just doesn't make sense that Marcus Eli Ravage, sitting in Romania, would get letters from immigrant relatives saying, 'America's this place where even a poor boy can become a doctor or a millionaire.' The book also said that sometimes the letters contained gold pieces from America. But then later in the book it tells of the story of Rose Cohen, who was twelve when she came to America who had to go to work at a garment shop, and went without food and wore the same thin dress for several months."

Listening to Sarah, I could have chosen several teaching points to proceed with. I could have worked with her to check out more sources to try to clarify her confusion. I could have asked her to conduct deeper research on Marcus Ravage and Rose Cohen. I decided however, that in order for Sarah to make sense of what she regarded as conflicting information, she needed deeper consideration of what each text was essentially saying.

"Sarah, that was smart work. You've immediately picked up where the text seems to offer conflicting information. Can I teach you something? Sometimes what we understand to be conflicting information is really two sides of a story—and both sides might be true. This means you may not have to just choose one idea over the other, but instead you can carry both perspectives with you, comparing them, and finding out information that supports both ideas. A text, or texts, often presents more than one angle."

In the end Sarah decided that some of the books in her bin were written to project America solely as the land of opportunity, glossing over the difficulties that many immigrants initially faced, while others presented both sides, opportunity and success along with hardship and challenges. From this work on considering opposing angles, Sarah was able to grow new thinking. "That's why it was known as the American dream," she announced triumphantly. "It was a dream that came true for some but not for everyone."

Clarifying a Group's Thinking By Using Graphic Organizers

Moving on to the group that had been reading the Young Reader's edition of Greg Mortenson's *Three Cups of Tea*, I found them poring over an atlas and a *New York Times* article entitled "Afghan Girls, Scarred by Acid, Defy Terror, Embracing School." Though not originally part of this club's text set, Brandon's mom had contributed this somber piece from the previous day's newspaper—an article about acid-throwing attacks on schoolgirls in Kandahar, Afghanistan. Judging from their stricken faces and grave tones, I could see that the article had affected all three. "What are you working on?" I asked.

"We're looking to see how far Kandahar (where these acid attacks happened) is from Korphe, where Greg (Mortenson) built his first school," offered Brandon, pointing out the map. "We've found Kandahar, but we can't find Korphe on any of these maps of Pakistan."

MID-WORKSHOP TEACHING POINT

continued from previous page

book make sharks seem vicious and the other book paint an entirely different picture? This question—'Why?'—is worth pondering."

I adopted a pensive air as if mulling this "why" over in my mind before adding, "Maybe one book uses the thrill value of fear as a marketing gimmick—like a movie that plays on our natural fear of monsters just to get audience attention and to create an exciting piece of cinema. On the other hand, the second book might be written by scientists or environmentalists who worry about animals being hunted unnecessarily and becoming extinct. So the authors of these two books have different motives.

"Readers, this is an important point to consider as you read on. When you notice that different books report differently on the same topic, do what Jack and Isaac did. That is, ask, 'Why?' Who benefits from reporting on this subject in this way? Read the author profile. Explore the author's motives for reporting in a certain way. Remember that nonfiction is written by people, and each person is driven by some motive to report in a certain way. I have written on this chart (I pointed to the questions) some questions that may help you think about the author's motives as you are reading. Take a second to read them over and then read for the rest of the time with these in your mind."

continued on next page

"Is Korphe the village that didn't have a bridge allowing people to reach it?" I asked. As the group nodded, I suggested, "That village, from the description in your book, is so small and remote that I doubt you'd see it on most maps. You'd need a very detailed map of that area to find it. On most maps, you'll find cities, not villages," I told the group. "But why are you looking for the distance between these places?"

"Well," began Jane. "In *Three Cups of Tea*, the villagers all wanted this school for their kids—their girls. But in this place, the girls are being attacked—motorcyclists sprayed acid on their faces. Just for going to school," the emotion in Jane's voice was palpable. "So we're trying to see how far apart these places are—whether Greg's schools, too, are in danger of being attacked in this way."

In a typical conference, I would have stopped the group right here to congratulate them on researching their reading in this way. In this instance, however, I stayed quiet, not wanting to break the group's momentum just yet. I noted that Jane, Brandon, and Danny were emotionally invested in the content of the article, horrified by the violence against girls and women, and genuinely worried about the fate of Mortenson's schools.

"Here is K2!" Danny piped up suddenly, pointing at a tiny black triangle on the map between them. "That's the mountain Greg was trying to climb—the second highest after Everest. He got lost near here, and this is probably where Korphe must be too." I watched all three kids trace their fingers over the paper, gauging the distance between K2 in Pakistan, where Mortenson built his first school, and Kandahar in Afghanistan, where the news article reported the acid terrorism to have occurred.

"You're thinking like a researcher, Danny," I praised before falling silent again, waiting to see where the group would take their conversation without my intervention.

"These guys who're trying to stop girls from going to school—they're nothing like Haji Ali and the villagers of Korphe that Greg met," Jane finally suggested. "Those villagers were ready to give up all they had for the school. They'd give things they worked hard for."

"So Greg's villager friends wanted schools more—more than these Kandahar guys?" Danny offered tentatively, adding after a pause, "'Cause there's no acid attacks mentioned in Greg's book."

"But the parents of these girls who've been attacked are the same way. The same way as Greg's villagers," Jane countered. "The parents refused to let those motorcyclist guys win. They kept sending their daughters to school even though they knew the dangers."

"This girl's uncle even said so—that if the girls don't go to school, then the enemy wins," said Brandon.

There was much to compliment in this group's work. They'd been reading like gold, visibly invested in their book. They had independently consulted an atlas to get a sense of the part of the world in which their story

was set. They were bringing in a new text and comparing and contrasting in their initial text. I could have taught them to continue researching strategically to answer their question of whether acid-throwing attacks had ever been tried against any student attending a school built by Mortenson. Instead, I aligned my teaching point with the larger direction that the group's discussion had taken.

"It sounds to me like you're comparing the situations in Korphe and in Kandahar," I suggested. "The way you've done this is impressive. You researched and compared their different geographic locations, and the different responses of the locals living in each village. I'm listening as you find similarities and differences between these two situations. I have a suggestion for how you can do this work more efficiently. May I teach it to you?" I picked up a pencil and paper and drew out a Venn diagram consisting of two large circles, labeling one circle Korphe and the other Kandahar.

"The things that are similar between Kandahar and Korphe can be written out in this space where the two circles overlap. The things that are exclusive to each can be written out in their own circle space.

MID-WORKSHOP TEACHING POINT

continued from previous page

Readers Ask Critical Questions About A Text ??

• Who is this author trying to get me to believe? What about that one?

• What has one author highlighted, either by putting it first, by writing about it most extensively, by using particular words? What has another author highlighted?

• How else could each of these texts been written so as to highlight something different? How are other texts on this topic written differently, conveying different beliefs on the subject?

• What do I know about these authors' backgrounds and roles that might help me to understand their different perspectives on this topic?

• How trustworthy is the information here? How convincing is the author's angle? What assumptions have each of these authors made and what do I think about those assumptions?

• What are my ideas on this topic? Where do I stand on it?

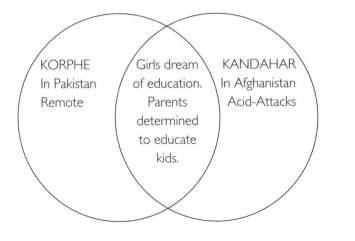

"I guess the two places don't have all that much in common," I heard Jane eventually mumble.

"When you organize your thinking as a group in this way," I added, "you'll get a much clearer picture than you would simply by talking. Talk generates ideas, but you need a system to hold and track those ideas so that you can look at them holistically."

"If you keep on filling in the Venn diagram, you'll not only keep track of all your thinking, but you'll be able to see, in a glance, how similar or dissimilar the two situations really are." I supervised a while longer, watching the group build up their Venn diagram as they noted that one location was war-ravaged, while the other location wasn't, that one had Taliban elements within its local population, while the other did not, and so forth.

TEACHING SHARE

Readers Recognize that Every Nonfiction Text Has a Purpose and an Intended Audience

Tell your students that their nonfiction books are written from particular angles, with certain readers' interests in mind.

"Readers, can I stop you for a moment? I've been watching you do this work today, and your conversations have been so thought-provoking. You noticed places where your sources say different things about the same topic, and you asked yourself, how are these sources different and why might they be different? What might the author be getting at here?

"An interesting thing happened when the Castles Group was working. Fallon came across a book that, to tell you the truth, I popped into their bin not sure if it would be helpful to them or not. The text itself is a bit hard, even for some adult readers. Anyway, Fallon realized that it had a lot of very technical descriptions of castle parts, and it even had explanations in it about how to build structures. Fallon and her group looked at it more closely and realized that it was a book written by an architect, someone who builds buildings, for people who wanted to know how castles were constructed.

"Fallon held this book against another book that talked about how people used parts of the castle for defense. So Fallon checked this source, and she saw that the author of this second book is a historian specializing in medieval warfare.

"Readers, what I want to share with you is this. One reason that texts are angled differently is that they are written by people with different expertise and meant for different purposes. As a reader, you can look for books that meet your purpose.

Ask your students to examine one of their nonfiction texts and to think and jot about its purpose. Then ask students to turn and talk about what they've noticed.

"Right now, look at one of the texts you were using today. Think to yourself or jot on a Post-it, 'What could be a purpose of this text? What might a reader who chooses this text want to know?'" *[Figs. XVII-2, XVII-3, and XVII-4]*

After a few moments, I asked the students to turn and talk to each other about what they were thinking. I circulated while they talked, and then I asked a few students to share their thinking.

Jasmine, from the Insects and Butterflies Research Group, volunteered. "I think someone who chooses this book might want to know about how to raise their own bees. This book is all about beekeepers and how they protect themselves as they gather honey."

Danny, from the *Three Cups of Tea* group, offered, "I think this book is for people who want to travel and help people of other countries. Like, it suggests that you have to really understand a person to help them. You have to respect them and also win their respect."

From the Penguin Research Group, Gabe piped up. "I think that this book about penguins is just to teach about penguin behavior for people who want to be scientists—zoologists." I gave Gabe a nod and a thumbs up for his effort at this precise word for scientist. He beamed and continued, "But this other penguin book tells about global warming, so its purpose is to get people to care about the environment."

"Readers, you're on the right track here. Thinking about a book's purpose, its intended audience, is an important part of understanding why a certain nonfiction text is written the way it's written. As we read, we keep asking, 'Who was this book written for? Who is the intended audience?'"

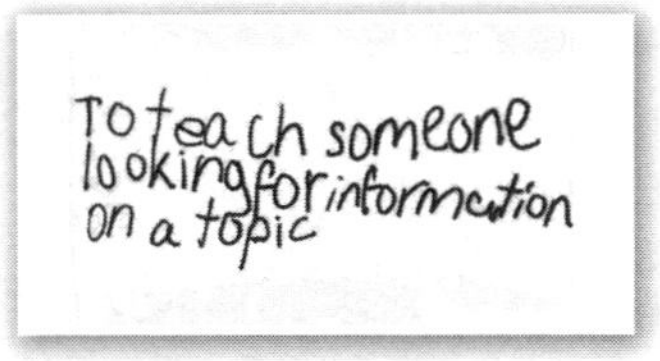

To teach someone looking for information on a topic

Figure XVII-2

To make us care and do something

Figure XVII-3

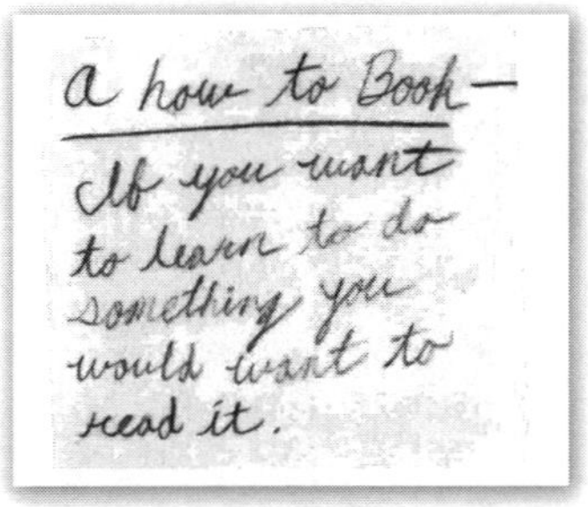

a how to Book—
If you want to learn to do something you would want to read it.

Figure XVII-4

Reading Critically: Why Is the Author Making Us Feel That Way?

When I was young, the nonfiction texts that were most important in my life were the large blue volumes that dominated the bookcase in a room that my parents called The Study. My parents purchased the set from a traveling salesman who convinced them that this would make us extra well educated. I never thought about those books as having authors. I think I assumed that a team of experts from across the world had convened to write each entry. The entry I remember the most was the ladder of animal intelligence that declared the pig wiser than a dog. I didn't question that ladder of intelligence. It was right there, in *The World Book*.

The word fiction comes from the Latin word *fictum*, meaning "created." By this definition, nonfiction means "not created." And that fits with the way I regarded those World Books. I imagined they were produced by a knowledge company rather than written by a lone person, sitting in his or her particular corner of the world.

Randy Pausch, a former computer science professor at Carnegie Mellon University, was diagnosed with a deadly cancer and then proceeded to give "The Last Lecture: Really Achieving Your Childhood Dreams." In that last lecture, he talked about how thrilled he had been, a few years earlier, when one of the editors of *The World Book* contacted him and asked if he would write an entry on his topic of expertise, virtual reality, for the encyclopedia. Randy must have been part of my generation because his family had also purchased *The World Book* from one of those traveling salesmen, and he'd also grown up worshiping the series. So he had been tickled when he was asked to be part of the process of writing an entry for the illustrious volume. Randy wrote the entry, submitted it, and waited for the reviews, the interrogations over his opinions, the fact checking. It is not that Randy thought his article was irresponsible—after all, he was an expert on the topic. But he knew full well the topic was a complex one, and that he was just one person

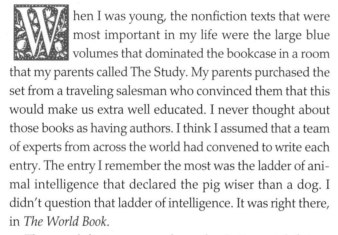

GETTING READY

- During the minilesson, you'll want to name some of your students and the feelings they've had in response to some of the nonfiction they've read.

- In this session, you'll read an article of your own choosing or the article included here and on the *Resources for Teaching Reading* CD-ROM titled "The Weird and Wonderful Octopus." You'll use this text to demonstrate noticing the emotions a text evokes in us and noticing the ways the author evokes those responses. It'd be helpful to copy a few lines of this onto chart paper so you can examine them closely.

- Make a chart of "Techniques Authors Use To Shape Readers' Thoughts and Feelings" to reveal in the teaching section of the minilesson. See the *Resources for Teaching Reading* CD-ROM for additional resources.

with one specific viewpoint, and he knew he had chosen to include some facts and exclude others. None of those choices are objective ones, and all of them can be questioned. So he waited for the review boards, the questions. But his article was never critically reviewed. A year later, a new edition of *The World Book* came out, and in it was the entry he'd whipped up that Saturday afternoon.

> *One of the biggest lessons that a reader of nonfiction can learn is that even sources of information that are regarded as reputable need to be read with skepticism.*

The realization that even *The World Book* is written by particular people with their particular biases was important enough to Randy that he included this story in his last lecture. His point wasn't to have one final chance to gripe— far from it! For Randy, this anecdote is an inspirational reminder that nonfiction texts, like fiction texts, are created by human beings who are each sitting in our little corner of the world, seeing through our own particular vantage point. Sometimes one sees little tags attached to Native American pottery or rugs, saying "Made by Hand." Tags like that belong even on entries in *The World Book*.

Children need to know this. First, as Randy points out, one of the biggest lessons that a reader of nonfiction can learn is that even sources of information that are regarded as reputable need to be read with skepticism. Then, too, the Internet has made it all the more necessary for readers to bring our own internal review boards to a text, investing our own time in determining whether or not a source is trustworthy. The Internet is a great democratizing force. Every person can now publish his or her opinions and knowledge, sending them out into the world. This makes it especially critical for all of us to approach texts with skepticism, asking, "What is the expertise on which this text stands? What evidence has this writer brought to bear? How trustworthy is this source? What assumptions and beliefs does the author hold, and do I accept them?"

Once children realize that nonfiction texts are made by hand, that they are created by a person with his or her own perspectives and passions, it is a small step before they also learn that many writers want not only to convey information but also to rally readers to feel and to care as the writer feels and cares. Many nonfiction texts are written in hopes that they will mobilize readers to care and to act. If reading non-fiction is a bit like taking a course, as I've suggested earlier, then students would be wise to register for these courses intending not only to learn something new but also to feel something new.

We've all had the experience of being deeply affected by nonfiction texts. My colleague Mary Ehrenworth recently told some middle school kids about her experience reading a book on tuna fish. The pictures in that book had gotten her to worry for dolphins. She said to the kids, "There was one picture of a tuna net being emptied on the deck of a huge fishing vessel, and wrapped into the netting, there were dolphins who had been caught in the net and had died." Then she explained to the kids, "That picture got me started reading a bit more, and I learned that some tuna fisheries use nets that aren't safe for dolphins."

Mary went on to say that she'd expected that reading a nonfiction text would teach her information on tuna fish, and instead she found that it had given her nightmares about dolphins. "That night I dreamed I was a young dol-phin, swimming with my mother in the cool blue ocean. She

was teaching me to dive deep. The water bubbled over us. Fish swam around us. And then, in my dream, a black net swept past us. It didn't catch me, but my mother was caught in it. Her tail tangled in the knots of the net. She tried desperately to get out, but she couldn't!" Mary continued, telling those middle schoolers about the dream she'd had as a consequence of reading that book. "And then the net was being pulled upward," she said, "and I watched my mother thrash." Mary told those young people that ever since reading that book, she'd vowed to never eat a can of tuna fish without checking first to see if the can included the label "Safe for Dolphins," a promise that the nets used to catch the tuna weren't ones that also caught dolphins.

This minilesson is a bit less graphic than that one, but it aims to bring home the same point. The minilesson is based on the fact that it is important for kids to know that all the experts in the world do not assemble together and hammer out right answers to allow a nonfiction book to be written. Instead, a specific person, writing from his or her specific vantage point, in hopes of making people care as that person cares, feel as that person feels, writes the nonfiction text. It is helpful, then, for readers to approach texts thinking, "What does this author want me to feel or do?" and asking, too, "How did the writer go about trying to make me think and feel in particular ways? What strategies did this author use to win me over?"

MINILESSON

Reading Critically: Why Is the Author Making Us Feel That Way?

CONNECTION

Tell children that you have something you are very eager to tell them.

"Readers, come close, I want to tell you something really important. Have you ever heard the saying, 'I've got some money burning a hole in my pocket?'"

The kids eyed each other and shrugged. They mostly had no clue what the phrase meant, although they enjoyed dramatizing what it might mean.

"People say, 'My money is burning a hole in my pocket,' and they mean that they've been carrying some money around for long enough that now they really want to spend it. They can think of little else and go around continually eyeing things they might buy and thinking over ways to spend the money. I think you already know that it's not dollars bills that are burning a hole in my pocket. Instead, it's an idea. I have an idea that I've been wanting to share with you for a long time, and I keep eyeing our minilessons to see if I can put the idea into them. By now, it's urgent that I bring this idea to you.

"You already know what I'm going to say, but it merits being said anyhow. Nonfiction books are not written by a committee of experts that convene from across the world to determine the right information on a topic. Instead they are written (most of the time) by one person who sits in his or her corner of the world and writes what he or she knows and thinks and believes. That's important. It is important especially because it sets the stage for the big thing I want to teach you today."

Name your teaching point. Tell readers that nonfiction books not only teach information; they also instill feelings. Tell children that readers note when an author is channeling us to feel and think in certain ways and mull over how the author has done that.

"I want to teach you that almost all nonfiction texts are written by people who hope not only to teach information but also to instill feelings. Readers are wise to approach

There is a lot of truth to my suggestion that the content of this minilesson has been burning a hole in my pocket. One of the challenges when designing a unit of study is to sequence and time instruction in such a way that kids are actually primed to make use of the teaching we do when they receive it. This means that I often rein myself in, not teaching something that would be easy for me to say, but that I believe would be hard for the kids to mobilize around at that moment. The challenge is to time teaching with an eye to what kids are already engaged in so that our teaching addresses the work that most of them are already doing and then takes that work just a wee bit further. In any case, for reasons such as these, I've postponed this important lesson on critical reading until this time, late in the game. You will absolutely want to teach another whole unit on this skill, and I highly suggest you lean on units in the Creating Curriculum: Alternate Units of Study. *Check out those on critical reading, on perspective, and on asking questions. All three of those units will extend the work of this minilesson in important ways.*

nonfiction texts thinking, 'What does this author want me to feel—to think?' and 'How did the author go about trying to make me feel and think in that particular way?'

TEACHING

Exclaim over the feelings that texts have generated in kids and then suggest that the feelings readers get have been engineered by choices the authors have made. Refer to a text that you shared earlier as an example.

"Readers, I've watched you poring over your nonfiction books, and I've seen you not only *learning* new things. I've also seen you *feeling* new things. I have seen some of you feel awe—like we'd feel if we walked outside and saw the most spectacular spread of snowcapped mountains—only this is awe at people and at creatures. I've seen you, Danny, awed at the passionate desire that the people in Pakistan have for a school—like the school we take for granted—and awed at the enormous lengths they are willing to go to to create a school. And José and Kwami, am I right that you were pretty impressed, even awed, at the intelligent design of some of those medieval weapons? I've seen some of you outraged, too—like over the difficulties immigrants in this country face. You've been reading texts by authors who not only give information. They also instill feelings. They encourage you to care.

"I am glad you are finding that we not only learn new facts, but we also learn new feelings from nonfiction texts. We may come to feel protective of the rain forest, to admire the villagers in Pakistan, to be afraid of great white sharks. I think you agree that nonfiction books can get us to feel as well as to know.

"Today, the really important thing for you to realize is that the feelings we end up having when we read aren't accidental. They don't come by chance. The author has engineered things so that we feel the ways we do when we read. You can think of the author of nonfiction texts as being a bit like those special effects guys who make movies. I picture those guys, behind the curtain, pulling levers and adding smoke and mirrors to stir all these feelings in viewers. I imagine that a special effects guy will call out, 'Okay, this next part is supposed to be scary—add some scary music, that's it! How about making a door creak in the distance? Let's change the weather—move in a cloud, that's it. Hide the sun, get the place to feel gloomy. You got it, you got it. This will work.'

I say all this as if I am simply admiring the work that kids have been doing, but of course, I am also scaffolding their work. I am building bridges between what they have been doing and what I am teaching. I'm also providing language for kids to borrow when talking about the feelings that books have instilled in them—awe or outrage.

I know, I know, I am repeating the same thing like a mantra. Of course, minilessons are a kind of nonfiction text, and I am engineering people's responses to this text by the craft decisions I make. One of those decisions is the decision to reiterate the main ideas.

I love this little bit of the minilesson. I know it is over the top, but I think it is fun, and it makes the point. You'll see that in upcoming sessions, I suggest that kids need to become writers as well as readers, generating their own perspectives and ideas and then putting these into the world in ways that make people feel what kids want them to feel about a topic. I hope I'll be able to refer back to this reference then, and certainly I'll do so in the writing workshop, so that kids get an insiders' understanding of what it means to craft texts to persuade, admonish, rally emotions, generate sympathy—to tug on our spirits in all the ways they can be tugged.

"I know, I know, authors aren't that intent on stirring up emotions, but authors definitely make all sorts of decisions over things like which details to include and which to exclude, and what comparisons to make—all in an effort to make readers think and feel in certain ways. For example, at the very start of this unit, when we read parts of *Bugwise*, I not only learned new facts about the bugs, but I also started to have different feelings about them. Instead of just thinking, 'Ew, bugs are gross,' I started to think of them as interesting, as impressive even. One way that *Bugwise* made me feel this way is that it compared bugs to people, to snorkelers and scuba divers. That text also included only the details that showed how ingenious the bugs' adaptations were. When you realize the author wanted us to feel in these ways, we can ask critical questions," I said referencing a chart we'd made earlier.

"And Jack, the book you were reading the other day that showed a shark with its great gaping mouth open and a woman swimming nearby with no protection—only a small bikini covering all that vulnerable skin. That picture wasn't there by accident. That author was trying to instill certain feelings in you!"

Jack, of course, responded, "He did!" and wrapped his arms around himself, shuddering at the thought of the gaping jaws of a shark.

Reread a bit of a familiar nonfiction text, spying aloud on your emotional response to it, and then reread that text to deconstruct how the author engineered that emotional response.

"Let me show you how we can be more alert to ways books instill feelings as well as give us facts. Remember earlier when we read about octopuses? As we read, we gathered all of this new information about octopuses that we didn't know before. We started to think about the octopus not just as a funny eight-armed creature, but as an amazing animal with many different talents. We started to feel differently about the octopus.

"Let me reread part of that article. Will you watch as I read, and this time, listen not so much to the boxes-and-bullet structure in the piece but, instead to my reactions, my feelings and thoughts. Get ready to help me ask not only 'What is the text making me feel about this topic, octopuses?' but also 'How is the text getting me to feel that?'" I read a snippet of the text, printed on chart paper.

> The octopus isn't just amazing physically. It's smart, too. Scientists have taught octopuses to learn to distinguish between shapes and patterns. Some octopuses in tanks have been observed "playing" games. They

I read a section of "The Weird and Wonderful Octopus," the text I'd read earlier in the unit when helping children make the transition from reading texts with clear heading to reading those without explicit headings. I picked this section because the ideas it introduces about octopus intelligence might lead readers to feel differently about octopuses than they once did.

throw objects into circular currents in the water and then catch them again.

"Wow, right now I'm going to stop and think, 'What am I feeling right now?' I'm feeling . . . um, let's see. I'm impressed by the intelligence of this creature and surprised, too.

"Readers, do you see that the text got me feeling some things? Can you help me research *how* the author got me to feel in those ways? What were the special effects that the author was throwing in there to engineer my feelings?" I gave children a second to reread and think. "If you are thinking, 'There are no special effects,' look closer. They are often hidden. What I do is I take just a line or two, and I say, 'Somewhere in here there are hidden ways to get me feeling certain things,' and then I look really closely and think about the decisions the author made and could have made." I drew my finger under the first sentences, pausing my finger under the word *scientists*.

> The octopus isn't just amazing physically. It's smart, too. Scientists have taught octopuses to learn to distinguish between shapes and patterns.

"Right there!" I pointed to the word scientist. "It says that *scientists* taught octopuses to distinguish between shapes and patterns. Because the text says that scientists did this work, it makes me more likely to believe it is true and that this was somehow very challenging work. If it had said, 'Other fish teach the octopus how to distinguish colors, that wouldn't have seemed so impressive. But these octopuses are being schooled by scientists. They seem smart already!

"I'm going to think about other ways that the text made me feel that octopuses are impressive. The way the text names what the octopus can do makes their skills sound like a big deal: they distinguish between shapes and patterns. You know, that sounds distinguished, doesn't it? And also, the author doesn't just say the octopuses are smart. He also gives examples—proof."

Chart the techniques you have noticed the author used to influence readers' thoughts and feelings.

"Let me record a few things I've noticed this author doing to make me feel what he wants me to feel."

It'd be helpful to have these sentences written on chart paper. Notice that although this is a demonstration, I recruit kids to help me. I want them to participate as much as possible in the demonstration so that I am able to be just one step ahead of them, showing them how to proceed. Our demonstrations will be vastly more powerful if kids are engaged alongside us.

When I point to the word scientists and say, "Right there!" I'm going to give a few seconds of time, long enough for kids to look at the word choice and to come to their own conclusions, if they can, about why this word is part of the special effects that have been so powerful. Leaving tiny spaces for kids to do the thinking you are about to do is very important.

You'll constantly be amazed at the amount of learning you can harvest from a tiny bit of reading and thinking aloud.

ACTIVE INVOLVEMENT

Invite students to try what you have just demonstrated, reading the next passage of the same text and setting them up to spy on their responses and deconstruct what the author did to make them respond that way.

"Let me read on, and this time, will you spy on the way this text makes you feel, and then in a moment you and your partner can unpack it, noticing particular ways the author engineered things to make you feel as you do.

> Research shows that octopuses may have emotions, too. Scientists believe that an octopus can change color depending on how it is feeling. An octopus is usually pale in color when it is relaxed. It becomes brightly colored when it is angry or scared.

"Turn and talk. How are you feeling, what made you feel that way?"

The room buzzed with talk. After a bit, I convened the class. "Fallon said that this made her feel close to an octopus, that she'd like one for a pet, even. Like an octopus is similar to a dog. I know each of you had your own feelings and that I asked you to pay attention to those, but let's talk not just about the feelings but also about what the author did to affect you. Okay, turn and talk."

I listened in as Grace said, "It also says *research*. 'Research shows.' This makes me think of us doing our research and becoming experts. I think if there's research, then it must be important. It makes me feel that someone knows a ton and is conducting experiments or something."

I then convened the class and recalled what I'd heard children saying, I added my own observation as well, aware that the personification of octopuses is subtle enough that the children were not likely to note it on their own. "I also noticed that the author uses words to describe the octopus that we would normally use to describe humans, like relaxed, angry, and scared. When I hear these words, I usually think of a person. When the author uses those words, it makes it more likely that we can relate to the octopus."

Again, it would be helpful to have these words visible on chart paper or in some other fashion to help students study the author's craftsmanship.

If you want to teach students about connotation, this minilesson sets up that work. For older students, you could simply tuck this term into your minilesson. Then again, you can always use small group work to extend the content of a minilesson.

LINK

Before dispersing kids, invite them to start rereading a text from their own inquiry, considering how that text makes them feel and reflecting on the techniques the author used to instill those responses.

"Readers, the most important thing I want to teach you today is that you can do this work with any nonfiction text. When you pay attention to the feelings that get stirred up as you read, like the feeling that you are fearful of the great white shark or inspired by the rugged resilience of the Pakistani villagers, then you can ask critical questions about the author's intention. 'What is the author trying to get us to feel or to believe? And how has the author engineered our reading experience?'

"How about we try reading like this with our own inquiry texts? Right now, grab a book from your bin that you've looked at before. As you scan your book, find a picture or a photo or a bit of text that makes you feel something."

I gave children a minute to do this. Then I said, "Now ask yourself, 'Is it possible that the author chose that picture or those words intentionally, hoping to engineer your response?' Turn and talk to your inquiry group."

I leaned in and heard Kadija say, "This family arriving at Ellis Island looks really exhausted. The text says that immigrants came to America to 'start fresh in a new land,' but this family doesn't look that hopeful. Maybe the picture tells more of the truth about immigrants' experience. Maybe America wasn't, like, this great place to come to."

Emma said, "Yeah, like after Hurricane Katrina there were commercials asking people to give money and donate time."

As children talked, I coached in, reminding them to ask themselves the questions on the chart, "Techniques Authors Use to Shape Readers Thoughts and Feelings." Then I reconvened the class. "Readers, nice work. Remember that we read nonfiction not only in this classroom but in the world, too. Any time you log onto the Internet and read about anything—a little article about skateboarding or chess or some kids' opinions about a new video game or a new movie—or when you read the menu at a restaurant, remember that authors of nonfiction texts each have their own angle, their own perspective on the topic, and the author wants you to feel or believe or act a certain way. Remember that nonfiction isn't just a string of factual evidence. It conveys a perspective."

You could easily extend this work into your social studies or science curriculum, looking at the way in which word choice reveals the author's perspective. Again, laying two texts that address the same subject alongside each other can be powerful because, this way, readers become aware that the information that is included and the words that are used reflect choices an author has made.

CONFERRING AND SMALL-GROUP WORK

Help Readers Read Critically

Critical reading requires a conscious decision on the part of the reader to step back from the text and to read against the grain of it. Instead of letting words and images wash over her, the reader makes the choice to study the more subtle factors that contribute to the way she responds to the text. This relationship to texts does not come easy to many readers. That is, this kind of reading requires teaching; it requires practice. But once a reader learns to read critically, this relationship to texts can exponentially deepen the reader's understanding not only of the text but also of herself and the world.

It follows, then, that conferring into this work requires a similar shift in focus. As teachers of critical reading, we must move from focusing on whether our readers are "getting it," whether they are comprehending all of the parts of the text, to focusing on whether they are analyzing the text. Peter Freebody and Allan Luke describe, in their Four-Resources model (1997), the importance of readers learning to assume the role of text analyst (understanding how texts work by engaging in a critical analysis). That's what we teach when we confer to support critical reading.

Help Your Students Shift the Way They Approach Their Texts by Channeling Them to Spy on the Feelings or Thoughts that Texts Generate in Them before Asking, "How Did the Author Do that?"

MID-WORKSHOP TEACHING POINT

Readers Notice the Feelings We Have in Response to Texts and Ask How the Text Cultivates that Response

"Readers, can I stop you for a second? I noticed that right away when you started doing this work, you almost exploded with different reactions you were having about your texts as you read. Some of you shared with each other what really struck you, and some of you began jotting notes down as you reacted to portions of your text. Can you try right now to name the feelings you were having as you responded so passionately to your books? Ask yourself, 'What is the feeling I'm having as I read this?' Try to name what you are feeling as you read on for a few minutes."

The children read on, and then I interrupted again. "Readers, now look back over what you were feeling and, now, think how does the text make you feel this way?" I pointed to the chart to remind them of some possibilities. "Is the author of your text bringing in the voice of an expert? Or is he or she acting like a trial lawyer, giving lots of examples to support their claims? Study the comparisons the author is making. What feelings are they evoking? Or do the words the author is using themselves evoke feelings or images? Do this work as you read for a few more minutes."

After a few more minutes, I said, "Readers, turn and talk to your group about what you just did. Tell them what feelings you were having as you read, and then tell them how the text was making you feel that way."

continued on next page

We can give fancy inspirational talks about critical reading, and doing this is helpful, but conferring provides us with a way not just to tell readers about the stance required to read critically but also to go a step further and give readers a sense of what it feels like to do this new kind of work.

The best way to shift the students themselves into this new relationship to texts is to do lots of coaching in as they read, providing lean prompts that get them going doing this work. This is not unlike the way you have taught your kids to read with more fluency. Later you can help your students step back and reflect on what they were able to do with your pointers, and this reflection will eventually allow them to do similar work without you. Approach this day of conferring by recalling what it was like when you circulated quickly among readers, leaning in to listen a bit as they read, and then whispering in to say things such as, "Put your words together," "Try reading it more smoothly," "That's it." You'll do a similar sort of teaching, only of course, your image of good work will be different, and your prompts will be different.

First, plan to coach readers to be aware of what the text makes them feel. For many it will be enough to say, "I see that you are thinking about not just what information your books are giving you but what feelings they are giving you as well. That's important." Next, you will want to coach readers to consider not just what the text is making them feel, but how the author channels them to feel that way. "What are the things the author does, the tools he or she uses, that are making you feel the way that you do?" For other readers, you'll want to say, "Can I read this too?" and then get your own reading aligned to the student's so that the two of you are making your way, side by side, through the text. As you read, let the text affect you and then voice your response aloud, saying things like, "Yikes, this is getting me worried," or "Oh, no!" Try to do this in a way that nudges the student to react—even if just to look up from the text or to gesture toward a particular part of the text. Help the student say what the text is making him feel or to at least nod in agreement when you put words to what you ascertain he is feeling.

Coach Readers to Notice Their Own Responses to Texts

I pulled my chair alongside the shark group just in time to hear Jack exclaim, "Whoa!" He and his inquiry group had a stack of books about

---

MID-WORKSHOP TEACHING POINT

continued from previous page

I listened in while the Insects and Butterflies Group shared what they had done.

"Well, I was reading about how a caterpillar makes a chrysalis," said Jasmine. "I didn't know that the chrysalis is under its skin, like part of its body. I always thought the caterpillar made it somehow. It says that the caterpillar has all of these things built in to help it turn into to a butterfly, kind of like tools. That made me feel pretty amazed by caterpillars. It made me think that they are smarter than I thought, maybe."

Jasmine seemed finished talking, and Brianna was on the verge of sharing what she experienced. I intervened to nudge Jasmine to try the second and more important part of the work. "So if I understand what you're saying, Jasmine, the text made you feel differently about caterpillars. It made you think that they are smart."

Jasmine nodded her head. "So how did the text do that? How did it make you feel differently about caterpillars?"

"Well, first it uses a lot of words like amazing and incredible. I never really thought of a caterpillar like that before. It also uses a lot of examples of kinds of tools the caterpillar has to turn into a butterfly."

Lily jumped in excitedly. "My book did kind of the same thing. I'm reading now about how a butterfly can remember things from when it was a caterpillar. That's a weird idea because a butterfly seems like a new kind of thing. Almost like a new animal. And I never thought of a butterfly as being able to remember. My book made me feel like a butterfly is more like a person or something, kind of like we talked about with the penguins. And also my book has scientists and research. It says that they think butterflies can remember because scientists did research that showed that butterflies stayed away from bad-smelling stuff that they smelled when they were a caterpillar. It proves that they can remember. So I think it's probably true."

continued on next page

---

sharks spread before them, many of them books far easier than those they usually read, and they had been milling through the pile. Jack had settled on *Shark Attack!*, and when I arrived, he was gaping at a picture of a shark chomping a surfer in half.

The other two boys looked up from their books to peer over his arm, and asked, "Is that real?!"

"Yeah, look at this!" Jack said and showed several photos of sharks in attack mode, their mouths gaping, full of razor-sharp teeth. He got a big rise out of the other two boys when he showed the real life photo of Rodney the surfer, with his 462 stitches that he received after four hours of surgery following a shark bite.

At this point, I knew I'd stumbled upon a very nice teachable moment. It would be no big deal to help a cluster of students see that this book had made Jack react in a certain way, to have a certain emotional response. My hunch was that Jack was thinking that all sharks are violent flesh-eating creatures, and I was quite sure I could bring him and others to a place where they saw that the author had engineered that response. "Readers, can I stop you for a second, and can you listen in as I talk to Jack? As I'm talking to Jack, think about how this might also apply to your book." Sam and Isaac put their books down and looked at me. Emma, from a nearby inquiry group, overheard us and she, too, put her text down. "Jack," I said, "What are you thinking and feeling right now?"

"This is sort of scary," he said. "If I was Rodney, I definitely wouldn't be surfing anymore!"

"Jack," I said. "Do you realize what you just did? It's so huge! You just looked at the photos and the words in your book, and you realized that the text had made you feel and think in a certain way. Nonfiction readers who want to think critically about their texts do the same thing—we spy on our own responses to texts, and we notice how texts make us feel."

I suggested the others could reread their books and see if their books, too, had made them feel in a specific way. As they started on this work, I circled to Emma, who didn't take as well to my prompt, "How is this text making you feel?"

"Well, I'm not really feeling anything. It is just is telling me how an earthquake happens—the tectonic plates that move and stuff. I don't really feel anything. I'm just sort of learning a bunch of facts."

I nodded. "Sometimes instead of noticing feelings we have as we read, we notice thoughts. Then we can still think about how the text inspires us to have those thoughts," I said and showed her that a part of my book said that penguin chicks chirp constantly and that each chick has a unique chirp. "I wasn't really thinking very much about this, but I decided to push myself to think, and when I pushed myself to have a thought, I realized I was thinking about how a book I read

once said that human babies each have their own cry, and that mothers respond to their own baby's cry differently than to anyone else's baby. So then, once I had an idea, I thought, 'What did this book do to get me comparing penguins and human babies?' Do you think you could try that? Try really pushing yourself to see what kind of thought you can make or hear in your own head, even if it's a faint thought!" Emma went off to try.

Coach Readers to Ask, "What Choices Might the Author Have Made that Have Contributed to the Way I Feel and Think As I Read This?"

Once you see students observing their own responses to texts, you are in a position to help them think about what the author has done to make them respond in this way. When I returned to the Shark Group, I found that all three of the boys had determined the way their text made them feel (and think). I asked Jack (and the others) if they had been trying to take their thinking to the next step. To help Jack experience critical reading, I suggested that right then, he could try looking at just the cover and the title to see if, even in that earliest part of the book, he could see evidence that the author had set him up to feel as he felt. I briefly showed the other kids the cover to Jack's book so they could try doing some of the same sort of thinking along with Jack.

MID-WORKSHOP TEACHING POINT

continued from previous page

As the members of Lily's club murmured over Lily's new information, I voiced over to the whole class, "You're in the middle of some very smart reading work here. Group members, support each other in this work. Remind each other to notice not only your feelings but how the text is making you feel this way. And remember you stop to do this kind of work always as you read something that is giving you information." *[Fig. XVIII-1]*

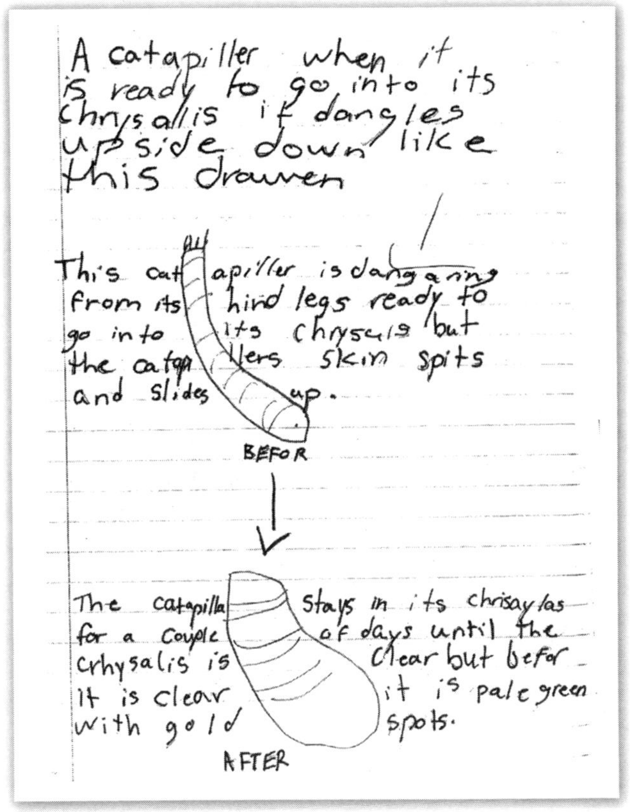

A catapiller when it is ready to go into its Chrysallis if dangles upside down like this drawen

This catapiller is dangaring from its hird legs ready to go into its chrysaus but the cataplters skin spits and slides up.

BEFOR

The catapilla for a couple crhysalis is It is clear with gold

stays in its chrisaylas of days until the clear but befor it is pale green spots.

AFTER

Figure XVIII-1

The boys realized right away that it was no accident that the book is called *Shark Attack!* even though it actually is an all-about-sharks book. What's more, they saw an exclamation point at the end of the title, which made them think these attacks are a big deal. Then Sam pointed out that the photo is of a shark with its mouth wide open, its teeth razor sharp. Isaac added, "Look! That shark has lines all over its face. I wonder if he got those in a fight." Jack said, "Guys! I noticed this before, but now I'm realizing it's not an accident it's here. There's a girl snorkeling in this picture. She's a goner!"

I jumped in. "What do you think this author, Cathy Dubowski, wants her readers to believe about sharks?"

The three boys agreed that she might have been out for some shock value. They wondered if she just wanted this as a grabber at the start of the book and began looking through the pages of the book to see if her stance was consistent throughout. They discovered lots of little stories of people losing limbs, or their lives, and concluded that this author definitely wanted people to believe that sharks are dangerous, attacking animals.

At this point, I needed to quickly extrapolate some lessons that I hoped would be transferable to another text and another day. "Did you remember how you started this work by, one, spying on your own reaction to the text. Then, two, you made that powerful, all-important move to ask, 'What did the author do to get me to feel this way?' And, three, you started looking over the text, noticing other decisions the author had made. Right now, Sam and Isaac, you might look at the books you're reading with this in mind and talk to your group about it."

I knew I would have to do some follow-up work with the boys to teach them that skimming a book is one way to begin ascertaining the author's angle on a topic, but that actually this requires a deep sort of reading because sometimes the text seems to say one thing and actually says something different. Meanwhile, I needed to hurry to some other readers.

Lily looked up from her book about earthquakes to tell me she felt very worried for the people of San Francisco and wondered why anyone would want to live there. I recruited the others at her table to listen in, and then I helped her think, "Why did the author get me so worried about the people that live near those earthquakes?" Lily realized that the text described one child's experience in the 1906 earthquake, and that probably made a difference for her. "That's it!" I said and helped Lily realize

that she had just done the work of reading critically. "You realized that you empathized with the people of San Francisco because the author included a story of a child like you, living through that earthquake." I then tried to help Lily name what the author had done in such a way that pertained not just to this book but to nonfiction books in general. "Lily, we can't say, then, that all authors can get readers to empathize by telling stories of kids in earthquakes, can we?" Then I nudged her to extract and name the principle she had found, but she struggled to understand, so I did this work for her. "Could we be saying that one way authors make readers sympathize and empathize with a story is by including characters that resemble the readers and showing those characters being affected in ways you want the readers to imagine being affected?" I could, of course, have labeled this in simpler terms (and probably should have done so). For example, I could have said, "The author included true stories of moments in individual people's lives."

Naming the text moves that authors make for children helps kids to then see evidence in texts that the author has done some engineering to affect readers' responses to the text. So just as it is helpful for readers to keep tabs on their own emotional responses to books and to then try to generate words for what the author did to create those feelings, readers can also begin by becoming skilled at noticing what an author has done.

That way, as students go off to read on their own, they can say things to themselves that sound like this: "Oh, there's one of those true stories of a person who resembles the reader. I wonder what the author is trying to get me to feel or believe with this story?" You can help students notice the connotations of words, notice the balance of attention given to one subtopic or another, and notice whose story is told and whose story is missing, for example.

Conferring: Comparing, Contrasting, and Growing Insights

As I moved on, I encountered the *Three Cups of Tea* group having a discussion as the gorgeously illustrated pages of Carmen Deedy's picture book, *14 Cows for America*, lay open between them. Danny had suggested to the group that the two books, *Three Cups of Tea* and *14 Cows*, provided opposite sides of a story. In the first case, he asserted, an American, Greg Mortenson, was giving a gift to another country—the gift of schools. In *14 Cows*, people from another country are giving a gift to America—the gift of fourteen cows as an act of compassion following the September 11 attacks.

Jane was having visible trouble accepting Danny's suggestion. "Yes, but the villagers in Pakistan saved Greg's life. He wasn't giving them a gift exactly. He felt he owed them. There's a difference."

After listening for a while longer as each defended their position, I eventually intervened. "I hear you both," I assured them. "It is surely true, Danny, that one book feels like it is about giving while the other is about receiving a gift, and it is also true, Jane, that Greg's relationship with the villagers was unique. They accepted him as their own." I had been about to add my teaching point, urging the group to consider the angles in

which each book viewed various common themes—giving, friendship, and America—when I was interrupted.

"They're more the same than different," Brandon spoke up. "The three cups of tea are just like the fourteen cows." When he noted us looking blankly at him, Brandon explained further. "The villagers gave Greg three cups of tea because they accepted him as family. Just as the Maasai gave America fourteen cows, a gift that they might give to their own family member."

Jane, Brandon, and I were quiet for a moment, exchanging glances. "Wow," he said. We talked for a bit about Brandon's brilliant idea, and I resolved to find a way to tell others about it. The best teaching sometimes merely catches a bit of brilliance and holds it up for others to see.

TEACHING SHARE

Readers Consider Authors' Biases

Consolidate what your students have learned about critical reading and name the next step: readers think not only about what the author makes them feel and how the author does it but also about why the author wants them to think or feel this.

"Readers, can we gather back at the meeting spot for a few minutes? There's one more idea that is burning a hole in my pocket, and I just have to share it with you.

"You've done important work today becoming not just gatherers but also analysts of information. I don't think you are any longer the kinds of readers who just let facts wash over you, believing everything you read. You are stopping to think, 'What does this author want me to believe?' And then, 'How is he or she getting me to believe this?' You're ready for the next level of this work. This involves asking not what or how, but why, as in, 'Why might the author want me to feel this way about this subject?'"

Tell a story about one time you read a text and were persuaded, until you investigated the author's biases, leading you to be more skeptical.

"Let me give you an example. Recently, I read an article in the newspaper about a charity organization that gives money to people who are struggling, helping those people start their own businesses. It wasn't an advertisement—it was a newspaper article. While I read the article, though, I was inspired to donate money to this charity because the cause made so much sense. Giving someone money to help that person start a business allows the person to earn his or her own money instead of just needing more charity, again and again.

"I thought about why I felt that way after reading the article, and realized I'd been touched because of the stories about individuals for whom this money made all the difference. I was also convinced by the statistics about the success rate of this charity versus other charities. But then I took a next step—the step I want to teach you that you can also take.

"I asked myself, 'Why is this article so strongly in favor of this charity?' So, I did a bit of research on the author. And I found out that even though the article was in the newspaper as if it had been written by a reporter, its author was actually one of the founding

If your students are getting to the point where they are ready to question not only how the text is making them feel but also why the author might have wanted to create that feeling, then (and only then) you might want to teach a variation on this share. This share aims to help readers consider who the author is and what background or motivations she might have in bringing forth this topic this way. This work is easier with higher-level texts and becomes crucial when students start to navigate the world of adult nonfiction, in which the author's particular thesis is almost always presented as truth.

Now that you've taught readers to research sources of information in this sort of way, be sure you show them that this research stance can influence not only their work in the reading workshop but also their lives. Do they wonder whether one hockey stick is any better than another? Do they wonder why one town salts its roads and another doesn't? Questions like these can spark research. Your children need to hear about your research, and they need to be encouraged to conduct their own similar investigations.

members of the charity! The article instead was not written by an objective reporter the way I assumed it had been. Whoa! Once I realized the article was actually written by someone whose job is to get people to contribute money to this particular charity, that made me much more skeptical about the whole thing. I'm not just going to jump in and give a bunch of money until I find a more objective source to read about this charity."

Remind children to continue reading critically that evening and for the rest of their lives.

"Some of you have found it easy to think about how the author engineered things to get you to think and feel particular ways, and you may be game for taking this work a step further. If you are, the next step is to think about why the author of your text might have been trying to convince you of something. For example, an author might be trying to get you to give money or buy something, or to join the author's side for or against a certain cause. You can do this sort of critical reading tonight, while you are reading at home, but more importantly, you can do this kind of critical reading for the rest of your lives!" *[Fig. XVIII-2]*

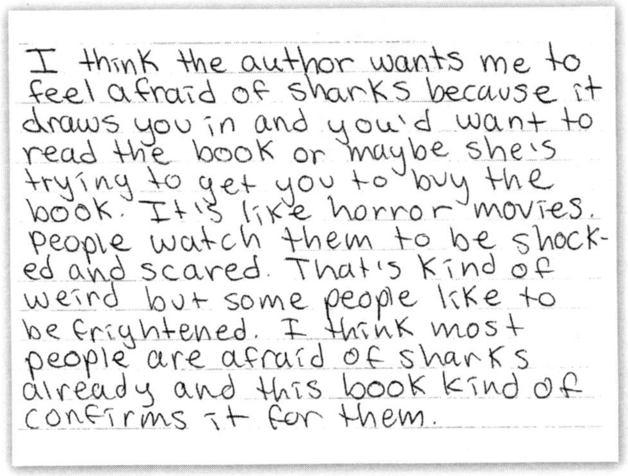

I think the author wants me to feel afraid of sharks because it draws you in and you'd want to read the book or maybe she's trying to get you to buy the book. It's like horror movies. People watch them to be shocked and scared. That's kind of weird but some people like to be frightened. I think most people are afraid of sharks already and this book kind of confirms it for them.

Figure XVIII-2
This is the result of critical reading.

Creating Our Own Responses to Nonfiction

riter and educator Ralph Fletcher begins *A Writer's Notebook* with an interesting story. Addressing an audience of young writers, he tells of an evening in his boyhood when telephone repairmen dug a ditch in front of his house to lay a line, leaving it gaping until they could return to fill it the next day. He talks of getting up at dawn the next day and running to the ditch, fascinated, peering inside. Two frogs, four toads—even a turtle—greeted him from the recesses of the ditch. They'd fallen in during the night and sat there, trapped. Ralph likens a writer's notebook to the ditch—a place to trap thoughts. Otherwise, he claims, thoughts pass through us like the air we breathe. We need to have a system to trap our thoughts, peer closely at them, and make more of them.

Ralph is right, of course, about us having thoughts that pass through us like air—thoughts of great potential consequence made inconsequential because we didn't hold onto them. Authors who scribble ideas on napkins in cafes or on the backs of grocery receipts know this well—we hang on to our thoughts, revisit them, make more of them. This is, in a nutshell, the writing process.

Nonfiction reading is a time when thoughts on a specific topic abound. As we read and process texts, we generate so much new thinking. And so it is inevitable that the teaching of reading taps into the rich process that occurs when readers take in external words and then respond. Reading is not only listening. It is also talking back; it is generating thinking that spins off from the texts we take in. It is inhale,

GETTING READY

- Bring white boards to the carpet for several students to use during the teaching phase of the minilesson.

- Be prepared to select two or three ideas from the class research project as examples of ideas that could be developed further. Each of these ideas will need to call for a particular common nonfiction text structure like problem and solution, compare and contrast, cause and effect, question and answer, narrative, or outright description.

- List these ideas on chart paper during the teaching section, soliciting more from the students as you do so.

- Create the chart "Common Nonfiction Text Structures." You will need to unveil this chart near the end of the teaching section.

- You'll need to hand the rest of the white boards and dry erase markers out during the active involvement section of the minilesson so the kids can try out ways the class topics might unfold in various text structures.

- In the active involvement, you'll need to create (or unveil) two different sets of notes. Each set of notes should list— perhaps with boxes and bullets—an idea from the list of class topic ideas, using a common text structure.

exhale. And yes, that response, like the air we exhale, can be carried away forever unless we somehow have systems for catching it—catching our thoughts, organizing those thoughts, and then making more of them. This session takes

> *Reading allows each of us to attend any university in the world, to apprentice ourselves to any authority, to stand on the shoulders of any giant.*

reader response beyond casually scribbled Post-its, beyond simply exhaling. This session is intended to teach readers that reading, and then reading and thinking, is actually—prewriting!

"If I have seen further, it is only by standing on the shoulders of giants," wrote that most original of nonfiction thinkers and writers, Isaac Newton, in a letter to another original nonfiction thinker and writer, Robert Hooke. Indeed, it is this that we are teaching in this session. Reading allows each of us to attend any university in the world, to apprentice ourselves to any world authority, to stand on the shoulders of any giant in a field. And for what purpose? We stand on the shoulders of giants to do as Isaac Newton did—to see further. Not only to inhale that person's knowledge, but also to exhale our own—to grow ideas that bear the mark of our knowledge, our own life experiences, our own beliefs and quirks and passions and memories and images.

Ironically, we read the ideas of others to grow our own original ideas. And it is that originality, that sense of per-

sonal investment and voice that matters most in this session. You are helping students make something of their responses to reading.

Again, we must do more than tell kids that this is the way to go. Once we point out the path, we want to hand kids some running shoes, get them started, and cover the first leg of the journey alongside them until they no longer need us. To say to kids "The more you read, the more you will find yourself becoming original text-creators" is not enough. We want to hand them the tools to actually do this complicated work.

Tucked into the session is the important news that writers and readers of nonfiction texts sometimes find it useful not just to think of the narrative and expository structures but also to think, more specifically, of the micro-structures that underlie all kinds of expository texts. By micro-structure I mean texts that are built on patterns: cause and effect, compare and contract, question and answer, and the like. Offering students these micro-structures to choose from may seem like a big new challenge, but we do it as a scaffold. We offer it here specifically because humans can make knowledge more easily when it's patterned. Once the "whole" of an idea is described, once the shape and scope of the text are laid out, then what we need to create, what we need to figure out to fill in the structure, becomes less abstract and more attainable—more manageable. These micro-structures are meant to be aids for readers new to fleshing out ideas about their nonfiction reading.

The fact remains that this is a complex topic to tuck into one of the final sessions of a unit, but keep in mind, every unit of study aims to initiate work that continues long after the unit, and every unit of study aims to allow for differentiated learning.

The session, then, first and foremost, rallies readers to construct their own points of view, their own ideas on a topic, and to begin the work of developing those ideas as they continue to read and reread.

MINILESSON

Creating Our Own Responses to Nonfiction

CONNECTION

COACHING TIPS

Suggest that during this session, children's research will turn an important corner: it will begin to feel as much like writing as like reading. They're constructing meaning.

"Researchers, I think holidays are important, especially holidays such as birthdays and New Year's Day that make us almost draw a line in the sand of our lives. I love the holidays that get us to think backward and forward and to resolve to do more.

"Do you remember that book we read earlier in the year, *I'm in Charge of Celebrations*, in which Byrd Baylor says that she's in charge of celebrations, and she makes a lot of them? She made a celebration called The Green Parrot Cloud Day to honor the day she saw a cloud in the sky that looked exactly like a green parrot.

"Well, I think we should be in charge of celebrations, and we should declare today's reading workshop (and tomorrow's, too) as New Year's Day for us as researchers. Because over the course of these days, each of us will draw a line in the sand of this unit and resolve to be a new kind of learner—similar to the way, at the end of our first unit of study, we resolved to read stories like they're gold.

This session represents yet another new way to convene children's attention. You'll see connections that draw students in by making them active, using their names, telling personal anecdotes, and reading aloud, but declaring the day a holiday is a new way to create a drumroll for the minilesson.

This idea of a New Year's Day in reading hearkens back to Unit 1, when children began resolutions in authoring their own reading lives. The idea is similar in this session, except that in this session, specifically, I want readers to author their own reading research lives.

Name your teaching point. Specifically, tell children that after reading what all the books have to say about a particular topic, we come up with something we want to say about the topic. Instead of just being a reader on our topic, we become a writer.

"Today I want to teach you that eventually, research begins to feel as much like writing as like reading. We do not necessarily do a lot of physical writing (researchers sometimes teach or draw or chart instead), but researchers at least develop a text in their mind (or a mental model, as some people call it). To do this, we bring the writing process to our reading. We not only select and gather ideas around an idea that matters to us; we also decide what we want to say and organize what we know."

TEACHING

Recruit a few kids to record on white boards the steps you take as you select an idea from the class research topic to develop and put forth. Brainstorm possible ideas, each suited to a different text structure.

"Let's return to the topic we've been studying all along, penguins, and think how we, as a class, might go about choosing what it is we want to teach others about penguins. Do you remember that in the writing process, we reread what we have been collecting around an idea, asking, 'Is there a particular seed idea in all this stuff that I could develop into something important that I could send into the world? We do the same in reading. Instead of collecting and looking across our notebook entries, we look across all we've read on our topic and all our jotted notes, culling out what we've learned from the books and what we've thought, so we decide what ideas we now want to develop and send forth into the world.

"I'm going to show you how we might start fashioning an idea we could develop pertaining to penguins. Can I have some volunteers to record the steps involved in organizing this project? I'll give you white boards so that later you can share the steps you record with the rest of us. We're all going to want to follow the same general pattern of work.

"In reading, as in writing, when we want to decide on an idea about a topic we care about, we reread and rethink, asking ourselves, 'What are some really important and interesting insights I have about this topic? What might I want to tell people, to help them feel, about this topic?'

"So let's look back over some of the books we've read, some of the conversations we've had. Hmm, . . ." Then, to engage the kids, I said, "I'll distribute some of our penguin books, and you can scan them too and help come up with ideas we've had that matter." I passed half a dozen books out into the meeting area and continued staring into space, modeling running through my mental files of the same books.

"Well, certainly one of the things we've learned is that penguins aren't much like the pigeons outside our school or anything. I mean, I thought ho hum, we'd be reading about just another bird, but these creatures are really different. And, yes, I do want to teach people how these birds are not much like pigeons." I jotted that on chart paper, starting a list of possible seed ideas for this research project.

You could, no doubt, think up numerous ideas for your project, and so might the kids. I want to caution you, though, that just any idea will not fit the planned path of this minilesson. I'm composing. I have selected ideas with an eye toward using those ideas to allow me to overview the micro-structures that one finds in nonfiction texts—problem and solution, compare and contrast, cause and effect, question and answer, narrative sequence, and description.

During the active involvement section of this minilesson, I'll ask children to turn to the note-taker nearest them and review what that person has recorded. If you plan to do this as well—a variation on turn and talk that I think kids will welcome—then make sure you distribute the white boards to all the corners of your meeting area so that every child will be able to convene around a note-taker. Be sure, too, that you select reliable and fairly proficient note-takers.

I spoke as if I had expected just a mundane research topic on the dullest thing in the world—a kind of bird. Then, carrying on, my inflection utterly changed to show that this bird is far from dull. I am, of course, using the same strategy my mother uses when she wants to make one of her nine kids feel really terrific. She contrasts us with all the others! Psychologists may not love this strategy, but it certainly is an effective way to pop out the unique characteristics of something. Note that the way I have worded this idea makes it suitable for a compare and contrast text structure—penguins are different from pigeons (though not entirely).

"Hmm, . . . What else?" I looked over my notes. "Oh—I know. I think we could teach others how a penguin's day goes, you know, 'A Day in the Life of a Penguin.'" I jotted that down, adding, "I'm not sure what I'd want people to feel. Maybe I'd want people to admire the way these birds work hard from morning to night." That topic, too, got added to a list.

I eyed the class to see if they had ideas. Malik said, "Remember we found out that all our penguin books have a chapter on the cold weather? We could say about how penguins have adapted to live in cold." That got added to the list.

I noted that Fallon was looking at a sketch of a penguin, and I said, "We have definitely learned some interesting stuff about the way a penguin looks, haven't we—with the brood pouch, the flaps over its legs, the crest. We could describe them, right? Telling about each part of their bodies?" Again, that joined the list.

"What else? Well, we could also teach others about how global warming is causing things to change for penguins, right?" Again I recorded this.

This topic is sequential, suitable for a narrative text structure. I worded the phrase "They work from morning to night" with special care to make sure I was highlighting the sequential nature of this topic. Later I will ask kids to help me think about how these different ideas might lead to mental models that would be structured differently.

Again, keep in mind that I'm hoping to create a list of possible penguin topics that can double as a lesson on text structuring.

> ## Possible Penguin Topics
>
> - Penguins are different than pigeons in more ways than they are the same
>
> - One day in the life of a penguin goes like this...
>
> - Freezing weather can be a problem. Penguins have adapted to solve these problems.
>
> - The penguin's body looks like...
>
> - Global warming is causing new challenges for the penguins.

Then I said, "Now that we have a whole bunch of possible seed ideas, we need to choose one and begin to organize our notes and our thoughts so that we could teach a class or write a paper on the idea we want to put out into the world."

Point out that once a person has an idea about a topic, the idea often implies a particular text structure. When the person anticipates not only the content but also the structure of what will be said, this helps that person organize his or her thinking.

"The other day I was working with Jane, Danny, and Brandon, who were trying to figure out how far Kandahar is from Korphe, where Greg Mortenson built his school. They were surprised that the people in Korphe embraced education for girls and welcomed Mortenson's efforts, whereas in Kandahar, girls were attacked for going to school. Jane, Danny, and Brandon were afraid that the girls in Korphe might be in danger, too. Because they were comparing two situations, I taught them how to use what's called a Venn diagram (I held up the Venn diagram that this group of kids made) to compare Korphe and Kandahar's respective situations.

"This reminded me that sometimes it helps to think about how we might organize a class, or a piece of writing, on the topic we're thinking about. And the first question to ask is, 'Would this be organized like a story or like an all-about, or expository, text? Let's see if any of these ideas of ours are sort of leaning toward being written in a narrative—a story sequence." I reread the list, leaving time for children to do the same. I hoped they were coming to their own answers.

I let the kids run their eyes over the list together. Yes, "A Day in the Life of a Penguin" would be a narrative. The other texts would all contain big ideas and supports.

"Readers, do you see that if I made a text (in my mind or on the paper) that was 'One Day in the Life of a Penguin,' then I'd be constructing a narrative? A story? So I could sort of make a timeline as an organizer for my notes and collect what happens early, later, and later still." Then I backed up for a moment and said to the class, "Do you see that I thought about how that sort of a text might be organized, and that helps me have a plan for organizing my notes?"

You may decide that this volume of information should not be tucked into a minor section of a minilesson, and you may decide to do otherwise. My own feeling is that these text structures mean the most to kids if they have talked and written into them first, as they'll be doing here, before they are asked to find these structures embedded under the surface of texts they are reading.

Summarize and post a chart listing some common nonfiction text structures.

"What you should know is that there are common ways that many nonfiction texts are organized. And it can help to be aware that our topic has a certain organizational structure to it. Here are some ways that texts are often structured.

You might decide to highlight just a few of these text structures. The most obvious one—other than the narrative or main idea with support structures—is that of comparing and contrasting. You might want to show your students how to structure their compare and contrast thinking.

Common Nonfiction Text Structures

- *Cause and effect (This happens, so then that—and that and that—happens.)*
- *Problem and solution (There is this problem. It gets solved in these four ways.)*
- *Question and answer (There is this question. Here is a long answer. Then, another question and another answer.)*

- Compare and contrast (This is the same as that in these ways. It is different in these ways.)
- Description (This looks like....)

ACTIVE INVOLVEMENT

Channel children to talk through the text structure that best matches each of the seed ideas you and the class have recorded. Do this with the class topic.

"Readers, will you and your partner see if you can imagine ways in which we might organize our ideas if we decide to not write 'One day in the life of a penguin' but instead to take on one of our other ideas? Think of how it might be organized."

The room filled with conversation, kids pointing at one chart and another. After a bit, I called over the hubbub, "Take one of these and imagine what your notes might look like if you were jotting down your ideas. I'm going to pass out the rest of these white boards. You and your partner can try sketching out whether you'd take notes in two columns or in boxes and bullets or some other way. You might need to talk out what those notes would be. This is complicated, so turn your brains on high."

Show the children the way that different ideas match different text structures through examples. Provide possible outlines for a text that compares and contrasts, one that cites a problem and provides solutions and so forth.

I convened the class and asked kids to display their white boards with lists of different ways that texts could be organized. Then I suggested that if I wanted to teach that the penguin is mostly different than the pigeon, I might take notes organized like this:

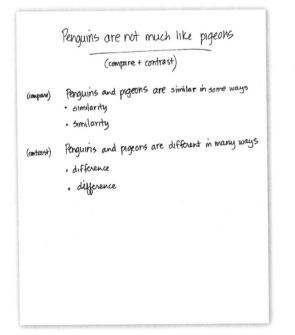

Penguins are not much like pigeons

(compare + contrast)

(compare) Penguins and pigeons are similar in some ways
- similarity
- similarity

(contrast) Penguins and pigeons are different in many ways
- difference
- difference

"If we wanted to talk about how the cold weather had caused adaptations in penguin bodies, we could organize our problem-solution information like this." I revealed another outline, this one on another sheet.

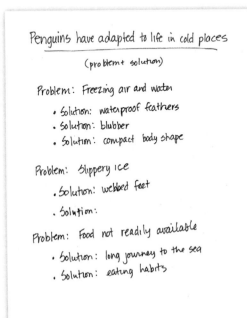

Penguins have adapted to life in cold places

(problem + solution)

Problem: Freezing air and water
- Solution: waterproof feathers
- Solution: blubber
- Solution: compact body shape

Problem: Slippery ice
- Solution: webbed feet
- Solution:

Problem: Food not readily available
- Solution: long journey to the sea
- Solution: eating habits

After walking through several more possibilities, the class decided to develop a descriptive essay, one that started with a diagram of the penguin's body, followed by a description of each of the body parts of a penguin.

LINK

Ask that all your readers choose an idea they want to advance, imagine an organizational structure for that idea, and begin collecting, thinking, and organizing toward a final presentation at the end of the unit.

"Readers, I do not usually tell you exactly what to do during one day's reading workshop, but in just a very short time you are going to teach other people what you have learned from your inquiry. So you're going to want to follow the steps that our recorders jotted down. (Can you hold those up so we can see them?)"

I read off the notes, paraphrasing as necessary: "First, reread your notes and your texts and think, 'What idea matters to me? What is it I want to say to the world about my topic?' Then think, 'How might the text I construct (in my mind or on the paper) be organized?' You can use this chart to think about possible ways that texts are structured." I pointed to the chart "Common Nonfiction Text Structures" again.

"And of course, you'll be readying yourself for teaching others, so remember to think, 'What do I want people to feel? What feelings am I trying to instill?' And then think about ways you can engineer things to make your listeners, your readers, think as you want them to think, feel as you want them to feel. That's what readers of nonfiction do when we have a topic we read a lot about. We make our own ideas about the topic and talk about them in the world, in ways that influence and affect others. Okay, off you go to begin trying that!"

Of course, I could have suggested that children record notes in Venn diagrams or matrixes of all sorts. You may decide to do so. I figured that it is also important to help children see that all of these structures fall under the broader category of an expository text, and all fit into the boxes-and-bullets work that students learned about earlier in the unit, so I mostly stayed aligned to that earlier work, for now.

This is an ambitious minilesson. In a sense, you are channeling children to go from collecting Post-its to making theory charts, only this time the work is not about characters but about their research topic. You'll suggest that the theories we develop tend to follow the commonplace structures of compare and contrast, cause and effect, question and answer, and so forth. Much of the most challenging intellectual cargo in the minilesson, then, revolves around the recognition that authors structure texts according to templates that are already out there in the world. Sending them off to read with those theories as lenses helps them collect new information and develop their initial ideas.

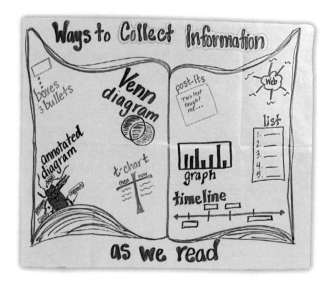

CONFERRING AND SMALL-GROUP WORK

Help Researchers Find Their Own Angles on Their Topics

Research to Understand What Children Are Already Doing

The children in the Castle Group were reading quietly when I approached them. Because I wanted to observe them talking together, I asked if they'd mind interacting now, while I was with them, and then they could read while other groups talked during the share session. They put down their books and pulled in their chairs, Josh keeping his thumb in the book as a page marker.

The rest of the group hadn't even settled into place before Fallon began, talking partly to her group members (though particularly to her partner Josh) and partly to me. "I was thinking our seed idea should be weapons and tools from medieval days because my book is good for that and aren't yours, too? 'Cause mine says how back then, they needed to farm and they needed to build castles, so they invented tools. It is like problem and solution. They had to build castles, so they had a mason. My book says in the thirteenth century, a mason— that's someone who makes things out of stone—used a pulley to haul baskets full of stone for the castle. So we know that they invented pulleys back then. I also read about them

using chisels. We still have both of those today, and masons, too. Only they don't really build castles," she added as an afterthought.

As Josh started talking, I whispered to Fallon to remember to talk to her entire group, not just to Josh. I knew that the two of them had a great rapport, but I wanted this group to function as a team rather than as two parallel sets of partners. Fallon nodded.

Josh said, "I wonder what they looked like, though, the chisels and pulleys. Did they seem the same as ones today? I haven't seen any pictures in my books. José, is that what you were drawing in your notebook?" [Figs. XIX-1a and XIX-1b]

José said he thought he had sketched chisels somewhere and paged through his rumpled notebook until he finally arrived at the page. "Here," he said, displaying the sketches he'd made. "I think the chisel was used with the bricks to put them where they go. There is another thing they used that we have now, and that was mortar, which is what sticks the bricks together." Glancing again at the picture that was now at the center of the table, he added, "Oh, and crowbars." [Fig. XIX-2]

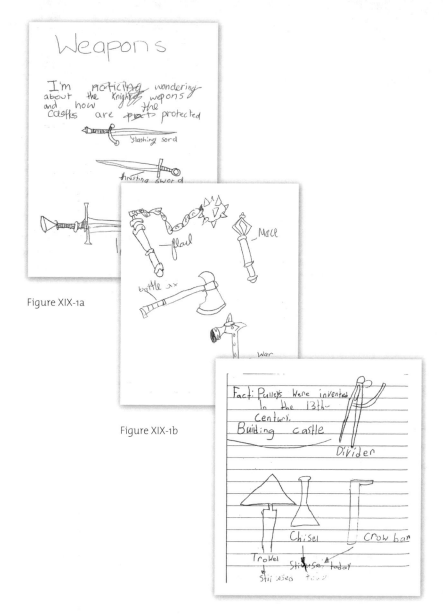

Figure XIX-1a

Figure XIX-1b

Figure XIX-2

accepted her suggestion that they talk about the problems back then and the way people invented tools to address those problems. In fact, it seemed to me that the conversation was actually becoming a compare and contrast conversation, juxtaposing tools from the medieval times with those used today.

Before I could intervene, however, José added a thought that quite literally put a new spin on matters. "But can we talk about weapons now?"

"Yeah!" said Kwami, jumping in. "One big idea I have is that catapults were so huge I wonder how they made them and how they moved them. They were more than 800 pounds! And you had to carry this one (he showed his group the picture) because it didn't have wheels. They needed over 100 people to carry it to the battle fortress."

Fallon piped in, "I saw a movie that had catapults in it. They fired rock balls. It's like the earliest version of a cannon ball, but no gunpowder, right?"

José, leafing through his book, said, "Yeah, Fallon, it said something like that in my book. I am not sure where, but it says catapults were the earliest kind of cannon." He found the page and showed it to the group.

Josh stole a glance at me, then said, "Wait guys, have we grown any ideas yet?"

I was glad that I had waited long enough for him to do this nudging. It can be tempting to seize every teachable moment that flies past us, but sometimes the best teaching move can be to wait an extra second or two. When listening to kids read, we all know to let them self-correct their miscues, but I think we sometimes forget to let kids self-correct their book talks.

A bit impatiently, Fallon rose to his challenge. "Well, I think people back then cared a lot about education because they needed educated people to invent all of these new things to build the castles, and they needed the castles to protect themselves from their enemies—so it was important that they had people who knew how to invent things and also to use them. So, education, that's my big idea. Anyone else?"

I was interested that she seemed to think that to generate "big ideas," it helped to go to an erudite topic such as the value of education.

José added slowly, unsure of his footing, "Well, this is sort of about weapons and sort of about education, too. It's about how they invented weapons. I think that people back then weren't that smart, but even though they weren't, some of them made really powerful weapons—like the hand-and-a-half sword. It could be nearly as tall as the knight who

At this point, I was about to intercede to suggest that the group spend a bit more time planning what idea they'd advance and which structure they might use. Fallon had suggested a general subject—weapons and tools—that the group seemed to endorse, but there is a difference between a topic and an idea, and I wasn't clear that the others had

carried it! And the flail was an iron ball, and it was changed to add a handle. The powerful weapons are increasing and increasing. And I didn't expect that in olden times, people could have ideas like that."

José seemed new to the academic dialect. "The powerful weapons are increasing and increasing." It felt a bit like he was dressing himself up in a grown-up's garb (which I loved). Of course, I'd been tempted to jump all over his comment about people "back then" not being smart, but I let that pass.

Kwami brought that topic to a close by saying that although the world back then may not have contained as much information, the people certainly made some cool stuff. He'd created some closure, so I took that as a sign that this was a good time to sift through all I'd seen and heard to do some teaching.

Decide What You'll Compliment and What You'll Teach

What would you teach at this point? My hunch is if I elbowed you and said, "You do the teaching," you'd probably feel unsure of what to say and you might well ask questions as a way to back yourself into a role in the conversation. If I was your staff developer, I'd very likely say, "By this time in this conference, nudge yourself to get past questions and push yourself to form a theory about these readers and what they are doing. You've got enough data in your in-box." The instinct to ask questions, at this point, probably comes because you want kids to name what their issues are for you. You want the theory to jump right out and hit you over the head. It usually doesn't go like that. You need to make meaning out of what you have heard—and it never stops feeling like you are taking a risk.

Of course, the best is for you to think with a colleague about what you'd do. Because I've transcribed the conference, you can flick your eyes up the page and reread, and while doing so you can nudge yourself to grow a theory about what the kids are doing—and are almost but not yet doing. The hardest part of a conference is this moment when the spotlight shifts to you, the teacher, and it is your turn to make something out of what you have seen. This always feel to me like I am taking a leap of faith, like I'm reaching up onto a rope swing and letting myself go flying into thin air. I generally have just a bit of a plan and hope things will sail along well.

Compliment in Ways that Lift the Level of What Readers Do on Even Another Day, with Even Another Text

"Can I tell you a few things?" I said to the group. "You know how you admire the capability of those people 'back then' because they invented those complicated tools and weapons? Well, I'm admiring the capability of you, because you have invented tools that really strengthened your conversation. I want to mention a couple tools I just saw you invent that I hope you use often."

Josh nudged his pal and said, "I bet you are going to say about José's drawings. He put detail in them, so we can picture how the different tools and weapons worked."

I nodded, although actually I hadn't made note of that. Now that Josh had reminded me, I heaped more specifics onto the compliment, thinking as I did that actually the kids' use of pictures was probably worth turning into a minilesson because certainly this would help kids integrate pictures and diagrams and call-out boxes in the text as they read. "That was a really smart thing, absolutely. And you not only created pictures and diagrams. You also referred to others that are in the books—you actually used visual tools to ground your talk. You put them in the center of the conversation and looked at them to get more ideas going. I definitely hope you do that often—with sketches, pictures, notes and charts.

"The second thing I want to compliment happened even before you brought out the pictures. You all worked together to decide on a shared subtopic, starting with Fallon, who remembered the charge from the minilesson—to look over your notes and your texts and come up with a topic you wanted to put forth to the world. She suggested that you could all think and talk about tools and weapons, and you actually did stay in that area for your whole conversation. Instead of skittering from one thing about the medieval times to another, you stayed with that one subtopic and talked about it in depth, combining one person's knowledge with another's."

Glancing at my scrawled notes, I added, "You also pushed yourself to get past listing information and to grow big ideas, as when you discussed the inventiveness of people back then.

"Another day, when I am not here, remember to continue putting pictures and diagrams (and texts, too) at the center of your conversation and let those tools keep you grounded, and continue to make that shift from listing specifics toward talking about big ideas, too."

Teach in Ways that Make a Lasting Difference

Because I'd spent a lot of time complimenting this group, I knew I'd earned the right to do some decisive teaching. "Can I do a bit of teaching?" I said, waiting for their consent—and their attention. "There are two related things I want to help you with, and one goes with what I said about readers needing to decide upon an idea that you want to put out into the world—sort of like writers decide on a seed idea—and then readers needing to take some time to reread and rethink, developing that idea. Do you have a sense of what the idea is that you have been thinking about, based on your reading, that you want to teach others?"

Fallon jumped in. "It's weapons and tools, really—both." She checked in with the others, and they agreed, qualifying that their idea actually was medieval weapons and tools.

I nodded. This was as I thought. "So my first tip is this. When you go to think, 'What is the idea I want to put forth into the world,' your idea can't be a topic: weapons and tools. It needs to be an idea, a claim, a thesis statement." I suggested the kids look again at the list of ideas we'd generated around the topic of penguins. After they reread that list, they started talking among themselves about what the idea was that they wanted it to be about. I jumped in. "This talk that you are having now—it is crucial. If you are studying a topic in a group, like you are, you need to take a bunch of time to talk over, 'What are we really wanting to say?' And if you are researching alone, you take lots of time to mull that over. In your talk, Fallon just said, "We're talking about the problems of farming and castles and how those problems led people to invent weapons." It was like that was the starting gun at the racetracks, and you all were off and running. Another time, take some time to discuss what you really are talking about.

"Right now, think about what the idea is, for now anyhow, that you do want to put forth into the world—the idea you really want to teach others."

The kids talked and decided they wanted to say, "People back then invented tools to build castles and weapons to protect themselves."

I pointed out that once a person has an idea, it can help to think, "How will I develop the idea?" And that often means thinking, "How will I organize my thinking about this?" They could start by deciding if their idea fit with a narrative or an expository structure. The group immediately decided it was the latter, so I suggested they could next think whether their boxes and bullets fit any of the structures we'd talked about in the minilesson. The kids weren't sure; they wondered if their idea fit into a problem and solution structure or a then to now structure (a compare and contrast structure.)

I agreed with their perplexity. "Usually we can think about a subject one way, then another way, then another way, and you are right that you can compare weapons then and now, or you can talk about the problems that led people to develop tools and weapons as solutions. But usually, it will help to choose one structure and stay in it for at least a while. And I should think that for kids who are so good at using visuals to ground your conversation, you might make a visual—some notes in a form that holds your talk in place."

I asked the children to restate what they thought their big idea was now, the idea they really wanted to project into the world, and they said, "People in the fourteenth century were inventive. They invented tools to help them build castles and weapons to keep themselves safe."

Together we turned that into boxes and bullets:

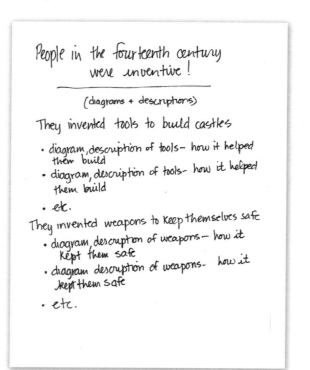

I told them, "These sorts of jotted notes can provide you with a plan for the teaching you'll do. And remember that you can always do this—side by side with the other great things you have already been doing—as a way to help you stay with and develop your ideas. Think of your conversations as chapters in the book you're together authoring about your topic."

TEACHING SHARE

Researchers Follow Trails of Thought

Highlight the trail of thought that the inquiry groups in your class have been pursuing, emphasizing the way each group worked for a while on one theory and then spun out into an extension of the first theory.

"Researchers, I want to be sure you know about the work your classmates are doing, because this is some of the most intellectually charged work I've seen us doing all year.

"The Penguin Research Group has chosen to develop the idea that penguins seem to have feelings for each other that are rather like the feelings that human beings have. The members of this group have been thinking and reading and talking about the great lengths that penguin parents go to for their children—about the long march for food, about their willingness to regurgitate food for their babies. And right now, I think they are investigating more about the feelings penguins have for their mates. Remember what we all learned earlier about their love songs?

"You'll remember that these readers made a web earlier, mapping out subtopics such as where the penguins lived and what their bodies are like. Then they put their first web aside, because they are no longer interested in giving equal attention to every single subtopic related to penguins. Now they have started a new flowchart, only the topic at the center of this flow chart is not 'All-About Penguins.' Instead, the topic at the center of their chart is this: 'Penguins have human-like feelings for each other.' [Fig. XIX-3]

"You'll see they have jotted some big ideas and supports under this new main idea, starting with the big idea 'Penguin parents do a lot for their chicks.' If they learn more that helps their idea, they'll record what they learn on their new web.

"My bigger point is that the focus of your research should be changing. The Shark Group started off interested in sharks' teeth, and now they are on the idea that some people stereotype sharks unfairly. The Castle Group started off learning all about fourteenth century castles, and now they are researching the idea that the people back then were inventive, inventing tools as well as weapons that they needed to live."

COACHING TIPS

Notice that I talk about intellectually charged ideas and then provide evidence by talking about the Penguin Group, which is a group containing a few of the readers who struggle. This is not empty flattery. Because the Penguin Group's topic is also the whole-class topic, that group is actually further along than most groups, and the work group members have done can help others.

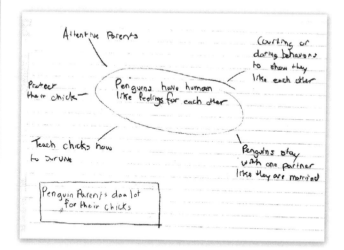

Figure XIX-3
This group recorded their learning on a new web.

Ask everyone to think and talk in their groups about the journey of their research, using the prompts "First we thought. . . . Then we realized. . . . Now we wonder. . . ."

"You know the prefix in the word research is re. What does re mean? Reread. Reheat? 'Re' means again, and research means to search again. To follow one idea, then another. So right now, with your group members, try saying, 'First we studied . . . , and now we are on about . . . .' They talked.

Then I voiced over, saying, "Talk about the journey of your research. Try saying, 'First we thought. . . . And then we realized. . . . And now we are wondering. . . .'" Again, the room was filled with a buzz. After a few minutes I ended the day by saying. "We need to stop now. But after this, remember that this is what nonfiction readers do. We follow our interests even as they change."

Using Lenses to See More in Nonfiction

e began this bend on an expansive note—opening up not one or two but multiple books on topics of inquiry and then grouping our children together to study these as if they contained hidden treasure. Children held conversations, they used open-ended writing to generate more ideas, they found contrasting points of view, and they dissected their reactions to the texts. Our young readers took on the garb of researchers and of critics. Nearer the end of the unit, however, this expansiveness converges into children's articulation of their own, individual stance on their topics. This move—from the generic to the specific—is common to all learning projects. We survey myriad possibilities—all we can find—and we weigh these against each other, considering details, sources, and perspectives until we know enough to narrow our research and to pick our own stance, making our inquiry lens more precise and personalized. This session aims to do just that, teaching children that after a general look at a subject, the photographer picks an angle and then fits in a zoom lens to frame and capture just what he has seen that encapsulates the essence of it all, for him or her. This is also what the can-

didate for a doctorate does or what I do when I assess a group of children: generalization, then a selection, and then specialization.

When I think about the lessons that have mattered to me as a researcher, there is one that towers above all the others. You may have heard me tell of it before, in *Units of Study for Teaching Writing*. Perhaps this lesson matters especially because it was the very first lesson I recall learning, on that first day when I left my role as a classroom teacher and became a research associate in Don Graves' giant National Institute of Education study of children as writers. But I like to think this lesson matters most because it is profound in its implications.

In any case, this is what happened. Don Graves, the senior member of our team, and I went into Pat Howard's classroom as researchers to record what a handful of case-study subjects did as writers. My job was to study these children as writers every day for two years, and on this day, Day 1, I was ready. I had my clipboard; I leaned against the radiator at the back of the classroom, ready to record anything the kids did. But they didn't do anything—they were all

GETTING READY

- You'll need to have two photos on hand for the minilesson today. Both should be related to the whole-class research topic. One photo should not relate in any obvious way to the angle the class will take on the whole-class topic, yet the photo should reveal something about that angle with some pushing. You may want to think this through ahead of time. The other photo should, in contrast, offer some obvious insight related to the class's angle on the class topic. If your whole-class research topic is penguins, you could use the photos and ideas included in this session.

busy copying math problems out of the math book. I roamed the aisles, looking for someone writing something. Nothing. Finally, I signaled to Graves, who'd been busying himself doing something or other, and we exited the room.

Before I could let out a weary sigh, Graves said, "Zowie. Wasn't that amazing! Chairs so high, desks so low. It was like they were writing around their knees. And other kids, with desks towering over them, sitting on those tiny chairs.

> *By altering—and zooming—the lens through which I look, I alter what I will see and learn to see things that would otherwise have been invisible to me.*

How could anyone write practically over their heads? And what'd you think of the way some of them copied those math problems?" Graves began dramatizing the child who'd read 37 + 64 aloud, then repeated the problem like a mantra, over and over, as he moved his eyes from the math book to his paper. Graves went on to comment on children whose pencils were tiny stubs, so small the child could barely grip them, and those with erasers the size of giant golf balls. "Wasn't it amazing?" Graves said. "What a gold mine!"

"Yes, amazing," I said, not wanting to let on that I'd spent the entire time waiting impatiently for some data to hit me over the head or to land at my feet. That day, I learned that I can't stroll through life, collecting learning as one might pick low-hanging fruit from an apple orchard. Learning requires that the learner—that's me—actively constructs meaning. And we do this to a large extent by altering the lens through which we look.

I can look at a classroom and just see, "Yup, the kids are reading." Or I can look at the same classroom and notice the girl giggling to herself in the corner as she reads. I can notice the boy hiding the *Magic Treehouse* book he's reading in the pages of a much fatter Harry Potter book. I can look again and this time see the same readers and note the relationships between genre and the reader's gender. Is fantasy unreasonably taboo for girls in this classroom? I can watch to see how often readers interrupt themselves while reading and note what readers seem to do during those interruptions. Are they writing? Talking? Drawing? My point is that by altering—and zooming—the lens through which I look, I alter what I will see and learn to see things that would otherwise have been invisible to me.

The process of picking a stance and zooming in—selecting and then specializing—will do more than merely converge our teaching into a point. It will allow kids to take control and add their voices to a topic that no longer daunts with its vastness. This technique, then, of selecting a specific point of interest from within a generic topic to zoom in on, allows for deeper, more specialized learning. The bigger message is that reading nonfiction is really all about authoring a learning life (not just a reading life), and doing this requires a person to take up a goal and then to set to work with deliberateness, hoping to learn from the process.

MINILESSON

Using Lenses to See More in Nonfiction

CONNECTION

Tell a story about a time in which you were at first too overwhelmed to take something in, but you selected a particular focus and that allowed you to take in much more than you otherwise could have.

"Readers, I want to tell you about a time I went to an art museum with a friend. She wanted to see some famous landscape paintings. When I saw the paintings, I had a hard time taking them all in. They were so huge, and there were so many of them, I hardly knew where to look. I felt ready to leave the museum! The paintings felt so overwhelming to me—there was so much to look at—that it was hard to enjoy them.

"But then, my friend started to explain how to really see the paintings. She told me many different ways to look at them. I could study how the artist used color to create a feeling of shadow and light. I could study the types of brush strokes the artist used. There were some paintings with long brush strokes that we could hardly see and one that I realized was actually only made of dots! She suggested I could even look in the backgrounds of the paintings and study all of the tiny details there, instead of only looking at the main subject.

"All these ideas helped me really study the paintings carefully. What really struck me is that even though I was looking at only one aspect of the paintings, instead of making me see less, it actually made me see more, because it focused my attention.

COACHING TIPS

You will have experienced other minilessons that invite readers to focus, to select, to cup one's hands around one thing or one part or one aspect of a work. The great American psychologist William Jones compared the stream of consciousness to a bird's life. "As we take, in fact, a general view of the wonderful stream of consciousness, what strikes us first is the different pace of its parts. Like a bird's life, it seems to be made of an alternation of flights and perches."

Explain how this analogy explains the next phase of nonfiction reading. In this case, explain how finding a particular focus or angle can help a reader see more in the text.

"Readers, this makes me think of the work that we're doing with nonfiction. You began this work with a wide range of possibilities of topics to study. You sifted through all of those possibilities, and you thought to yourself, what do I really want to know about? What really matters to me? Then you threw yourselves into your topics, finding out as much as you could about them. You lost yourselves in your texts, letting the feelings you were having wash over you. I watched some of you react to your texts with surprise, amazement, and delight, and also with fear, anger, and disgust.

"Then you began the work of noticing not only feelings you were having as you read, but also how your texts made you feel the way that you did. You began to notice ways that your texts convinced you to feel or think a certain way about your topic. You realized that the authors of nonfiction texts have some ideas about their subject that they really want their readers to know or understand. And do you know what? Because of this, books on the same subject can often give us different feelings about that subject. Think of the books that the shark group is reading. Some of their books give readers the feeling that sharks are vicious, bloodthirsty killers. They do this by including scary images and pictures of shark attacks. Some of their books, though, give readers the feeling that sharks are not really that dangerous and that they are more often the victims of vicious attacks. They get readers to want to protect sharks from illegal hunting and pollution that damages their habitats. That's very powerful stuff—to feel so differently about one topic, to be totally on the other side of the fence just based on how the author presents the facts.

"Today's session is going to be about giving you that power that authors have. It is going to be about you deciding what you feel about your topic, what stance you are going to take on it. Then, as you choose your stance, you can actually look for facts that support your stance, much as these nonfiction authors undoubtedly did when they began the research for the books they wrote.

"The stance that you take on your topic will help you to focus on certain parts of your topic that interest you."

In her book Notebooks of the Mind, *Vera John Steiner discusses the set of "invisible tools" that a creative person—a scientist, a writer, an artist—draws upon within the creative process. She summarizes her findings in an introduction, which ends with this thought: "To think, it seems to me, is to hold an idea long enough to unlock and shape its power in the varied contexts of human knowledge. There are differences among human beings in their willingness to pursue and hold the power of ideas, and it is within this domain that the similarities and differences between thought in its mundane and creative forms lie." This session helps learners hold and pursue ideas, helping them understand that the creative process is as much about composition as it is about comprehension. Experienced thinkers construct ideas. We are pro-active. We make choices. We do this even as we choose the lens through which we will look.*

Name your teaching point. Tell children that nonfiction readers and researchers construct lenses through which to conduct research that influence what we study. Researchers often record our thinking in writing.

"The important thing that I want to teach you is that researchers don't just take in knowledge. We also decide on the lens through which we will research the topic. This lens represents our particular interest in our topic. And the lenses that we are in the midst of constructing influence which parts of the information we notice, what we record, and what we think as we read our nonfiction texts. As we start researching through particular lenses, things become significant to us that we might not otherwise notice. We get thoughts we might not otherwise have."

TEACHING

Tell the story of a time you and a child learned to use lenses as a way to see more and learn more about a nonfiction topic.

"Let me tell you a true story of a time I taught a girl who is just your age how to research using a lens. (I think you'll see that this story relates to your own research.) Dori's class had made terrariums of different ecosystems, and her terrarium contained a desert ecosystem, complete with a couple of geckos (a sort of desert lizard). Dori's teacher asked each member of the class to study his or her ecosystem. Nothing much was happening in Dori's miniature world. The gecko walked about, blinked, turned this way, turned that way, stuck its tongue out, blinked again. For a few minutes, Dori essentially followed her subject. She waited for the gecko to do stuff and then wrote down what it did. But the gecko didn't do all that much. 'What's there to research about this creature?' Dori asked."

"Dori and I met, and I taught her something that researchers need to know. This is it. When studying a subject, you can actively build ideas. You can decide what, specifically, you'll learn! Then, you go out and make that learning happen. And if you approach something—a book, a photo, even a gecko—as an active, constructive learner who has decided on something to learn, you actually see a whole lot more.

"I showed Dori that while still looking at her gecko, she could decide to research one particular part of the gecko—like gecko legs, or gecko eyes. And if she did that, she might then go on to give herself the job of comparing the gecko's eyes (or legs or

Isn't it true? When we read nonfiction with a topic in mind, we see things that relate to that topic wherever we go. If we carry a big idea with us as we read, then we'll notice information related to our idea, ignoring information that seems unrelated. This, of course, is not unique to reading. It is also about living. My son is moving to Seattle, so all of a sudden I notice Seattle everywhere: Morning Joe is telecast from Seattle, my book by Annie Dillard, The Living, is set near Seattle, I get my coffee from a sister cafe to the original cafe in Seattle. I doubt that Seattle has just recently become especially prominent. Instead, I'm just now noticing the prominence it's had all along. Similarly, when I'm in the market for a new car, all I can see on the road are the cars that I'm considering buying. They seem to be everywhere! The same is true when we have a certain lens through which we read and research nonfiction texts.

whatever) to the cricket's eyes (or legs or whatever). Or she could broaden her research so geckos were just a part of it, and study 'legs across the desert' or 'legs across the whole world,' looking at the legs of every creature in her ecosystem or the legs of animals across all the different ecosystems represented in her classroom."

ACTIVE INVOLVEMENT

Relate your anecdote to children's inquiries by suggesting that if you were researching the class topic, you could glance past a lot of texts, thinking they weren't "about" your subject, or you could look again and develop insights.

"I think if I was in the Penguin Group, I might look at a picture of penguins and think the same thing Dori did at first. Like, I might look at this photo," I said, holding up a photo of penguins populating an icy landscape, "and think, 'Okay. Got it. There's a slew of penguins there—miles of them.' Then I might look up as if to say, 'Next? What other stuff is there for me to see?' That is how researchers act if we are just passively waiting for our subject to jump up and teach us something, to hit us over the head with something that we then record. But most learning doesn't happen that way. A lot of times learning requires the learner to construct meaning."

Recruit children to join you in looking at a photograph that at first seems to show little. Aloud, mine the photograph for insights it can yield if you look at it through a particular lens.

"How does Dori's story pertain to your own approach to research? Pretend the mini-lesson is over and it is reading time. Pretend you are in the Penguin Group—our class group. Pretend that yesterday you did some writing about penguin relationships and how those seem almost like human relationships. Now you are going to look through your book for sections that might go with that idea, 'cause you are gathering more stuff for your chart on that idea.

"Say you open *The Penguin* by Béatrice Fontanel to that photo we looked at earlier. You glance at it. You are looking for stuff on penguin relationships. Is it here? Or should we turn the page, looking for a picture about relationships? Thumbs up if you think there's stuff on this page about relationships. Thumbs down if we better search for another photo."

The kids' responses were mixed. "You are saying different things, and no wonder. This picture is probably not intended as a picture about penguin relationships. You have seen the ones that are, like this." I showed the familiar penguin family portrait.

"But what I want to teach you is that learning doesn't always jump up and hit you over the head. Sometimes you, the reader, the learner, need to take what the text says and find ideas and information in the text that the author didn't even make a point of pointing out.

"You can approach this photo with your theories about penguin relationships in mind, and you can use this photograph to get you thinking and wondering a lot more stuff about that topic. Try it. Decide that absolutely, this one photo says a ton about penguin family relationships, and then tell the person beside you what this says to you about penguin relationships."

Demonstrate the way a researcher can actively construct meaning pertinent to the researcher's subject, using the photograph mentioned above as a source of insight on the class topic.

The children tried this, but it was not easy for them. After letting them struggle a bit, but not too long, I demonstrated. "In a minute, I'm going to show you how I think about this photograph, and when I do that, you'll see that one secret to learning a lot *from the page* is that the reader needs to bring a lot *to that page*. Right now, continue to look at the page, thinking about penguin relationships, but as you look, be sure you draw on everything you already know about penguin relationships to see stuff, and to ask stuff."

I let the children again talk to each other about the meaning they constructed from studying the photo.

After a bit, I demonstrated. "Listen, now, to the meaning that I made of this photograph, and notice whether there are ways in which you can learn something about research by studying what I do.

We want to seize every opportunity to tap into children's prior knowledge. Teaching children that they can angle the way they look at a picture or photograph and see what the viewer wants to see and not simply what the author intended for the viewer to see will be challenging work. What you're doing today by having children fill in ideas about a picture is something that you can extend beyond reading workshop. During read-aloud time, you are probably reading nonfiction books as well, and after you've read a few books on a topic, let's say whales, you can then read an easy-reader book on whales and ask kids to fill in information they know on this topic that the author did not include in this easy-reader book. Children can even be sitting with their research group during read-aloud time while you do this, turning and talking to each other about everything they know about whales and building ideas off the beautiful photographs and illustrations.

"Hmm, . . . I've seen a number of photographs of penguin colonies that look like this. It is interesting because although we read so much about penguin relationships, I've often seen pictures of their colonies that look like this, with each penguin, thousands of them, sitting on a separate nest, as if oblivious of all the other penguins even though they are just two feet away. It seems as if the only relationship that matters to penguins is the nuclear family. I mean—I do not even know if penguin colonies have leaders, if some penguins are more dominant than others. I want to learn about the relationships they have outside the immediate family, within their colonies."

Set children up to practice what you have demonstrated. Give groups of kids a different lens through which to view the data (the photograph) and ask them to work together to see what they can see, applying their designated lens.

"Researchers, it's important for you to realize that we could have studied this photo using different lenses. Let's imagine you (I gestured to one chunk of the class) were studying penguins' food. What would you make of this? And (gesturing to another chunk of the class) you were studying penguins' enemies. That's a hard one. And you (gesturing to the final swatch of the class), the climate in which penguins live. Each of you tell the person beside you the meaning you would construct if you approached the picture wanting to construct theories about those topics. And remember to bring information to as well as to draw information from what you read."

LINK

Ask children to "read" a photograph related to their own topic, and encourage them to grow ideas related to their angle from that photograph.

"Right now, put a photograph related to your topic in front of you. And think about the line of thinking you've chosen and see if you can construct meaning related to that as you 'read' your photo. Don't let yourself swish your photograph out of sight saying, 'There is nothing here to see.' Instead, look again! List some of your ideas or thoughts across your fingers."

After a moment, I said, "Now show your research mates what you made of what you studied. What ideas did you construct?"

My point here is that I want readers to realize that the mental models we construct about our topics can influence what we notice and what theories we grow about our topics. In the same way, our theories also influence our mental models and what lens we use to take in the information we learn.

Students who are studying penguin's food might notice that the terrain seems barren and overpopulated. Might this be why penguins need to journey so far for food? The group studying climate might be intrigued to notice that penguins don't always live in snowy conditions. The group studying enemies might wonder if penguins ever work in concert to fight against an attacking animal—after all, there could be strength in numbers.

Tell children that we can read text in that same way we've been reading photos—to learn something in particular about our topics, even when that topic was the not author's main point.

"Readers, today, of course, you won't just be reading photographs, you'll be reading print texts. You all have some ideas, lenses in a way, that you are carrying with you as you approach your materials—and your temptation might be to take your lens, your big idea, in one hand, and then to scan through your materials thinking, 'Does this go with my main interest?' You might then flick past one page, another, and another, saying, 'No, no, no.' If you did that, you'd be looking for the texts where the information that is related to your interest jumps up and hits you on the head. Remember, if you were looking at our photo (I showed the initial photo) to grow ideas about penguin's families, you probably would initially have passed it by, thinking, 'Nothing here.' But there is more to see than first meets the eye. There is more in what you read than what you read at first, too.

"So remember, today you'll continue to do your research in preparation for teaching others about your topic. Your learning will feel as if you are writing a text—maybe an all-about text, maybe an essay text on an idea you are forming. You'll collect stuff on charts or mark stuff with Post-its, or write to grow journeys of thought, and by tomorrow's reading workshop, *you'll* be the author, the one to teach people about a topic that has enthralled you.

"The most important thing for you to remember is that today and every day for the rest of your life, you can make new meaning, see more than what's just laid out there, if you take a lens, take your own agenda, and look through that to see what you can see that speaks to your ideas. That's a lesson that can last your whole life—in reading and in living!"

This session helped readers to approach photographs and printed texts, both, expecting to find meaning and information that furthers an inquiry. If you have time to do so, you might want to extend this session with another that supports visual literacy. Nonfiction readers synthesize information from charts, timelines, diagrams, and photographs with the information gleaned from print. Graphics are an important source of information, and researchers not only read graphics, but also interpret them, distill them, and synthesize them.

CONFERRING AND SMALL-GROUP WORK

Support Kids' Book Talks with High-Voltage Teaching

Coaching to Help Children Use Note-Taking to Hold Their Conversations on a Course

In the far corner of the room, the Shark Group had become embroiled in a heated conversation. As I made my way toward them from across the room, I could tell that something had fired up this group. They were climbing out of their seats—first kneeling on their chairs, then standing around their table, and finally pacing around the table, opening one book and then another, shoving pictures in front of each other, and all the while, gesticulating wildly and talking rapid-fire. When I got close enough to hear, I heard comments flying back and forth.

"Only a dozen people get attacked by sharks in a year. A dozen," Jack exclaimed.

"Yeah," José added. "People say, 'They are vicious, they should be killed.' People are always talking about their teeth—but it is not their fault they have two rows of 300 teeth."

Sam added, "I can see why people would be afraid of sharks because their teeth are three hundred times

harder than the teeth of humans. But the thing is—I also learned that to a shark, a surfer looks like a seal." He returned to the picture I'd seen often before of a shark swimming near a bikini-clad swimmer. "It is not that the sharks have killer instincts so much as they just get mixed up and think the surfer is dinner."

"And they don't bite bit by bit," Isaac pointed out, "like the way some of the books say."

Listening, it was apparent that the boys, once eager to pronounce sharks violent and bloodthirsty were considering a new angle with equal ardor. They had several books open before them—one open to a page whose heading read "Sharks in Trouble" and the other, "Sharks Under Attack."

Jack had meanwhile extended his friend's comment, adding, "The sharks are just like humans. It's like us eating a burger."

Sam jumped in. "I agree. And you notice how humans talk about how sharks attack humans, and how cruel the sharks are to do that, but we kill cows and eat them. So. . . ." He pushed back from the table and took to the floor. "Stop stereotyping sharks!" *[Fig. XX-1]*

MID-WORKSHOP TEACHING POINT

By Reflecting, We Consolidate New Learning

"Readers, can I stop you for a minute?" I paused until all eyes were on me. "I want to take a moment to help us all look back and realize all we've done and learned in this unit so far. People all take time to step back once in a while to review and celebrate what they've learned. Readers do this, too.

"You have all learned that the strongest nonfiction readers read like experts and researchers. Experts don't just consult one source or read one book on a topic to regurgitate what that one book says. Experts read several texts on a topic and begin talking in expert ways about that subject, using an insider's lingo. That's the first stage of truly researching and acquiring expertise. And you've all worked hard and learned to do this!

"And then we went a step further, comparing and contrasting the different books on our topic. 'How does this book want me to feel?' we thought, and 'What angle does that book report from?' Once we began reading in this critical way, weighing our sources against each other, we developed seeds for thinking. We found questions and ideas that we wanted to develop. But we didn't just let these questions and ideas pass through us. We jotted them down. We used graphic organizers to make more of them. In a way, our reading began to feel more and more like writing, because after reading about our topic, we now had something of our own to say, questions of our own to ask. And these somethings that we wanted to say or ask became the lenses through which we read further. That's a lot of reading work, isn't it?!

"Right now, after having watched everyone do this amazing work of constructing lenses through which to research your topic and then writing long about that, I have to say, look at all we've done! Congratulations for working so hard and doing so much outstanding nonfiction reading work."

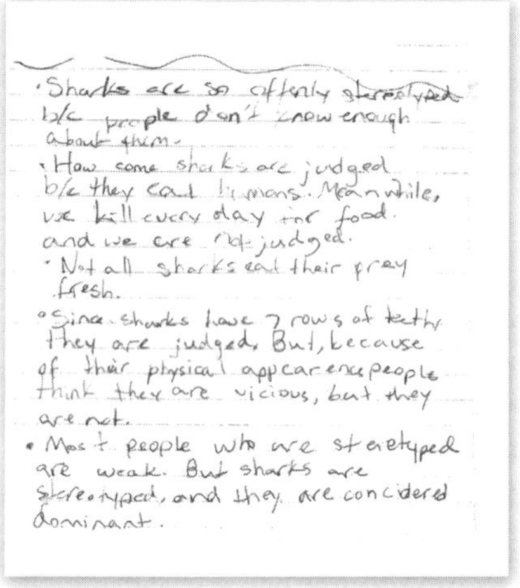

Figure XX-1
Sam's writing helped mobilize an energetic
discussion.

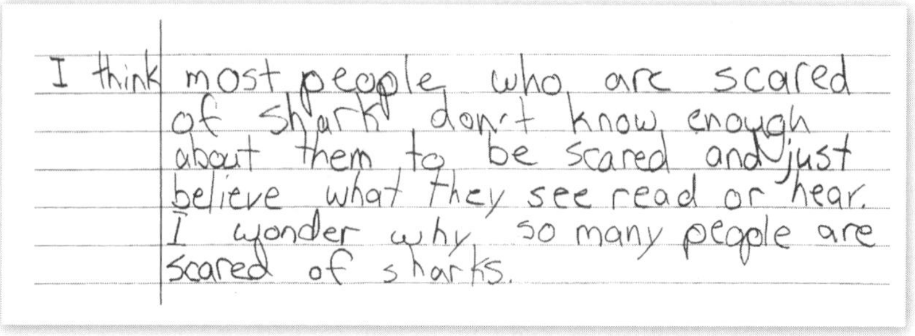

Figure XX-2
When readers have time to delve into deep conversations, they ask more
probing questions.

Isaac said, "Wait, wait guys. So why? That's the question. Why are people afraid of sharks, because you aren't that afraid of being hit by lightening, but it is more likely that you'll be hit by lightning than killed by a shark? And we have a better chance of being hit by a car than being killed by a shark." [Fig. XX-2]

Jack added, "Or even that you'll drown. You have a better chance of drowning than of a shark attack."

Detouring, Sam pointed out, "It does partly depend where you live. Where my dad grew up, in Australia, is different because the ocean is around people."

"Yeah, you are right. For sharks don't attack in Europe. We saw a map locating shark attacks, and it's not evenly spread around." I laughed at this comment, because most of Europe is land-bound, but didn't want to develop that idea anyhow, so let the comment go.

I did want to pick up on a bigger concern, so I called for the boys' attention. "Boys, sometimes when our thinking or talking gets going fast and furious, we lose track of our line of thinking, and our thoughts or comments start popping all over the place in a sort of random popcorning like fashion, with a few comments about this, a few about that, and it is hard to make your thinking deep. I'm going to replay for you what I've heard you say so far, and you can chart the main ideas you've talked about right on this paper—all of you combining your efforts—and then decide what your focus is for the upcoming talk, and try to stay on that focus 'til it feels right to move to the next focus. Does that sound okay?"

The boys agreed, so I read aloud the gist of this transcript, my voice accentuating when I felt as if the conversation had popped to a new subtopic. Soon they'd recorded (on a single sheet of paper at the center of their group) a trail of thought like this:

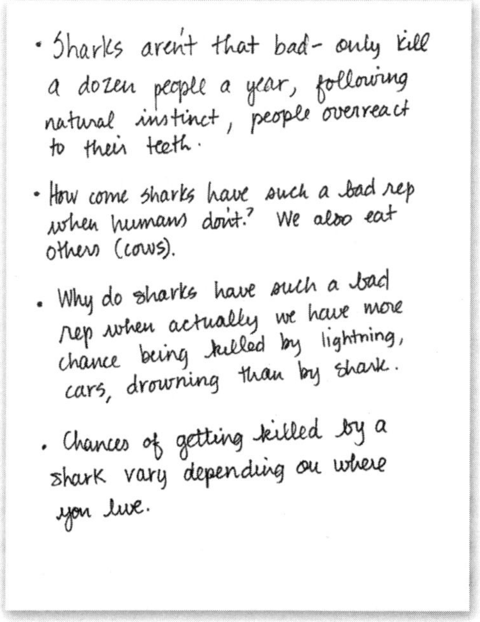

The boys talked among themselves and agreed that they wanted to talk about why the world is so unfair to sharks, wrongly stereotyping them. Why sharks? As Sam put it, "Okay so we are gonna talk about 'Why sharks?' I mean, why are sharks the big bad animal. Why not tigers or rhinoceros? And how do people stereotype them?"

Just articulating the idea got the kids wound up again, and they returned to the theme of collecting evidence that sharks are maligned, rather than trying to figure out why sharks are the ones to receive this treatment. "See, here it says that '100 million sharks are caught each year for food and fun,'" Isaac said, quoting directly from one of the books. "That's like thousands of times more sharks killed by people than the other way around!"

"Yeah," Jack said. "And listen to this." From another book, he read, "'For centuries people have feared sharks. But, today, sharks have much more to fear from people. Overfishing is threatening many species with extinction.'"

There was a short silence as the boys reflected. Then Jack broke the silence suddenly. "This makes me mad!" he said. "It's like sharks have this bad reputation for being vicious killers when we're killing them!"

I interrupted. "So, you have your angle. You are mad that the world stereotypes sharks. You said you want to talk about why it's sharks that get this bad treatment and how the world maligns them—but after making that decision, your conversation hasn't been about the exact topic you chose. Instead you've kept piling up evidence that sharks are stereotyped. That's different than thinking about *why* they are stereotyped. You could take on either topic, but one huge thing to learn about thinking deeply, talking deeply, is that it helps to spy on the conversation as it unrolls, almost taking notes on the subtopics being addressed like you just did when I reread your transcript. Only, people do this 'keeping tabs' while we talk. And we don't just record our subtopics as we address one and then another. We control them. We choose them. We can say, 'Wait, we decided to talk about such and such. Let's get back to that.'

"So keep talking but continue recording the subtopics of your conversation. One of you can be the record keeper, okay?"

The boys nodded in agreement, and I said I'd get them started by rewinding the conversation back to the part when they decided the subtopic they wanted to address. I read from my transcript, "Okay so we are gonna talk about 'Why sharks?' I mean, why are sharks the big bad animal? Why not tigers or rhinoceros? And how do people stereotype them?"

Isaac took control of the group at this point. "Hold it, hold it," he said, "We gotta get our idea going of why." As he said this, I took a marker and wrote a big why at the center of their table. He noted the word and said, "I think, why people are afraid of them is because people just don't know. Ignorance. Like a lot of people think they only eat meat, but some sharks just swim around on the bottom of the ocean and are bottom-feeders. Only most people do not believe that. They think they eat meat. And actually, only one in twenty species of sharks in the world actually eat meat. Most sharks eat leftovers." Meanwhile Sam recorded, "Ignorance. People think meat eaters."

Jack, still very conscious of the topic—Why?—added, "Okay, I agree. I agree about the ignorance, but also, the great white shark. That's it. That's their total image of sharks. And that is the one kind that does kill people."

Again Sam recorded a phrase. I considered pointing out that ideally there are a few comments exchanged for every new word added to the record of their subtopics, but didn't.

Sam said, "Well . . . I think the reason we are so afraid of sharks is they live in a habitat that is not natural to us. Land is our natural habitat. We don't live on the moon or in the jungle or on the bottom of the sea. We are not all that afraid of tigers—'cause they live on the land. When we see a shark, we think, 'He's going to eat me.' When we see a lion, we think, 'How noble.'"

He elaborated. "We are more afraid of sharks because their habitat is not natural to us. We feel like we have more options on land. If a land animal attacked us, we'd have ways to get away." *[Fig. XX-3]*

Jack extended this. "In the sea, all we could do would be to swim, and we wouldn't feel at home, swimming away from them. And in the ocean, we're scared of eels, of the octopus. We're not scared of elephants. When we look at photographs of an octopus, we don't think, 'How beautiful.' Our sense of beauty is not ocean beauty."

I wasn't wild about the topic of their conversation, but was glad they'd talked for what amounted to half a page in my notes, all on one smallish point. I gave them a quick compliment for this, burying a tip into the compliment: Talk for as long as you can about each one of the points in the record of your conversation.

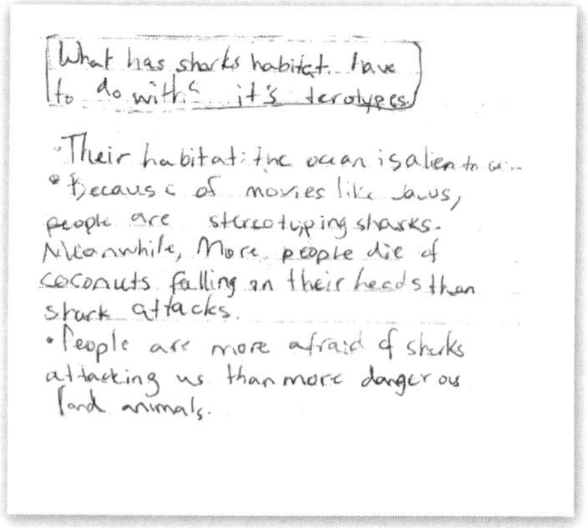
What has sharks habitat have to do with it's sterotypes

- Their habitat: the ocean is alien to us
- Because of movies like Jaws, people are stereotyping sharks. Meanwhile, More people die of coconuts falling on their heads than shark attacks.
- People are more afraid of sharks attacking us than more dangerous land animals.

Figure XX-3
Sam later captured his idea about habitats onto paper.

I didn't want this to sway the boys into talking a whole lot more about the idea that the human unease with the ocean had contributed to our stereotyping of sharks, so I reiterated the larger terrain of their conversation, relying on Sam's notes in a way that essentially asked, "What else do you want to say about why sharks are stereotyped?"

Isaac took the ball and ran with it. "Plus it's a circle. People are afraid of sharks so people make them look physically like they are scary. I mean we even name them with scary names—the hammerhead shark. That shark is not really a hammerhead. The bull shark. The sharks didn't name themselves that. Those are human names. The names are even scary. People who have stereotypes about sharks name them."

Jack said, "I agree. Human beings are why people are afraid of sharks. Humans name them and humans decide what pictures to show and all." Taking hold of a book, he said, "Like this book shows a shark and it is called *Chomp!* But if the book had an elephant, would it be named '*Crunch*?' Or a book about human beings—it doesn't show you times when the humans are violent and name itself '*Bang*.'"

"People get influenced. Books and movies influence people, too," Sam said. At this point I left the conversation for a bit. When I circled back, the boys explained they had done some writing to think and walked me through it. Sam began. I smiled at how easily they threw around this newly learned term, writing to think, and scanned a bit of it.

Isaac, for example, had written his thoughts down on paper. He had used a boxes-and-bullets format. One box said, "People are putting bad images in people's minds," and another said, "People are afraid of sharks because at a young age people put images in front of their minds that are not true." *[Fig. XX-4]*

Jack, meanwhile, was holding a book written for first-graders featuring a shark on its cover. "Look how authors present sharks—to children even! Young kids look at this image, and the image gets recorded in their minds—sharks are scary—and those images stay with them through their whole lives. It's like the images on women's magazines. The images make people look better than they are. Then people look at those images and think, 'Am I like that? If I don't look like that, am I not okay?'"

Isaac said, "This, about the sharks, is the opposite. This makes things look different—worse—and puts those images in people's minds."

Sam held up another book, this one geared more toward third-graders, but again, one showing a violent picture. "Look what they are publishing on a grade three level! This is sick."

Now from all sides of the table, more examples emerged. "That guy in the picture—he got 462 stitches!" Jack exclaimed.

I tucked in a comment. "Do you see how you are all staying on one topic and adding to each other's thinking about the one subtopic? (I ges-

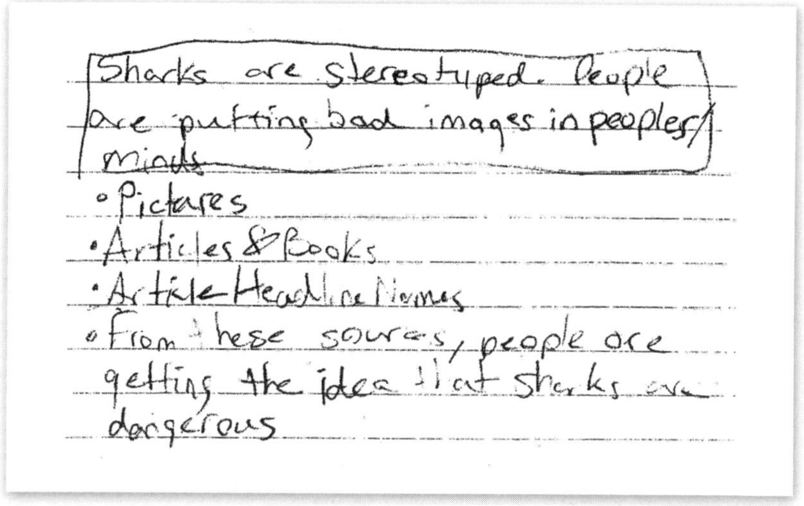
Sharks are stereotyped. People are putting bad images in peoples minds

- Pictures
- Articles & Books
- Article Headline Names
- From these sources, people are getting the idea that sharks are dangerous

Figure XX-4
Isaac borrowed a familiar structure to organize his ideas.

tured to the page on which they'd been recording notes.) Nice work. Keep it up."

Turning to an interior page, Isaac showed another photo. "They didn't have to choose this photo. This guy's leg is being ripped off. Mind you—this is for third-graders. It puts these images in your mind, and people grow up with them."

"And it's not just the words. It's the photos," Sam added. "These books—we are reading them for information but I notice the headings alone: 'Chomp' or 'What's for Dinner' or 'Deadly Jaws.' It's absolutely ridiculous. Or take this book." Sam read aloud from a Scholastic publication: "The shark rips off a large chunk of flesh. Gulp. The shark swallows it."

Jack concurred. "People are putting images in other people's minds that aren't true."

Isaac piped in with, "But we are fascinated by scary things, and those images make us fascinated by sharks. People almost like to be scared."

I gestured to the note page at the center of the table. "Nice work. You established your point—that books create the stereotype—and now you extended it. It is not just books that do this. It is also our response to books, our love of violence."

Nodding, Sam said, "Yes, we are interested, human beings are interested, in stuff that is scary. If there was a picture of a shark with his mouth closed, it might be dull for us. To make it interesting they open the mouth and show the teeth."

Sam hit the nail on the head, I thought. "Maybe people make it violent to make money."

"I notice when they write books for kids who are just learning to read, they need to make them especially violent. I don't know why," Isaac said.

"We should warn the little kids who are reading this book," Jack said. Soon the boys had gotten all wound up over the idea of traveling to the classrooms containing younger kids and teaching them a course: Beware of the Stereotyping That's Happening in Your Books.

I didn't want to talk, at that point, about the lessons I hoped they'd learned that could be transferred to another day and another book. But I made notes of those lessons and planned to definitely discuss them another day.

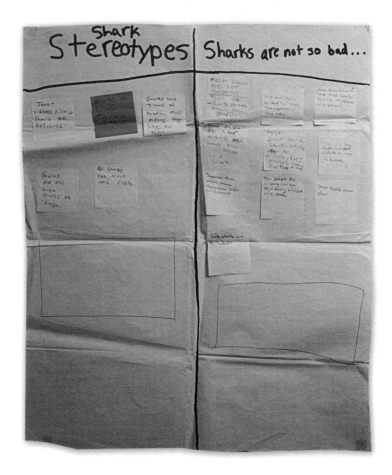

TEACHING SHARE

Readers Can Use Prompts to Grow Our Thinking

As children write ideas based on their research, let them know that they can insert thinking prompts to help them develop their ideas.

"Readers, can I stop you for a moment? I've just been thinking about the writing you've been doing to grow your ideas as you research. I noticed that you are writing long about your topics and you are writing a lot of facts that you find. You are thinking about how those facts might be connected to the idea you are growing about your topic.

"Right now, let's try something together. As you write, I'm going to say some prompts that you can insert into your writing as you go, just like we did when we were growing ideas for personal essays. Keep writing, and as I say a phrase, just write that phrase and then keep writing off of it. Don't worry if you don't think your writing makes sense. In the end, you can look back over it and see what ideas you can pull out.

"Start with the phrase, 'What I believe about my topic is. . . .'"

After a few minutes of furious scribbling, I interjected, "What I really want the world to know about my topic is. . . ."

Then after a few more minutes, I said, "I think this is important because. . . ."

Then I said, "Other people may disagree because. . . ."

And finally, "I would say to those who disagree that. . . ."

Ask children to share their writing with their group members.

After letting the students write for a bit longer, I said, "Readers, look over what you just wrote. What ideas did you grow about your topic? Did any of you write anything that surprised you? Share now with your group some of what you noticed as you wrote."

Highlight the work of a group whose conversation was deepened by their writing work.

After the students talked in groups for a few minutes, I asked the butterflies and insects group to share what they had talked about because their conversation had been particularly powerful.

Brianna was one of the first to want to share. "I was writing about all of these insects

Teachers, if you have taught the Breathing Life into Essays *unit of study in your writing workshop, then you know how using writing prompts can grow student thinking exponentially. You can use any of the prompts suggested in that unit here as well. I chose these because I wanted to set the students up to deal with multiple viewpoints and to understand why they chose the viewpoints that they did.*

we read about that are endangered. I thought about some of the bugs that are dying out because their habitats aren't protected. When I wrote about other people disagreeing, I realized that a lot of people, and me too, before, might not really care about saving bugs. Most people think bugs are gross. But then when I wrote about what I would say to those people, I would say that we have to protect the bugs because bugs deserve to live, just like any other animal or person."

"Yeah," interjected Lily. "And then when Brianna told us that, I remembered something else I read about why we should save bugs. I read that many bugs are food for things like birds and lizards, and without those bugs, the other animals would die, and then others, and others. And see, people don't think about bugs being important, but actually if we didn't save them, then lots of other animals could die."

"So we decided to research why it's important to save bugs," said Jasmine, completing the journey that the girls had undertaken.

"Girls, you have done such smart work. By thinking about what other people might say about your topic, you decided on your lens, which is clearly something you all really care about. So readers, as you go forward with this work, keep in mind, you can always use prompts like this to push your thinking. Then you can go back and ask yourself, 'What are the ideas that are really important here? What do I really care about?'"

IN THIS SESSION,

you will celebrate, with students, all they've learned about their topics and about nonfiction reading by structuring an opportunity for them to teach others.

Celebration

onsider this for a moment. Presumably neither you nor I have sailed an oil tanker through icebergs or watched penguins make the long trek to the sea or built a bridge across a mountain ravine or witnessed a saguaro cactus grow from a seed to a plant so large that it becomes a hotel for hosts of other creatures. By the end of this unit, however, you and your young readers will have experienced and learned from all this and much more. Pakistan will no longer be an obscure location on a map; penguins will be more than those charming creatures that somehow managed to thrive in Mr. Popper's basement. Nonfiction reading does this.

The allure of nonfiction is that it pushes readers into deeper connections with the very real world around us. From the true story in a magazine that inspires its reader to pledge the donation of a heart or an eye, to the book on teaching reading that helps a teacher reimagine the tone and texture of life within her classroom, nonfiction reading has the power to spill out of its covers to affect what readers think about their world.

What opportunity this unit provides! How important it is for nonfiction reading to help your children connect to that big wide world out there. If we conceive of a unit of study as being a vehicle that drives children's consciousness down a path of learning, we might regard the skills and strategies involved in reading nonfiction texts as the starting point of this journey. The strategies are important, but the lasting influence that this (indeed any) unit will exert in your children's lives will depend on whether their "skilled" reading allows them to build relationships to texts that are deep enough to change your children's perceptions of the world and of their places within it. If teaching is going to be as powerful as it can be, all the strategies need to leverage very real results in the world. This unit should be a passage into an entirely other way of being, seeing, and reading. With passion and ambition, then, we aim to send our children off,

GETTING READY

- Prepare a chart on which you've written out points for coming up with a teaching point about the topic of one's nonfiction reading.

- Have children sit with their inquiry groups at the start of the lesson. Later, you'll use a jigsaw teaching technique to split groups up so that "experts" can teach others.

giving them the conviction that passionate nonfiction reading can inspire the sort of actions that will change the world.

> *The allure of nonfiction is that it pushes readers into deeper connections with the very real world around us.*

On this final day of the unit, you and your children will celebrate the information they have gathered, the ideas they've grown, and the traces that all this new learning has left in their lives. The concept of celebration itself suffers from a connection to firecrackers and confetti. A celebration actually denotes something far deeper, something often missed. Any thesaurus tells us: to celebrate is to mark, honor, keep, remember, and memorialize. Toward the end of the unit, therefore, the question that we might ask ourselves is "What, in this month's work of teaching and learning, is most worthy of honoring, keeping, and memorializing?"

Certainly strategies are precious, especially those that have the transferability to can propel kids onto a higher plane of thinking. But more than this, we'll want to honor the joy of learning, the thrill of being one who can launch learning expeditions of our own. We will want to memorialize ways that nonfiction reading can spur a legacy of thought and action in the reader.

As you close the door on the last chapter of this unit, gather your children close together and issue them an invitation. Say, "Children, today we celebrate not only the end of this unit but a beginning, too. It's the beginning of taking this new knowledge and thinking with us wherever we go, whatever we do in the world. This is the beginning of living differently because of all we've learned."

# MINILESSON

Celebration

CONNECTION

Share with children that reading about a nonfiction topic never has to end, nor does letting what you know influence your life.

"When I'm reading a fiction book that I love, I sometimes feel like I never want it to end! When I feel the thinning sheaf of pages left to read, I think 'Oh no,' because I know the story will soon be over. 'Goodbye Harry Potter. Rowling says the series is over. I'm going to miss you.'

"Readers, we've been looking at all kinds of nonfiction texts this past month: expository, narrative, achievement stories, disaster stories, magazines, newspapers, reference books. All these texts have something in common: they don't just stay inside the covers of their books. They spill out into the real world. And so, nonfiction readers, know this: nonfiction texts don't end when you close the book or turn off the screen.

"After reading one book about King Tut, I can get ten more. I can Google King Tut. I can visit a museum exhibit and look at some of King Tut's actual treasure. If I ever travel to Egypt, I will plan my trip with King Tut in mind. There are so many ways to let the topic continue in my life.

"A famous writer named Annie Dillard wrote about how, when she was ten, she got hold of a nonfiction book called *The Natural Way to Draw*, and that one book changed her life. She writes:

> . . . this book would ignite my fervor for conscious drawing . . . For the rest of August, and all fall, this urgent, hortatory book ran my life. I tried to follow its schedule: every day, sixty-five gesture drawings, fifteen memory drawings, an hour-long contour drawing . . . I outfitted an attic bedroom as a studio and moved in. Every summer or weekend morning at eight o'clock, I taped that day's drawing schedule to a wall (1987, p. 78).

"That's what nonfiction reading can do!

I often say that the skills we teach need to cumulate, traveling with our students as they progress from unit to unit, year to year. But there are other things than skills that need to leave a lasting legacy. The identities that are cultivated within units of study are ones we hope children can inhabit forever. James Gee has helped all of us realize that students and teachers have identity kits or ways of being in the world. Sometimes when I am speaking to teachers at a conference, I arrive at a nearby hotel the evening before, and as I check in, I see people sitting in clusters throughout the lobby. I can spot the teachers among those people. They have that identity kit of being a teacher. Students try on multiple identities while in our classrooms and come to recognize themselves as certain kinds of people. How important it is that children decide that among other things, they are the kinds of people who read. This minilesson aims to help children know that reading itself can give them a world of other identities, too. Reading can invite them to be entomologists, archeologists, and activists. Reading can give them passions and causes.

Name your teaching point. Specifically, teach children that the characters and themes in nonfiction texts travel with us into the real world, changing the way we live.

"Readers, what I want to teach you today—on the day of our celebration, on the day when we say goodbye to this unit on nonfiction reading—is this. When we finish reading nonfiction texts about topics we come to care about, those texts and, even more, those topics live with us. Those texts and those topics walk through our lives with us. We carry our nonfiction reading with us, using it to find direction in our world."

TEACHING

Offer readers an analogy for bringing their nonfiction knowledge and passions with them through life, even as they finish reading the texts they have.

"Have you seen an adult on the bus, the subway—perhaps it is a woman—and she reads the newspaper, then folds it up, sticks it under an arm, and then she carries that nonfiction reading down the sidewalk. That reading gives her direction: about the day's weather, the stock market, the world events, the opening of a 'green' supermarket, the newest book by a favorite author. And these directions help steer decisions—her actions. Should she pack an umbrella? How should she vote?

"Today, even though you may not take the actual texts with you, you'll fold up your nonfiction reading, tuck it under your arm, and you'll walk out of this classroom 'carrying' that nonfiction with you, as readers do. And two things will happen. First, you'll find yourself teaching others what you know. And second, you'll find others teaching you. That is, you'll leave here, with your nonfiction under your arm (in your mind), and you'll go through life continuing to be part of conversations about the reading you've begun here."

The truth is that nonfiction reading has changed my life in a way that is not dissimilar to what Annie Dillard describes. I remember as a new graduate from college, teaching in a teacher corp program (not unlike today's version of Teach for America*) and being disillusioned with what I encountered at Weaver High School, the urban school where I was trying to learn to teach. I read Charles Silberman's* Crisis in the Classroom, *a book about the British primary schools, where an image of education was alive and well, and hope stirred inside me. At the end of that school year, I flew to London, hitchhiked to Oxfordshire, and waited outside the office of John Coe, the senior education advisor who had been described in that book. When I finally met Coe, I told him I'd come to apprentice for the year in these schools that I'd read about. "I'll work anywhere, do anything," I said. "I just need to see with my own eyes what I've been reading." Later, in a similar way, the books by Donald Murray drew me into the field of teaching writing—and into writing. I suppose in my heart of hearts I am hoping that this series might be a way to give back, a way to participate in the grand conversation.*

Invite children to see themselves as participants in an intellectual community, a grand conversation that traverses lifetimes.

"Readers, the one thing that I have loved most about this unit of study that we've done together has been the conversations we've all had. I'm not a big fan of yackety-yak kind of talking, but I am a huge fan of real conversations—the kind where someone puts forth information or a point of view and others lean in, faces rapt, listening really closely, and then one of those listeners picks up what's been said (with one hand I gestured as if I've picked up something and held it high) to build upon it by adding something new (with my other hand I gestured as if I've balanced something new atop whatever I just picked up). Conversations like that really tower over other kinds of talk because each new input is like a building block that adds to what came before. (I motioned as though I was placing block above block above block to build a tower.) I love to watch and listen in when you're in real intellectual conversations with each other.

"It occurs to me as we end this unit on nonfiction reading that all of you have become part of something. We can call it the grand conversation. It is a conversation that began with the dawn of history and continues today, and it occurs not so much through the spoken word, as through the written word. Picture this. When a person writes a book about a topic, he or she basically says something about that topic, gives the world a perspective or an idea or new information about that topic. Then, along comes another person who also writes about this topic, and what this new person does is to build on what previous books say and also add something of his own—kind of like when you all engage in a conversation and you build on what has been said before and say something new. Later, when somebody else responds, that carries the conversation forward.

"When someone writes a book on philosophy, they essentially add a word into the grand conversation started by Plato and Aristotle, the first writers to write about philosophy.

"Passionate, ambitious nonfiction reading means participating in the grand conversation about our topic. We don't have to write a whole new book to enter this conversation. We can become a spokesperson for the topic, teaching it to others. We can become an activist and find a life cause in some urgent aspect of our topic. Passionate, ambitious nonfiction reading means saying to ourselves, 'My nonfiction reading has changed the way I think about this topic, and in turn, I can educate others or change others or convince others to take some positive action on this topic.' Instead of being a passive eavesdropper on a grand conversation, standing outside looking in on what

Have you ever seen the classrooms where children literally organize their whole-class conversations by building a tower as they talk together? One child speaks and puts out a block. The next child adds to what the first has said and represents that he has done this by putting his block on top of the first. After a bit, a child may venture to suggest a related but different topic, and so she puts her block on the floor, not on top of the others. I've got that image in my mind as I talk to children about the way the grand conversation goes.

You could, of course, continue. When someone writes a book about architecture, they enter a conversation started by Imhotep, the architect of the pyramids. When someone writes a book about psychoanalytic thought, they carry forward the grand conversation started by Sigmund Freud. Of course, referencing names such as Plato, Aristotle, Imhotep, and Freud within the same breath is saying a lot—name-dropping intellectual giants. Even if the children do not entirely grasp who Plato is, they'll get the gist that the agenda for today is lofty. In referencing a grand conversation, we're also slipping in the sense of what comprises true scholarship—deep nonfiction reading on a topic to acquire expertise before articulating one's own opinion, an opinion that carries the weight of research and reflection and contributes to the conversation.

others have written and said, we can be the kind of active readers who carry this forward out there into the world."

Set each inquiry group up to disperse to a different audience and to spend some time teaching that audience about their topic, bringing those people into the grand conversation on the topic.

"Readers, in this past month, some of you have been listening in on the grand conversation about fighting terrorism by building schools instead of bombs, some about immigration, penguins, about ways animals are stereotyped.

"Today, as we end this unit of study, each of your inquiry groups will put your topic and your texts under your arm and head out across this school with the mission to participate in the grand conversation about your topic. So listen up to the plan. Specifically, I've arranged for you to head to different places around the school, where people will be waiting for you eighteen minutes from now. Before you head out into the world of this school, you'll need to think with your group mates about how you can bring these people who have not been part of your conversation into it.

"So, members of the Shark Group, you're expected in Ms. Grimes' second-grade classroom, where a group of kids have been in a nonfiction center on sharks. I've got a couple of the books that they have been reading here so you can look them over before you arrive and prepare for what you'll teach those youngsters. And members of the Extreme Weather Group, there's a group of children who can't find anything of interest to study, and Ms. Grimes is really hoping you could talk up your topic and get them excited about some books on it. Again, I brought a few of the possible books for you to look at.

"Members of the Insect Group, the kindergarten teachers are expecting you. I don't know if you remember, but every year they've hatched monarch butterflies, and they'll want to learn whatever you want to teach them about the monarchs and to hear any ideas you have for what they might do with their class this year.

"Members of the Penguin Group, I'm thinking that your topic belongs to all of us. We all love your topic. Before we have our parent-teacher conference night in a week, it would be terrific if you could think about what could go into this room that would show the parents a bit about this topic. Maybe it could be a bulletin board, or a mural, or a collection of books with notes on them about things parents might want to notice. You'll start work on it today, but the work will need to continue past today.

We've referenced sharks, penguins, and Greg Mortenson because these are some of the inquiry topics that our kids have been working on in the past few days. You, of course, will insert your own children's inquiry topics as a reference.

I'm reminded of Erik Erikson's quotation, "Human beings are so constituted so as to need to teach because ideas are kept alive by being shared, truths by being professed." If you recall the way teaching ignited your own learning when you were first called upon to teach, you'll have some sense for the energy source today's celebration will tap into. Notice the children are teaching in small groups so the stakes aren't high enough to create stress. Excitement, yes; stress, no.

"And the Greg Mortenson group, I haven't figured out who you could talk with, but I figured that you could come up with a plan, and I'll help make it happen.

"So all of you, get with your groups and plan like crazy for how you are going to bring others into the grand conversation that you've been in. You have exactly eighteen minutes for planning, and then you're expected in your various places, and you'll have fifteen minute to bring those others into the conversation."

As groups plan for their teaching, coach into their work in ways that remind them to advance main ideas and organize subtopics to support those ideas and to draw on all they know about teaching well.

The room erupted as children began planning what they would say to these different audiences. After they'd gotten well started in their conversations, I intervened to coach the entire class.

"Readers, let me give you a few tips. Like you, I have some topics I've been focused on. You could say that I'm something of an expert on the role that dogs can play in a family, and frankly, I don't just know about this. I care about it too. I have my own ideas about this that matter to me, so I think, 'When I participate in the grand conversation about dogs, what is it that I want to say? What will my contribution be?'

"One thing I might say is, 'The most important way to teach your dog to behave well is to keep your dog with you as often as possible.' That's sort of like my box—my main idea. And I'd want to think about the points I could make that relate to that big idea. To prepare for talking, I might list these across my fingers. Like, right now I'm thinking that for starts, if you want your dog to behave well, then when company comes to visit, you can't shut your dog up in the bedroom. The dog needs to be out, with the company (and of course that means you need to teach the dog not to jump up on people, not to run around in circles). I'd think about if I have any examples—times when I wanted to shut my puppy up but forced myself to not do so and was glad afterward."

Then I paused to extrapolate the general point I hoped I was making. "So each of you, think, 'What do we really want our contribution to be in the grand conversation about this topic?' Figure out what your main idea is, and think, 'What points do we have that go with that idea?'"

The truth is that I have a pretty good idea that the kids in this group are itching to rally the class to raise money for schools in Pakistan, so when I say that I don't know who they'll want to talk with, I actually do know they'll want to talk with the class as a whole, and I've built this into my sense for how this final day will unfold. But I know they'll get extra pleasure from initiating this idea.

I decided not to present too glamorous a topic because, after all, the children have really just been reading on their inquiry topics for a little while, and it is a bit of a stretch to think that these topics will be for them like education has been for me. I'd rather show them that a seemingly small topic can be handled well than pump this up too much. You could, of course, decide differently. I'm not entirely sure I've made the right choice.

Again I let children talk, and as they talked, I circled among them. I reminded some children that they knew how to teach and would want to use that knowledge—using gestures and drama and references to pictures to make their information come to life. I reminded anther group that they needed to think about their audience and to be sure they were taking into account what their audience would want to know. I encouraged a third group to share precise bits of fascinating information and to use the lingo of their topic.

Follow kids when you can and eavesdrop a bit on what they do when invited to teach others. Don't coach into this work. Don't worry about it being perfect. Give the kids this time in the sun.

The Shark Group was in the middle of their presentation to second graders. Jack said, "We know you're just starting your shark study, and we're wondering what you think sharks are like and why you think that."

Jack called on a few of the kids, who all said that they thought sharks were scary and mean and that they eat people.

After the second graders spoke, Isaac said, "We used to think the same thing! But then we learned the truth. We're going to teach you a little bit about how sharks are stereotyped." He referred to the charts the group had created and taped to the wall.

"One of the big things we realized is that the pictures in our books make us think that sharks are vicious and that they attack all the time, but we know now that that's not true. It's a stereotype," Isaac continued.

Sam added, "We looked at your books and we found the same thing. We found pictures of sharks being aggressive." Each of the boys held up one of the second grade books that had a picture of a vicious-looking shark.

Jack said, "Sometimes pictures make you think one thing, so it's important to check the words to make sure the pictures match 'cause we found that isn't always the case."

Jack continued, "There are many reasons why people are afraid of sharks. One reason is because at a young age images are put in our minds that are not true. Like in movies and pictures and on the news. And like in your books!"

The boys continued to talk off their chart, and I quickly scampered to the next room.

One teacher I know talked to children about how her passion for the topic of food and diet inspired her to make a change in their school. She said, "I've read up on Atkins, Ornish, Pritikin, South Beach—you could say I'm kind of a diet expert. I haven't read just one book on nutrition. I've studied as many as I could find; I've accessed the grand conversation on healthy eating. When the school cafeteria committee decided on the menu for your lunches, and all I saw were hot dogs, fries, mayo-rich salads, I couldn't be passive. I had to join that committee and change that menu so that it included more fruit, more veggies. I didn't change the whole world, but I changed my small part of it. I changed my school—made it a bit healthier."

In one of the kindergarten classrooms, the Insect Group was standing in front of a chart titled, "No More Insecticides! Reasons to Save Bugs!!!"

The girls were talking off their notes about how monarch butterflies are endangered and need to be saved. Lily was saying, "Another reason why you guys need to care about monarch butterflies is because a lot of people give money to save animals that are cute, like pandas and dolphins and whales! But nobody really hears about how monarch butterflies need protecting, too!"

"I agree!" said Brianna. "They need protection from pollutants that threaten them, cause it spoils their nectar, which they need to live. And they need to be protected from their predators."

Jasmine added, "And parasites and pesticides threaten monarch butterflies, too!"

The girls listed other reasons why monarch butterflies need protection. Then Grace said, "You can help. Anyone can. There are organizations that maybe your class might want to join or give money to that will help monarch butterflies."

As Grace was passing out a flier with the organizations, Lily quickly called the kids' attention to the chart the group had created on the dangers of pesticides not to just monarch butterflies but to all bugs.

I entered a fourth-grade classroom just as Aly was pretending to weep at "the stairs of separation (a few chairs the immigration group had put together to represent a staircase). The girls had created an imaginary immigrant girl named Hannah and had drawn a picture of her journey through Ellis Island, listing the steps and tests immigrant families had to take to enter New York. I noticed thought bubbles conveying Hannah's feelings at each step.

"Don't leave me, Mama," Aly called out dramatically to Sarah, who held out her hand as Kadija (in the role of the test administrator) pointed to an eye test on the wall and said sternly, "Read!" Hannah's mother did pass the test, and the family of two trotted down the "staircase," off the island to New York.

I stayed long enough to hear Aly say to the fourth graders, "Even though it was hard being an immigrant, there was hope, too, and sometimes families did end up together in the new country."

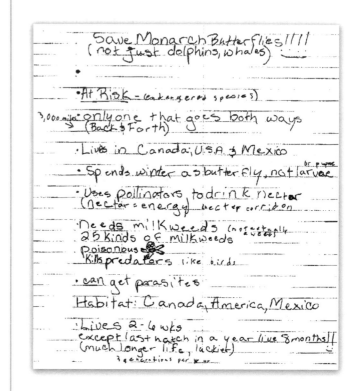

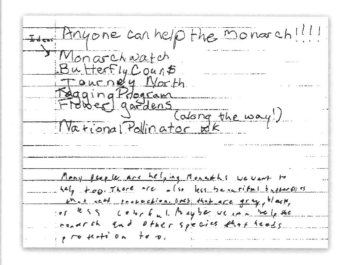

Reconvene the class and find a way to cumulate all that occurred. Then give one group the chance to teach the class as a whole, bringing the whole class into the grand conversation on one topic that can evolve into a class service project.

When children returned—well after the ending time of a usual reading workshop, I reconvened them, and for a few moments they shared stories about how their preparations for teaching had gone. Then I pointed out that the making a difference group had decided that it would present their ideas to the class. They did so by telling about the journey of their research, starting with an article they had read about a librarian from Iraq, Alia Muhammad Baker, who so treasured books that she moved out as many as she could—approximately 30,000!—from Basra's central library to her home, to save them from destruction. They'd then drawn pictures of the Librarian of Basra, which they now shared with the class—images that showed a woman racing between the library and her home, her arms laden with books. "We learned that somewhere in the middle of Iraq," Jane said, "there is a house full of books; there are books on shelves, books on countertops, books on windowsills blocking the view, books piled up in an old refrigerator even . . . everywhere in that house are mountains and mountains of books."

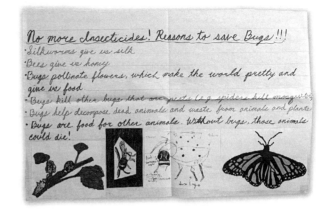

The kids then went on to tell children that they had carried that story into their lives and had conversations around it. "We found that loads of people are helping get books to kids in countries where there have been lots of wars," Danny said. Brandon then talked to the class about an idea: What if the entire class joined the international movement called Pennies for Peace, collecting pennies to help build schools.

"We can't do it alone, we need your help!" the three kids said.

Jane added, "So bring in your pennies, dollars, and coins to help."

Soon the class was working together to generate a plan for involving the larger school. They'd soon planned who might stay in from recess that day to make fliers, who might travel to other classrooms, and what those speakers might say to the children in those rooms.

Name what has happened that you hope affects what kids do—this day and always.

Time had long since run out. I needed to add some benedictory words. "Do you see what has happened? We've all become part of the grand conversation about building schools to educate others. And there are seven-year-olds in this school who are part of the grand conversation about sharks and hurricanes. And kindergarteners who'll soon be rallying to protect another insect, as the world is already working to protect the monarch butterflies.

"You or I could come from our reading, deciding that we want to become the kind of person who makes it easier for immigrants who come to America, to work on behalf of global warming so creatures who rely on the arctic cold aren't at risk. Reading non-fiction passes an invisible legacy onto us. One of us could decide, years from now, to go to meet that librarian, who has since distributed those books to friends, schools, and the new library in Basra. One of us could look at the beautiful photographs in this book (I held up one of the books on penguins) and decide to become a photographer of nature. That would be an entirely different legacy.

"What I want to point out is that in some way, as our nonfiction reading ends, it leaves us thinking of what we could do differently in our own lives as a result of this reading. This is how readers truly make words our own. We develop reactions and actions in response to whatever we read, picking up some personal legacy from the text, letting it guide our futures. Here is a reader's secret; listen closely. (This is something that I am telling you at the end of the unit rather than at the start because you wouldn't have understood me if I had told you earlier.) Reading changes people's lives."

By this point, your celebratory message should be clear. On this final day of the unit, you and your children will celebrate that today's readers and thinkers are tomorrow's movers and shakers. The concept of celebration itself suffers from a connection to fire-crackers and confetti. A celebration actually denotes something far deeper, something often missed. Any thesaurus tells us: To celebrate is to mark, honor, keep, remember, memorialize. Toward the end of any unit in the reading workshop, the question that guides us in choosing our final teaching point must be, "What in this month's work of teaching and learning is most worthy of honoring, keeping, and memorializing?" Our teaching point and the fervor of our teaching itself must reflect this.

This work is not dissimilar to pausing at the end of a well-told story to contemplate its larger and enduring meaning. Deeper contemplation doesn't always happen on the go. It often requires the intervention of the teacher to insert a quiet space in the hum-drum of an active school day for kids to think deeply, in silence, amid the collective energy of peers engaged in similar work. Usually we say to kids, "Stop daydreaming and pay attention to what I'm telling you." But now, perhaps what we are saying is, "Stop listening to what I'm saying so you can explore what you think. Then tell others. Tell me."

Adler, David A. 1999. *A Picture Book of Amelia Earhart*. New York: Holiday House.

Allington, R. L. 2006. *What Really Matters for Struggling Readers: Designing Research-Based Programs*. New York: Pearson Education.

Aloian, Molly, and Bobbie Kalman. 2004. *The Life Cycle of a Flower*. New York: Crabtree.

Atwater, Richard, and Florence Atwater. 1992. *Mr. Popper's Penguins*. Boston: Little Brown Books for Young Readers.

Bartoletti, Susan Campbell. 2005. *Black Potatoes: The Story of the Great Irish Famine, 1845–1850*. Boston: Sandpiper.

Baylor, Byrd. 1995. *I'm in Charge of Celebrations*. Fullerton, CA: Aladdin.

Beck, I. L., and M. G. McKeown. 2006. *Improving Comprehension with Questioning the Author: A Fresh and Expanded View of a Powerful Approach*. New York: Scholastic.

Beck, Isabel L., Margaret G. McKeown, and Linda Kucan. 2002. *Bringing Words to Life: Robust Vocabulary Instruction*. New York: The Guilford Press.

Berger, Melvin. 1999. *Chomp! A Book About Sharks*. New York: Cartwheel.

Brooks-Simon, Barbara. 2004. *Escape to Freedom*. Des Moines, IA: National Geographic Children's Books.

Brown, David West. 2009. *In Other Words: Lessons on Grammar, Code-Switching, and Academic Writing*. Portsmouth, NH: Heinemann.

Bruner, Jerome. 1977. *The Process of Education*. Cambridge, MA: Harvard University Press.

Calkins, Lucy. 2007. *Units of Study for Teaching Writing*. Portsmouth, NH: Heinemann.

Calkins, Lucy. 2000. *The Art of Teaching Reading*. Boston: Allyn and Bacon.

Calkins, Lucy. 1994. *The Art of Teaching Writing*. Portsmouth, NH: Heinemann.

Cleary, Beverly. 1990. *Socks*. New York: HarperCollins.

Coburn, Broughton. 1997. *Everest: Mountain without Mercy*. New York: National Geographic Society.

Cole, Joanna. 1990. *The Magic School Bus Inside the Human Body*. New York: Scholastic Press.

Covey, Steven R. 1990. *The 7 Habits of Highly Effective People*. New York: Free Press.

Darling-Hammond, Linda. 2008. *Powerful Learning: What We Know About Teaching for Understanding*. San Francisco, CA: Jossey-Bass.

Deedy, Carmen Agra. 2009. *14 Cows for America*. Atlanta, GA: Peachtree.

DiCamillo, Kate. 2001. *The Tiger Rising*. Somerville, MA: Candlewick.

Dillard, Annie. 1990. *The Living*. New York: Harper Perennial.

DK Reader. Donkin, Andrew. 2000. *The Bermuda Triangle*. London: Dorling Kindersley.

———. 2001. *Disasters at Sea*. London: Dorling Kindersley.

DK Reader. Dubowski, Cathy East. 2000. *Shark Attack!* London: Dorling Kindersley.

DK Reader. Ganeri, Anita. 2001. *Eruptions! The Story of Volcanoes*. London: Dorling Kindersley.

DK Reader. Griffey, Harriet. 1998. *Secrets of the Mummies*. London: Dorling Kindersley.

Donovan, M. Suzanne, and John D. Bransford, editors. 2005. *How Students Learn: Science in the Classroom*. Washington DC: National Academies Press.

Durrell, Gerald. 2006. *The Whispering Land*. New York: Penguin.

Erikson, Erik, and Robert Coles. 2000. *The Erik Erikson Reader*. New York: W. W. Norton & Company.

Felps, Will. 2008. Interviewed by Ira Glass on "The Bad Apple," *This American Life*, National Public Radio. Aired December 19, 2008.

Fletcher, Ralph. 1996. *A Writer's Notebook: Unlocking the Writer Within You*. New York: HarperCollins.

Fontanel, Beatrice. 2004. *The Penguin: A Funny Bird*. Watertown, MA: Charlesbridge.

Freebody, Peter, and Allan Luke. 1990. "Literacies Programs: Debates and Demands in Cultural Context." *Prospect: Australian Journal of TESOL* 5(7): 7–16.

Fullan, Michael, Peter Hill, and Carmen Crevola. 2006. *Breakthrough*. Thousand Oaks, CA: Corwin.

Gardiner, John Reynolds. 1999. *Stone Fox*. New York: Scholastic.

Gardner, Howard. 1983. *Frames of Mind: The Theory of Multiple Intelligences*. New York: Basic Books.

Gee, James Paul. 2007. *Social Linguistics and Literacies: Ideology in Discourses*. London: Taylor & Francis.

Gibbons, Pauline. 2009. *English Language Learners, Academic Literacy, and Thinking: Learning in the Challenge Zone*. Portsmouth, NH: Heinemann.

Gillman, Leni, and Peter Gillman, Eds. 2001. *Everest: Eighty Years of Triumph and Tragedy*. Seattle: Mountaineers Books.

Gladwell, Malcom. 2008. *Outliers: The Story of Success*. New York: Hatchette Book Group.

Goodall, Jane. 1997. *The Chimpanzee Family Book*. New York: North-South Books.

Gourley, Catherine. 2002. *Who Was Maria Tallchief?* New York: Grosset & Dunlap.

Guiberson, Brenda Z. 2007. *Cactus Hotel*. New York: Henry Holt and Co.

Halberstam, David. 2003. *Firehouse*. New York: Hyperion.

Hall, Donald. 1979. *String Too Short to Be Saved*. Boston: David R. Godine.

Hart, B., and T. R. Risley. 1995. *Meaningful Differences in the Everyday Experience of Young American Children*. Baltimore: Paul H. Brooks.

Heifetz, Ronald A., and Linsky, Marty. 2002. *Leadership on the Line: Staying Alive Through the Dangers of Leading*. Cambridge: Harvard Business School Press.

Hickman, Pamela. 1990. *Bugwise: Thirty Incredible Insect Investigations and Arachnid Activities*. Reading, MA: Addison-Wesley.

Hopkinson, Deborah. 2003. *Shutting Out the Sky: Life in the Tenements of New York, 1880–1924*. London: Orchard.

Jenkins, Steve. 2002. *The Top of the World: Climbing Mount Everest*. Boston: Sandpiper.

Jerome, Kate Boehm. 2003. *Understanding the Brain*. New York: National Geographic Society.

John-Steiner, Vera. 1997. *Notebooks of the Mind: Explorations of Thinking*. New York: Oxford University Press.

Johnston, Peter. 2004. *Choice Words: How Our Language Affects Children's Learning*. Portland, ME: Stenhouse.

Kalman, Bobbie. 1994. *Frogs and Toads*. New York: Crabtree.

Kalman, Bobbie, and Robin Johnson. 2006. *The Life Cycle of an Emperor Penguin*. New York: Crabtree.

Kelso, Richard. 1992. *Walking for Freedom: The Montgomery Bus Boycott*. Orlando, FL: Steck-Vaughn.

Kidder, Tracy. 2009. *Mountains Beyond Mountains: The Quest of Paul Farmer, a Man Who Would Cure the World*. New York: Random House.

Kodas, Michael. 2009. *High Crimes: The Fate of Everest in an Age of Greed*. New York: Hyperion.

Koestler-Grack, Rachel. 2004. *Sacagawea: Native American Biographies*. Chicago: Heinemann Library.

Kramer, Mark, and Wendy Louise Call. 2007. *Telling True Stories: A Nonfiction Writers' Guide*. Nieman Foundation for Journalism, Harvard University. New York: Penguin.

Lasky, Kathyryn. 1993. *Monarchs*. New York: Gulliver.

Lauber, Patricia. 1990. *Lost Star: The Story of Amelia Earhart*. New York: Scholastic.

Lauber, Patricia. 1996. *An Octopus Is Amazing*. New York: HarperCollins.

Lewis, C.S. 2001. *The Chronicles of Narnia*. New York: HarperCollins.

Lionni, Leo. 2009. *Swimmy*. New York: Scholastic.

Lyman, Peter, and Hal R. Varian. 2003. "How Much Information," Retrieved January 2010 from http://www.sims.berkeley.edu/how-much-info.

Lyon, Elizabeth. 2003. *A Writer's Guide to Nonfiction*. New York: Penguin Putnam.

Maathai, Wangari. 2008. *Planting the Trees of Kenya*. New York: Farrar, Straus and Giroux.

Medearis, Angela. 1999. *Dare to Dream: Coretta Scott King and the Civil Rights Movement*. New York: Puffin.

Mortenson, Greg. 2009. *Listen to the Wind*. New York: Dial.

Mortenson, Greg, David Oliver Relin, and Sarah Thomson. 2009. *Three Cups of Tea* (Young Reader's Edition). New York: Puffin.

New Skete Monks. 1991. *The Art of Raising a Puppy*. Published in the United States.

Nelson, Robin. 2003. *From Cocoa Bean to Chocolate*. Minnesota: Lerner.

Nicolaides, Kimon. 1975. *The Natural Way to Draw*. New York: Houghton Mifflin.

Nivola, Claire A. 2008. *Planting the Trees of Kenya: The Story of Wangari Maathai*. New York: Farrar, Straus and Giroux.

Osbourne, Mary Pope, Sal Murdocca, and Will Osbourne. 2000. *Knights and Castles*. New York: Random House Books for Young Readers.

Osbourne, Mary Pope, and Will Osbourne. 2004. *The Magic Tree House Research Guide: Twisters and Other Terrible Storms*. New York: Scholastic.

Pausch, Randy. 2008. *The Last Lecture*. New York: Hyperion.

Perkins, David. 2010. "Making Thinking Visible." New Horizons for Learning. Retrieved January 2010 from http://www.newhorizons.org/strategies/thinking/perkins.htm.

Pianta, Robert C., Jay Belsky, Renate Houts, and Fred Morrison. 2007. "Teaching: Opportunities to Learn in America's Elementary Classrooms." *Science* 315 (March): 1795–96.

Richardson, Will. 2008. "Footprints in the Digital Age." *Educational Leadership* 66(2): 16–19.

Ross, Stewart. 1997. *Charlotte Brontë and Jane Eyre*. New York: Viking.

Rowling, J.K. The Harry Potter series. New York: Scholastic.

Royal Geographic Society. 2003. *Everest: The Summit of Achievement*. New York: Simon & Schuster.

Ryan, Pam Muñoz. 2002. *When Marian Sang: The True Recital of Marian Anderson*. New York: Scholastic Press.

Sewell, Anna. 2008. *Black Beauty*. New York: Puffin.

Silberman, Charles. 1973. *Crisis in the Classroom: The Remaking of American Education*. London: Wildwood House.

Simon, Seymour. 2006. *Earthquakes*. New York: HarperCollins.

Squire, Ann O. 2002. *Animal Babies*. Danbury, CT: Children's Press.

Tangborn, Wendell V. 1988. *Glaciers*. New York: T.Y. Crowell Junior Books.

White, E.B. 2004. *Charlotte's Web*. New York: Scholastic.

Wilcox, Charlotte. 2000. *Mummies, Bones, and Body Parts*. New York: Scholastic.